THE REAL MAKING OF
THE PRESIDENT

American Presidential Elections

MICHAEL NELSON

JOHN M. MCCARDELL, JR.

THE REAL MAKING OF
THE PRESIDENT

KENNEDY, NIXON, AND
THE 1960 ELECTION

W. J. RORABAUGH

UNIVERSITY PRESS OF KANSAS

Published
by the
University
Press of Kansas
(Lawrence,
Kansas 66045),
which was
organized by the
Kansas Board of
Regents and is
operated and
funded by
Emporia State
University,
Fort Hays State
University,
Kansas State
University,
Pittsburg State
University,
the University
of Kansas, and
Wichita State
University

© 2009 by the University Press of Kansas

Library of Congress Cataloging-in-Publication Data

Rorabaugh, W. J.
    The real making of the president : Kennedy, Nixon, and the
1960 election / W. J. Rorabaugh.
        p.   cm. (American Presidential Elections)
    Includes bibliographical references and index.
    ISBN 978-0-7006-1639-8 (cloth : alk. paper)
    1. Presidents—United States—Election—1960. 2. Political
campaigns—United States—History—20th century. 3. Kennedy,
John F. (John Fitzgerald), 1917–1963. 4. Nixon, Richard M.
(Richard Milhous), 1913–1994. 5. United States—Politics and
government—1953–1961. I. Title.
    E837.7.R67 2009
    324.973′0921—dc22   2008044566

British Library Cataloguing-in-Publication Data is available.

Printed in the United States of America

10 9 8 7 6 5 4 3 2 1

The paper used in this publication is recycled and contains
30 percent postconsumer waste. It is acid free and meets the
minimum requirements of the American National Standard
for Permanence of Paper for Printed Library Materials
Z39.48-1992.

CONTENTS

Like Hector and Achilles, Grant and Lee, even Nicklaus and Palmer, Richard Nixon and John F. Kennedy were strikingly similar figures who are remembered for their differences. As W. J. Rorabaugh observes, both Kennedy and Nixon were Washington politicians who never served in state or local government; they were young (Kennedy was 43, Nixon only four years older), ideological moderates, Navy veterans, and family men whose main interests were in foreign rather than domestic affairs. They ran against each other in 1960 in a contest that was closely fought throughout the campaign and ended with Kennedy winning by a margin of about one-half vote per precinct.

Despite the similarities between the two candidates, their contest came to be defined by the differences between them. After eight years as vice president to President Dwight D. Eisenhower, Nixon made "experience" the theme of his campaign. "Kennedy," writes Rorabaugh, "countered with the theme of getting the country 'moving again.'" More significant, perhaps, was the difference between the two in upbringing and temperament. Nixon came up hard, the son of a struggling, quick-tempered, small businessman father and a mother who was often absent, busy taking care of Richard's two sickly brothers. From youth until the end of his political career, Nixon was transparently insecure and driven to succeed. Kennedy was born to wealth and raised to serene self-assurance.

To an unprecedented degree, the temperamental differences between the two candidates were on naked display during the election because of the spread of television. In 1950 only about one in ten American homes had a television set; by 1960 only about one in ten homes did not have one. Four live televised debates, the first in history, took place between the candidates. It is hard to recall a single important issue on which Kennedy and Nixon disagreed in these debates, but everyone remembers the contrast between Kennedy's coolly assured manner and Nixon nervous insecurity.

Politically, Nixon and Kennedy faced different challenges in 1960. The Republican Nixon was competing to win in a country that remained strongly Democratic. The Roman Catholic Kennedy strove to be elected by a country that was overwhelmingly Protestant. Nixon came as close as he did by making inroads among conservative Democrats in the previously solid South. Kennedy lost votes because he was a Catholic, but he also gained some, and the latter tended to be concentrated in the large industrial states that ultimately provided his margin of victory.

Rorabaugh describes the presidential candidates with evenhanded depth and insight. Unlike Theodore White, the author of *The Making of the President 1960,* he does not succumb to Kennedy romanticism. He also pays particular regard to the critical role played by Kennedy's running mate, Lyndon B. Johnson of Texas, who managed to keep most of the South in the Democratic column. Kennedy faced two threats in the region: not just Nixon, but also a movement among some anti–civil rights southern Democratic leaders, which Johnson largely suppressed, to withhold electoral votes from both major-party nominees and throw the election into the House of Representatives. Never before or since has a vice presidential candidate had as great an effect on the outcome of a presidential election as Johnson did in 1960.

AUTHOR'S PREFACE

This book began when Fred Woodward of the University Press of Kansas told me about the press's new series on presidential elections. I became interested in writing about the 1960 election after I published *Kennedy and the Promise of the Sixties* (2002), a book that only briefly discussed John Kennedy's election. Many of the social and cultural changes that the United States underwent during the first years of that fascinating, tumultuous decade could be traced to the 1960 election campaign.

In the present volume, I have reexamined terrain that the journalist Theodore White covered many years ago in *The Making of the President, 1960* (1961). A young reader will find it difficult to understand that very dated work, and many sources closed at that time are now available. In addition, White had his own prejudices and too often took campaign "spin" at face value. The present book, a corrective to White, is a reevaluation of the 1960 election and its place in American history.

This book owes much to the John F. Kennedy Library in Boston, where I held the Theodore Sorensen Fellowship in 1992. On that visit, as well as on a later one, I became well acquainted with many materials, including oral histories, about the 1960 election. However, the Kennedy side of the story is often told best in secondary publications.

The losers' papers are more interesting because they have not been the basis for as much scholarship: Adlai Stevenson's at Princeton, Hubert Humphrey's at the Minnesota Historical Society, Lyndon Johnson's at the Johnson Library, and Richard Nixon's at Laguna Niguel, California, recently transferred to the Nixon Library in Yorba Linda. Photographs appear courtesy of the Johnson Library, Harry S. Truman Library, Dwight D. Eisenhower Library, Minnesota Historical Society, Wisconsin Historical Society, George Mason University, and Corbis.

In many ways, this book began in 2004, when, largely through the generosity of Professor Hugh West, I was the Visiting NEH Professor at the University of Richmond. While in Virginia, I dug deep into Senator Harry F. Byrd's remarkable papers at the University of Virginia. The largely untold story about the South's role in the 1960 election that appeared in Byrd's papers led to the decision to write a book about the election. Senator Richard Russell's papers also proved to be a rich source.

The South, to a great extent, was the key to Kennedy's victory, and this book's chapter on the South is the book's most original contribution.

I would like to thank my colleagues Robert Stacey and John Findlay for helping to arrange a University of Washington paid leave for 2006–2007. Several chapters benefited from the Department of History's History Research Group, and especially from Dick Kirkendall's insights. I would also like to express appreciation to Don Critchlow at Saint Louis University for reading an early draft. Finally, at the University Press of Kansas, I wish to thank Fred Woodward, the series editors, Susan McRory, Susan Schott, and Jennifer Dropkin.

I would like to dedicate this book to Hugh and Rosalie West and to Richard Johnson and Carol Thomas, all fellow toilers in the vineyard of scholarship.

Reexamination of the 1960 election is in order. Today, the popular image is that the election was about John Fitzgerald Kennedy as a dashing liberal knight, playing Luke Skywalker to Richard Nixon's Darth Vader. The 1960 campaign certainly helped produce this distorted image, but careful study of the facts reveals that Kennedy and Nixon had much in common. With no ideological differences, these two moderate contenders in this close contest shared a generational outlook. World War II shaped both Kennedy and Nixon. Shortly after the two former junior naval officers won election to the House of Representatives in 1946, observers concluded that both would gain higher office. In 1950 Nixon moved up to the Senate, and Kennedy followed two years later, when Nixon became vice president. In the 1950s the two rising stars had offices across the hall from each other and frequently visited together. Both were cold warriors, both advocated moderate domestic policies, and both tepidly endorsed civil rights.

It is time to go behind the image to examine the evidence about the 1960 election. However, writing honestly about Kennedy is difficult. His popularity while president hinders discovery of the truth. Then, too, Kennedy was enigmatic, even for a political figure. Throughout his life, he routinely dodged questions either with wit or by asking questions to avoid giving answers. This evasiveness created an aura of mystery, which was part of Kennedy's charm, but it also left listeners with misimpressions. Fortunately, Kennedy's popularity means that sources documenting his career are abundant. The larger problem, however, is that even after sifting through the evidence, the sum of the historical parts fails to rise to the level of the heroic myth that surrounds this beloved American martyr. What are mere "facts" when one is trying to come to terms with a man who has become a legend so powerful that he has achieved mythic proportions?

Much of what we "know" about John Kennedy, it turns out on close scrutiny, is less about the real man, his principles, or his politics, including the presidential election of 1960, than it is about our collective socially constructed memory of Kennedy. In this sense, what we "know" is not necessarily that which is true. This memory, in turn, is rooted less in fact than in emotionally based images, often derived from television, where Kennedy first entered into the national consciousness. In our collective memory, he is an earnest student, rugged athlete, brilliant intellectual, heroic warrior, dutiful husband, proud father, urbane liberal, honest public servant, ardent defender of freedom at home and abroad, and crusader for social justice. Even though he has been dead for more than forty years, he is still all of these, more often than not in the present tense. Like Marilyn Monroe, another iconic public figure from the same period, he remains forever young. In reality, if Kennedy were alive today, he would be past ninety.

Nor can we escape the memory of Kennedy's sudden, grotesque departure from the public stage in the moment of horror that is his assassination. That scarring event continues to give contour and meaning to our memory of the glamorous young president. The tragedy both contradicted and reinforced the collective positive memories so vividly established during Kennedy's presidential election campaign and brief presidency. The murder contrasted starkly with preassassination images of a noble chevalier blessed with brains, money, courage, wit, creativity, and political skill, not to mention a beautiful wife, who was so loved by the public at home and around the world that many felt that he could do no wrong and that no wrong could be done to him. Sacrificed in blood in a public setting, Kennedy ascended to martyrdom, and his senseless death, when counterposed against his life, caused his image-driven virtues to be seen as manifestations of perfection.

Although positive images about Kennedy as athlete, intellectual, war hero, family man, and passionate liberal have some basis in reality, the truth, we have learned increasingly in recent decades, was sometimes more complicated than the image that simple memory would provide. And, in some respects, the image has been just plain wrong. Today we know that Kennedy's lifelong poor health prevented him from ever being a rugged athlete, and he was not a dutiful husband. On the other hand, he was a war hero, he was proud of his children, and he did earnestly seek to defend freedom. Although he had a fine wit, much of what passed for intellect came from his ability to utilize excellent speeches crafted by others, his liberalism was more cautious than robust, and his commitment to social justice was ambiguous. Part Harvard-educated patrician and part tough Boston Irish politician, Kennedy often felt more at home with the latter role, but he knew that the image of an Irish machine politician would never lead to the White House. Ambition dictated that Kennedy construct an image that paid homage to, but was somewhat distanced from, Irish roots.

Much of what became the Kennedy myth began with the 1960 presidential election, when, according to legend, the beloved knight in shining armor conquered the body politic with charm and panache. The truth was more complicated. Not well known at the beginning of the year, Senator John Kennedy of Massachusetts used the Democratic primaries to gain both votes and public notice. To win, he used hordes of money, an efficient organization, and television image making, but he also manipulated politicians and the media and ruthlessly attacked opponents, including the use of dirty tricks. Despite Kennedy's charm, he was no virtuous white knight, even if he tried to present that image. After Kennedy won the nomination in July, he ran all out against his much better-known Republican opponent, Vice President Richard Nixon.

The psychology of Nixon's campaign is fascinating. Nixon's quiet, self-contained brooding darkened his effort just as it did his later presidency. A poor political strategist but a brilliant tactician, Nixon may have concluded that he could not win the election at an early date. He certainly knew that he faced an uphill battle against a telegenic opponent who represented the majority Democratic Party and had unlimited family money, an excellent personal staff, and a superb nationwide organization. After the election, Nixon coldly concluded that the main reason for his loss was Kennedy's four-year head start. There is much truth in that analysis, although it ignores Nixon's own shortcomings. Despite Kennedy's advantages, he would never have won in 1960, given peace and prosperity, if there had not been widespread discomfort with Nixon.

Nixon campaigned on the theme of his "experience" in high office, which Kennedy countered with the theme of getting the country "moving again." In contrast with Nixon's static defense of the status quo, Kennedy's rhetorical device captured a mood of restlessness that gripped many Americans in the late 1950s. Intellectuals, in particular, were dissatisfied with the era's crass materialism and with the sense of complacency that Eisenhower's administration seemed to project. Even though Kennedy's Senate record was only moderately liberal, he offered a dynamic politics in which liberal programs might flourish. Although Kennedy's decision to use the "moving again" theme enabled him to excite the Democratic Party base, Eisenhower's popularity might have given Kennedy pause, had he reflected upon it. If Eisenhower had been eligible to run for a third term, polls showed that he would have won in a landslide. Americans liked Eisenhower's middle-of-the-road approach to governance.

Without television, Kennedy would have been neither nominated nor elected. A natural performer in the new medium, he also worked hard to develop an effective on-air persona. Both talent and effort were necessary to achieve success in television. Kennedy used television to win votes, but in doing so he established a majestic public presence that transcended mere political needs. Kennedy invented the concept of the handsome, glamorous, exciting political celebrity. The senator built this image upon a substantive foundation as a war hero, as a well-informed world traveler, as a labor law reformer, and as a Pulitzer Prize–winning author. Little interested in expressing a political philosophy or championing a set of programs, he offered charismatic personal leadership that could appeal to persons of diverse views. This image making was crucial to the formation of the Kennedy myth.

Like all successful American politicians, Kennedy was self-made, both in the sense that he had proved himself in the democratic political arena by winning elections and in the sense that he had, throughout his political life, artfully constructed for public consumption a set of images about himself. Kennedy had abundant help in this ambitious project. First, the senator's wealthy father, Joseph Kennedy, had been a Hollywood film-maker who understood the mechanics of manufacturing a star. Second, Kennedy's talented staff, led by the brilliant speechwriter Ted Sorensen, cultivated public recognition of Kennedy's name over several years both by crafting excellent speeches and by placing thoughtful articles carrying Kennedy's byline in leading periodicals. Third, Kennedy, as a former reporter, understood the needs of the press, and he personally gave reporters juicy tidbits. Today, these items would be called "spin." His successful manipulation of the press would be one of the hallmarks of the 1960 campaign.

As it turned out, no one played a more important role in creating the Kennedy myth than the journalist Teddy White, author of *The Making of the President, 1960* (1961). This widely read best seller became a major source, both then and now, about Kennedy's campaign and about the new president's emerging public image. During the fall, White spent about twice as much time with the Kennedy campaign as he did with the Nixon effort. In part, White did so because Kennedy and his staff fed White, as well as other journalists, fascinating details; Nixon and his staff provided little help. Kennedy's staff passed on anecdotes that promoted Kennedy while withholding material that showed the candidate in a bad light. Somewhat naively, White did not seem to realize that he was being used to further Kennedy's image.

On election night, White gambled that Kennedy would win by spending the night at the Kennedy compound in Hyannis Port, Massachusetts. Richard Nixon was in California, so there was no way that White could be at both headquarters. The author wanted to capture the flavor of the moment in which the voters willed a president into existence. White's riveting election night account, by far the most interesting part of his book, was used as a prologue. Even on election night the Kennedy campaign continued to manipulate White. The Kennedy pollster, Louis Harris, reported excitedly to White about counties that seemed to be going surprisingly for Kennedy. There were many other counties where Kennedy underperformed, and although Harris reported this sobering news to the campaign manager, Robert Kennedy, White was kept in the dark.

White's best seller, heavily influenced by his closeness to the Kennedy campaign, has shaped our conception of the 1960 election since its publication in 1961. The author presented the story of the election as a joust, as the white knight besting the black knight, as the triumph of the virtuous Kennedy over the morally ambiguous Nixon, as the resumption of America's inevitable progressive course, and as the success of a resurgent liberalism against the exhausted conservatism of Eisenhower's presidency. To heighten the sense of drama, White chose to write about the campaign mostly as a horse race, which became a common journalistic practice in covering later presidential elections. If the election was seen mostly as an exciting contest, then Kennedy's victory was in and of itself the significant story. Winning, according to this line of thought, is mostly about winning. White told the story as a liberal triumph, a view that was difficult to challenge at that time. In the 1960s, it was also hard to dispute White's interpretation because the author had enjoyed unique (if partial) access to many materials that were unavailable to other scholars, in some cases for decades.

The most important clue that White's interpretation of the 1960 election is flawed comes from the election returns themselves. Only 112,803 votes separated John Kennedy's 34,221,349 from Richard Nixon's 34,108,546—49.7 percent to 49.6 percent. Diehard segregationists in the South cast most of the remaining 503,348 votes (for details, see Appendix D). In a nation where the number of Democrats exceeded the number of Republicans by a margin of roughly three to two, how could

Vice President Richard Nixon, a man who was widely detested, gain almost as many votes as the intelligent, charming, courageous Senator John Kennedy of Massachusetts? Was not Kennedy the more compelling candidate? Was he not also the better campaigner? Had he not won the crucial first-ever televised presidential debate?

The close result raises other questions. Had peace, prosperity, and affection for the popular Eisenhower generated a lot of votes for Nixon? Did Kennedy's inexperience trouble many voters? Did Kennedy's Catholicism lose votes? Why did Kennedy, by historical norms, perform poorly in the traditionally Democratic South? Was the country, in fact, perhaps not eager to embark upon a new liberal era? Rather than being troubled by these questions, White and other originators of the Kennedy myth largely ignored the election returns. Although Kennedy narrowly edged Nixon in the popular vote, the winner did not gain a majority of the overall popular vote, he carried fewer states than his rival, and he won fewer congressional districts. The Democrats lost twenty-one seats in the House of Representatives and two seats in the Senate, which could hardly be construed as the sign of a new liberal age.

The 1960 presidential election was not a "critical election" marking the beginning of a new election cycle. Its voting patterns fitted quite well with the close elections of 1948 and 1968. Although the 1960 election was not about resurgent liberalism, it was about the continuing dominance of the Democratic Party. Kennedy's narrow victory reaffirmed that Americans preferred the Democrats, who had governed the country more or less continuously since 1932. Inside this party coalition, both northern liberals and southern conservatives were important. In some ways, it was an odd coalition, but intense party loyalty in the South meant that national Democratic rule was the only way that southerners could participate in governance, and northern liberals were too weak to govern by themselves. This unnatural alliance, which would fall apart over racial issues at the end of the 1960s, enabled Democrats to win all of the presidential elections except Eisenhower's two victories from 1932 through 1964. For all but four years, the Democrats controlled Congress. In 1968 the Democratic Party's two wings split, and northern liberals gained control of the party. In presidential elections, the South turned to the Republicans and started a new political cycle. Republicans would win seven of ten presidential elections from 1968 through 2004.

Why, then, is the 1960 election significant? First, Kennedy has remained a person of unusual historical interest. He wears well on videotape and is vividly remembered by millions born after his death. Second, it is time to go beyond the myth that White and others established as early as 1961 in order to understand better the realities about this important election contest. To find the truth, it is crucial to explore the nuts-and-bolts nature of politics in 1960. Third, Kennedy's election as the first Catholic president did represent a breakthrough that inspired millions of Americans to believe that the country was ready to move beyond prejudice. Some of Teddy White's excitement about Kennedy's election came from the fact that White was Jewish, and even more than Catholics, Jews long had been excluded from important American institutions. By the time that the Kennedy-Johnson years were over, the power of the white, Anglo-Saxon Protestant establishment had been broken. John Kennedy's election in 1960 began to open doors to many people previously shut out, and the novelty of Catholics and Jews in high places quickly gave way to the possibility of African Americans and other persons of color, as well as women, entering into positions previously unimagined.

As chapter 1 shows, understanding a bit about Eisenhower, his popularity, Nixon's baggage from the 1952 campaign, Kennedy's near miss running for vice president in 1956, and the Democratic midterm election victories in 1958 are all necessary background to the 1960 campaign. Older Democratic Party leaders greeted Kennedy's candidacy with scorn. Considered a lightweight in Congress, the senator seemed too green for the highest post. These leaders did not grasp that Kennedy astutely had figured out how to circumvent their opposition. Kennedy planned nothing less than to reinvent the nomination system. It was the only way he could be nominated. He cultivated the persons who would be delegates to the 1960 Democratic National Convention and quietly wooed the still-important party bosses. He knew that he needed to win primaries in 1960 to convince the bosses that, in addition to money, organization, and television appeal, he had real popularity and could handle the campaign trail.

Chapter 2 tells how Kennedy used a large personal organization, polls, and television advertising to win the primaries. Money, much of it supplied by Kennedy's supremely wealthy father, was necessary for all of these purposes. Kennedy's victories over Hubert Humphrey in Wisconsin and, especially, in West Virginia made his nomination all but inevitable. Tricks played on Humphrey in West Virginia have been underemphasized in most previous accounts. The knight rode deep in campaign mud, which the starry-eyed press ignored. Charming and manipulating the media were Kennedy specialties. After Kennedy swept the primaries, the Democratic Party could hardly deny him the presidential nomination without appearing to be anti-Catholic. In effect, Kennedy changed how presidential politics worked. After 1960, it was difficult to run for president without huge financial resources. Whether this money-driven politics has given us better presidents is an open question.

At the Democratic National Convention, covered in chapter 3, Kennedy narrowly prevailed on the first ballot. The election of 1960 would mark the last time in the twentieth century that a ballot for president would make news at a national convention. After 1960, primaries and caucuses that committed delegates before the convention would settle nominations ahead of the meeting. The most important event at the convention, other than Kennedy's nomination, was the adoption of an exceptionally strong civil rights plank in the platform. Kennedy signaled that the Democratic Party would seek black votes in the North, even if it had to risk losing white votes in the South. To counteract the civil rights plank, Kennedy put Lyndon Johnson on the ticket to try to hold part of the South. Politics is often about implausible political coalitions, and the Kennedy-Johnson ticket running on a strong civil rights plank was just such an example.

As seen in chapter 4, Vice President Richard Nixon was the Eisenhower administration's designated heir, but he found the position inherently frustrating. An aggressive politician who had made his fame attacking Communism in the 1940s, Nixon instinctively preferred going on the offensive. Instead, he had to defend an administration whose policies he did not always like. To win the election, Nixon had to combine Republicans with about one-fifth of Democrats and about one-half of independents. To unite Republicans, Nixon had to make a deal with liberal governor Nelson Rockefeller of New York on the party platform on the eve of the Republican National Convention. Rockefeller forced Nixon to accept a liberal civil rights plank. This deal enraged Senator Barry Goldwater of Arizona and the party's other conservatives. Nixon had to base his campaign solely on "experience." It was the only way Nixon could hold Republicans while trying to appeal to Democrats and independents.

As chapter 5 shows, the South played a key role in this election. In 1960, restless southerners threatened to bolt from the Democratic Party. Archsegregationists plotted to use unpledged electors running as Democrats to sabotage Kennedy's candidacy. Most historians have ignored this movement because it took place in backwater locales, but Mississippi's ultimate rejection of Kennedy in favor of unpledged electors shows how serious the race issue was in some areas of the South. To win, Kennedy knew that he needed to carry part of the South. Accordingly, Lyndon Johnson was put on the ticket. Johnson's role has been understated in previous studies, which have focused mostly on Kennedy and Nixon. The Texan was Kennedy's secret weapon. Johnson used both high-level personal contacts with key southern Democrats and his considerable charm with fellow southerners on the campaign trail to win Texas and several other states. Without Johnson, Kennedy would have lost.

The fall campaign is covered in chapter 6. In September, the religious issue dominated. Using television to address a gathering of Protestant ministers in Houston, Kennedy powerfully defended separation of church and state to help defuse the religious issue. It was the most effective speech by either candidate during the fall, and the Kennedy campaign widely rebroadcast the tape on local stations. From late September through mid-October, Americans watched the first-ever television debates between two presidential candidates. These debates helped establish a precedent that would take root from 1976 on. Nixon's weak performance in the first debate was devastating. Kennedy executed brilliantly and went into the lead in the polls. In the final phase of the campaign, Nixon surged to all but tie the contest by massive television advertising and by campaigning with Eisenhower.

As the last chapter demonstrates, Kennedy's narrow victory suggested that Americans were fairly satisfied in 1960. It turned out that "moving again" held only a slight edge over "experience." Outside the Northeast, Kennedy ran poorly, and the improbable combination of the liberal Northeast and the conservative South was a poor basis for successful governance. Nixon ran well in the Midwest, which would be the battleground for the next forty years, and he won the West, his home region. Kennedy won with the only possible political combination that he could put together, but it was an unstable combination that would not hold long. In 1968 Hubert Humphrey and George Wallace split the Democratic Party vote along liberal-conservative, North-South lines. The South's growing alienation from the Democrats is one of the most important lessons of the 1960 election. Nixon's ability to contest the previously one-party South gave the Republicans hope for the future in that region.

Overall, the 1960 election is, as Teddy White suggested, an inspirational story about how a young challenger fearlessly battled against stodgy, entrenched forces inside his own party, gradually persuaded them that he was a master politician and star vote-getter, gained the party nomination, and went on to slay the dragon, Richard Nixon. That version of the tale became the easily recognized myth about the election of 1960, but the truth was more complex. The election is also the nuts-and-bolts story, as told in this book, about how family wealth, political organization, television, good looks, charm, and a quick wit could go far in politics, especially when the money was used effectively. The darker side of the story is how money was used to prod, buy, or intimidate, how the media was charmed and shamelessly manipulated, how opponents were ruthlessly bulldozed, and how charisma, money, organization, and manipulation could be used to gain power.

For Kennedy and Nixon, ideas hardly mattered: Note the contrast with Woodrow Wilson or Ronald Reagan, two presidents for whom ideas mattered a great deal. Although Nixon's lack of an intellectual mooring has long been noticed, Kennedy's similar position has mostly gone unrecognized. In evading any commitment rooted in ideas, Kennedy was as smooth as Nixon was clumsy. Each of these opaque, nonideological politicians ran a campaign that largely avoided ideas. The absence of ideas did have an ironic side, since it enabled White to spin his myth about Kennedy as a liberal crusader. In reality, White concocted a story line that was poorly rooted in fact. The purpose of this book is to strip away the myth, examine the evidence, and explain the nuts-and-bolts operations of Kennedy, Nixon, and all of the other contenders in one of the closest and most exciting presidential elections in American history.

EISENHOWER'S AMERICA

The jockeying and maneuvering for the election of 1960 began well before the year of the election. Much of politics is about loyalties, patronage, rising through the ranks, and maintenance of past alliances. Individuals' worldviews tend to be constant, political issues often remain alive for years, and personal grudges can linger for a long time. On the other hand, successful political practice requires innovation. New political combinations are important, and new alliances can lead to big victories. All of the major presidential candidates in 1960 were well rooted in the politics of the 1950s. To understand what they did in 1960, it is necessary to review how they pursued politics before 1960, which is the focus of this chapter. On the Republican side, Richard Nixon became a presidential hopeful when he was tapped to be vice president in 1952, and the controversy surrounding him in that campaign continued to dog Nixon in 1960. In contrast, Governor Nelson Rockefeller only emerged as a possible contender after winning a stunning victory in New York in 1958.

Five Democrats vied for the nomination in 1960. Former governor Adlai Stevenson's presidential bids in 1952 and 1956 stimulated fan support but left him with the image of a two-time loser. Senator Hubert Humphrey of Minnesota first gained national visibility in 1948 when he had persuaded the Democrats to adopt a liberal civil rights plank. Senator Lyndon Johnson's effectiveness as Senate majority leader in the fifties had made the Texan the most powerful Democrat in the country. Senator John Kennedy of Massachusetts established his popularity by coming within a few votes of winning the vice presidential nomination in 1956. In the late fifties, Senator Stuart Symington of Missouri had received much media attention as an expert on defense.

Each of these candidates had been forced during the fifties to operate in the shadow of President Dwight D. Eisenhower. The overwhelmingly popular president set a middle-of-the-road tone. What was unusual about his unique approach to politics was the way he, at first glance, appeared to disdain politics. Ike's popularity and particular political style made most politicians uneasy, in large part because they knew that they lacked any capacity to duplicate Ike's success. Barred from running again in 1960, Eisenhower played only a minor formal role in the 1960 election, but the election was in some sense a referendum upon his administration. Politically, Ike both personified and represented public opinion. This is a balancing act harder to accomplish than one might think.

The president's grin was real, but behind the wide smile was as canny a political brain as ever existed, a fact that Ike successfully kept hidden from view. Eisenhower's enemies often felt sorry for the poor inept president, while he secretly guffawed at how he had once again outfoxed them. Like many other politicians, he used deception as a favorite mode. Ike was also a first-rate bridge player and enjoyed playing hands with that game's champions. He kept track of the cards exceedingly well. And Ike had launched the first successful cross-channel invasion since William the Conqueror in 1066. Neither Napoleon nor Hitler had been able to do so, and the odds were that long after Ike's presidency had been forgotten, D-day would still be remembered.

Ike had come to the presidency in an unorthodox fashion. He was not the first military hero to be elected commander in chief, but his nomination and election in 1952 did have a curious and roundabout quality. From 1945 on, his name had been prominently mentioned as a presidential possibility. In 1948 President Harry Truman, facing what looked like defeat, had asked Ike to run in his place as a Democrat. Ike declined. Only after Truman's stunning upset victory over Thomas Dewey that year did Republicans begin to recruit Ike. He met a lot of prominent Republicans while serving as president of Columbia University. Ike, however, did not announce that he was a Republican until 1952.

Truman's presidency after 1948 had not gone well. A conservative Congress had failed to pass Truman's liberal domestic proposals, including national health insurance, and the president's badgering of suspected Communists had enraged civil libertarians. A product of the notoriously crooked Pendergast machine in Kansas City, Truman ran an administration that suffered numerous scandals. Despite these problems, Truman's reputation might have survived if it had not been for the war in Korea. In 1950 North Korea had attacked South Korea, and Truman immediately intervened with large numbers of U.S. troops. Unfortunately, the war was poorly managed, produced high casualties, and dragged on through the remainder of Truman's presidency.

By early 1952 Truman stood at 25 percent approval in the polls. His reelection prospects were even worse than in 1948. After Senator Estes Kefauver, a liberal Tennesseean, upset Truman in the New Hampshire primary, Truman abruptly announced his retirement. He did so because, like almost all high-level politicians, he despised the popular Kefauver, whom he did not want nominated. Truman tried to recruit Adlai Stevenson, but the Illinois governor refused the offer. Stevenson had been elected in 1948, and he wanted to be reelected to advance his agenda. At the same time, Stevenson shrewdly recognized that being touted as Truman's candidate, although it would help get delegate votes that Truman controlled in the convention, would prove a powerful negative in the fall campaign.

The Truman administration went to the convention with no candidate. Only twice in the twentieth century, in 1920 and 1952, has the party in power entered a presidential election with neither an incumbent nor an incumbent-picked successor. The Democratic Party bosses, still important in 1952, were determined to stop Kefauver. His constant womanizing, chronic heavy drinking, and graft probably did not bother them. (When he died suddenly in 1963, he left behind $300,000 in stock from the pharmaceutical companies that he had been investigating.) Mostly, the bosses opposed him because in 1950 he had staged an antiracketeering Senate hearing in Chicago just before the midterm election that helped defeat Scott Lucas, the Democratic Party's Senate leader. Kefauver's cheap shot had been payback for Lucas's refusal to give the pushy Kefauver choice committee assignments.

At the 1952 Democratic National Convention, in Chicago, a coalition of party bosses, Truman supporters, and southerners picked Adlai Stevenson to be the presidential nominee on the third ballot. Many southerners saw Stevenson, correctly, as more moderate on civil rights than other northern candidates. Given the fact that Ike was likely to win the election, the Democrats' choice of Stevenson was smart. Adlai Stevenson ran an unusually cerebral campaign. Franklin Roosevelt had brought intellectuals, especially academics, into his orbit in the thirties, but many intellectuals remained Republicans, even when they supported Roosevelt. Stevenson largely converted the next generation of intellectuals into Democrats. Drawing often on speeches crafted by Professor Arthur M. Schlesinger Jr. of Harvard, Stevenson projected an image of a just world to be mastered by application of reason and logic. (Both Stevenson and Schlesinger were Unitarians.)

Much of Stevenson's campaign dealt with foreign policy. Since it was politically impossible to defend Truman, Stevenson pushed peace. He stressed confidence in the United Nations, then a major theme among liberals, and hope for negotiated solutions to global conflicts rather than further wars. Although this approach struck the average American as lofty and airy, it cemented young intellectuals to both Stevenson and to the Democratic Party. Adlai Stevenson became their hero. Many, especially women, were "madly for Adlai." A surprising number of Democrats who became important in politics in the late 1950s and in the 1960s first got their start in politics in the Stevenson campaign of 1952. This cohort would play an important role in the election of 1960.

The Republican National Convention in 1952 also cast a long shadow. For decades, Republicans had been bitterly divided into two factions, generally called conservatives and liberals. In 1952 Senator Robert Taft of Ohio, son of President William Howard Taft, led the conservatives as the Republican Party's Senate leader. Colleagues considered Taft to be a brilliant man, an effective senator, and a cold fish. Awkward with crowds, Taft seemed to lack a presidential temperament. He was not, however, so conservative as some opponents suggested. Sometimes enjoying support from the American Federation of Labor (but never from the Congress of Industrial Organizations), Taft supported public housing. From the industrial state of Ohio, he also favored a high tariff to keep out cheap imports. Most important, he advocated disengagement from the world, a form of isolationism sometimes called Fortress America.

As a senator from a key state with a famous name, Taft had been a formidable presidential contender in both 1944 and 1948. Both times he had enjoyed strong support from the Midwest, the most Republican part of the nation, and both times he had lost the nomination to the more liberal Thomas Dewey, the crime-busting district attorney turned governor of New York. What Dewey had that Taft lacked was ties to the Wall Street and corporate interests that financially controlled the Republican Party. Prominent among these backers was the Rockefeller family. After

1940, liberals controlled the national party machinery, even though conservative Republicans dominated in Congress. When Dewey beat Taft for the nomination in 1944, Ohio's consolation prize was to have Senator John Bricker picked for the vice presidency. In 1948 no such prize had been given, and 300,000 Ohioans cast blank ballots for president. Most were conservative Republicans. As a result, the state voted for Truman, a strong indicator that the Midwest was tired of playing second fiddle to the richer, more powerful, and more populous East.

Robert Taft knew that age was catching up with him and that 1952 would be his last chance to win the presidency. Taft never outgrew his narrow midwestern roots, and Dewey, a successful New York politician, played a masterful game. Dewey's candidate in 1952 was Eisenhower, whose popularity would not just guarantee a Republican presidential victory but would perhaps enable the party to regain its traditional majority status. Assisting Dewey's efforts to nominate Ike was Senator Henry Cabot Lodge of Massachusetts, a northeastern liberal internationalist. To demonstrate popularity among Republicans, Ike's backers launched an invisible campaign to win the New Hampshire primary. The overwhelming victory that resulted had the desired electrifying effect. While Lodge worked party leaders from the more liberal industrial states with the argument that only Ike could win such areas, Dewey operatives nailed down as many of the southern states as they could.

A crucial state turned out to be Texas. The issue there was the Truman administration's attempt to tax oil that was beginning to be developed offshore. Ike, a Texas native, indicated that he was sympathetic to Texas, not the federal government, controlling tidelands oil. On the basis of this policy position, a Texas delegation was arranged for Ike in opposition to the rival patronage-oriented Taft delegation, which argued that Ike's delegates were Democrats. Indeed they were. The gambit was not just to win Texas for Ike at the Republican convention but also to use the tidelands issue to put Texas in the Republican column in November. The key player who would bring Texas along was Democratic governor Allan Shivers, who endorsed Eisenhower and rallied what were called the Shivercrats.

Despite these strenuous efforts on Ike's behalf, it was clear to both the Eisenhower and the Taft forces that neither had a solid majority for the nomination as the 1952 Republican convention opened in Chicago. Several southern states sent rival delegations, and it seemed that which delegation was seated might well determine the outcome of the battle for the nomination. In addition, Earl Warren, the wily liberal Republican governor of California, whose reputation had been tarnished by losing his home state as Dewey's vice presidential running mate in 1948, had managed to hold on to the large California delegation as a presidential contender. Warren had little interest in another vice presidential run, but he could imagine a deadlocked convention in which he would emerge as the compromise presidential choice. Warren was correct that Dewey and his operatives, including Lodge, would prefer Warren to Taft, if Eisenhower could not be nominated. Furthermore, Warren was a formidable vote getter in his own right, and polls suggested that he would run stronger than Taft, although perhaps not so well as Eisenhower.

The key to Warren's chances was to cast California's vote in favor of seating the Eisenhower-backed southern delegations, because if Taft won those contested states he would almost certainly have enough delegates to be nominated. At the same time, Warren had to hold his state's delegates for his own candidacy, at least through the first ballot. California did back the Eisenhower-oriented southern delegations, the Eisenhower forces did win on that issue, and Taft's hopes for an easy majority were dashed. But the second part of Warren's plan failed when California senator Richard Nixon began to undercut Warren's candidacy inside the California delegation. Nixon liked Ike, and rumors circulated of an Eisenhower-Nixon ticket. Without unity inside his own delegation, Warren's deadlock strategy could not work, either numerically or psychologically. Eisenhower and Nixon were nominated, and Eisenhower later declared that he would appoint Warren to the first vacancy on the U.S. Supreme Court.[1]

Warren was livid at Nixon's perfidy. They had never been friends or even political allies. In 1946, when Nixon had come out of nowhere to defeat Democratic representative Jerry Voorhis in a famous upset, Warren had given no help to Nixon. Warren respected the unusually hardworking Voorhis, who was, like Warren, a fellow liberal. When Nixon indicated that he wanted to run for the U.S. Senate in 1950, Governor Warren had given the upstart no encouragement. In fact, Warren might well have voted for Nixon's Democratic opponent, Helen Gahagan Douglas. Warren was on the ballot with Nixon in that election, and he bitterly resented Nixon's red-baiting in the campaign. (Nixon famously said that Douglas was "pink right down to her underwear.") During the campaign, Douglas began to call Nixon "Tricky Dick," a name that stuck. For the rest of his life, Warren referred to Nixon never by name but only as "Tricky."[2]

To Warren, Nixon's insistence that he control a portion of the 1952 California delegation was itself an effrontery, since governors traditionally controlled state delegations to presidential conventions. The governor, however, humored the young senator because Warren valued harmony, and he took seriously Nixon's pledge that he would support Warren so long as Warren was a candidate for president. Both agreed that in a showdown Eisenhower was to be preferred to Taft. Imagine Warren's shock when he discovered that Nixon had been working the delegates, both his own and Warren's, on board the train from California to Chicago, telling them that Warren could not possibly be nominated, that Eisenhower had the nomination all but locked up, and that the smart thing for the Californians to do was to cut a deal with Dewey to get as much as possible in return for their support.

So Eisenhower, the benign beneficiary of these behind-the-scene maneuvers, found himself in 1952 with the thirty-nine-year-old Senator Nixon as his running mate. Born in 1913, twenty-three years after Eisenhower, Nixon had risen rapidly in politics. The son of a cold, devout Quaker mother and a mercurial, violent father who had fared poorly in a smattering of business ventures, young Nixon was eager to escape Whittier, California. Memories of his father's small grocery store, where he had been forced to work long hours, mingled with a pall that came from the slow deaths of two brothers from tuberculosis. From his mother, Nixon learned emotional repression and stoicism; from his father, he got ambition, hustling, and belligerence. After attending the local Quaker college, where he was a top scholar, a bad football player, student body president, and founder of a social fraternity for outsiders, Nixon won a scholarship to Duke University Law School. Although third in his class, this bright, socially stiff young man got no offers from top New York law firms. So Nixon returned to California to practice law.

Around the time that Dick Nixon's effort to launch a frozen orange juice business went bankrupt, he began to act part-time in a community theater. Like many shy people, Nixon found acting a wonderful way to be noticed. He met Pat Ryan when both were cast in the same play. The daughter of a Nevada miner, Pat had lived as a child in a tar paper shack with an outhouse, but she managed to rise above her surroundings and win a college scholarship. Dick and Pat married in 1940. They shared enormous ambition and a desire to escape painful pasts. In times of trouble, Pat showed backbone and was Dick's only true confidante. Despite family pressure, Nixon rejected Quaker pacifism to join the U.S. Navy in World War II. A junior officer in the South Pacific, Nixon built island airstrips. He was popular because he allowed his unit to operate a snack bar, which sometimes provided alcohol, and he won a lot of money playing poker. After the war, the young veteran plunged quickly into politics.

Nixon could not be seen as a conservative, since he had backed Eisenhower over Taft, but his anti-Communist credentials, especially in helping to expose Alger Hiss as a Communist in 1948, had greatly pleased conservatives. Although Nixon's strident anti-Communism had angered many liberal Democrats, it gave Nixon a certain amount of political credit with conservatives and thus allowed him to be more liberal on other issues. For example, he had accepted honorary membership in the National Association for the Advancement of Colored People (NAACP), thus signaling that he was sympathetic to civil rights. Throughout his career, Nixon pursued moderate, nonideological politics.

As the 1952 campaign began, however, Nixon was almost forced off the ticket. The then-liberal *New York Post* disclosed that Nixon had been the beneficiary of a slush fund, and many, including Dewey, demanded that Nixon resign from the ticket. The media kept up the pressure, but Democrats began to grow silent after Stevenson admitted that he also had a fund. Both funds were, in fact, legal. Eisenhower seemed especially upset by Nixon's fund and declared that his running mate must be "clean as a hound's tooth." Nixon insisted that he be allowed to defend himself on television, and he gave the brilliant Checkers Speech, in which he refused to give back the dog Checkers and praised his wife's "respectable Republican cloth coat." After 300,000 pro-Nixon telegrams and letters were sent to the Republican National Committee, where Nixon had allies, Eisenhower embraced Nixon: "You're my boy." Still, it had been a close call for Nixon.[3]

Nixon never forgave the northeastern liberals who had tried to oust him, and he spent the next eight years preparing for the presidential run that he believed he had earned. He worked to project a warmer personality. "It doesn't come natural to me to be a buddy-buddy boy," he conceded. He relished sadistically destroying his opponents. "Without enemies," Nixon admitted, "my life would be dull as hell." To many politicians, Nixon was always going too far. Robert Taft said that Nixon was "a little man in a big hurry." Nixon called Truman, former secretary of state Dean Acheson, and Adlai Stevenson "traitors to the high principles in which many of the nation's Democrats believe." Although the remark had not literally labeled anyone a traitor to the United States, the sentence was artfully constructed so the word "traitor" stuck in the mind. Stevenson said that the Republican candidate was "the kind of politician who would cut down a redwood tree, and then mount the stump and make a speech for conservation." Nixon dismissed Stevenson as "shallow, flippant, and indecisive." An infuriated Truman told Tip O'Neill that Nixon was a "dirty, no-good son of a bitch." Truman refused to be in the same room with Nixon. In 1956 there was another attempt to remove Nixon from the ticket, but the vice president had many close party ties, no obvious replacement was in sight, and he remained on the ticket.[4]

Eisenhower's presidency had proved to be a mixed blessing for the Republican Party. In 1952 Ike won 55 percent of the vote and carried thirty-nine states, losing only nine southern or border states. Despite this impressive landslide, the president had short coattails, and the party gained only the narrowest of margins in the Senate (49 to 47) and in the House (221 to 213). After Robert Taft died of cancer in 1953, the party's Senate leadership fell to California's arrogant, pig-headed William Knowland, whose weekly meetings with Ike proved so frustrating that the president, just out of earshot, asked, "How stupid can *you* get?" Eisenhower preferred dealing with Democratic leader Lyndon Johnson, who was able to pass legislation; Knowland mostly just blustered.[5]

Ike ended the Korean War, kept his cabinet on a short leash, and gave firm orders behind the scenes in what became a hidden-hand presidency. It was a good thing that the president kept the administration on a short leash. In 1954 both Nixon and Secretary of State John Foster Dulles, an internationalist anti-Communist and brother of Allen Dulles of the Central Intelligence Agency, urged Eisenhower to intervene in France's war in Vietnam. Ike declined either to send U.S. troops or to drop nuclear bombs. Several times the president vetoed nuclear war recommended by his advisers. Ike had the confidence and serenity befitting the hero of D-day. He did not mind when the media accused him of being befuddled. In fact, he rather enjoyed holding press conferences at which he gave nonsensical utterances to questions that he did not wish to answer. The press tried to discern meaning where there was none, and Ike and his press secretary, Jim Hagerty, laughed.

In 1954 there was a recession, and Democrats regained narrow control of the Senate (49 to 47) and the House (232 to 203). Sam Rayburn, a moderate Texan from a rural district, had been House Speaker off and on since 1941. He ran a stable House with leadership from conservative southern Democratic committee chairs. A conservative coalition of southern Democrats and Republicans often prevailed, but the southerners, being better politicians and having more seniority as well as control of committees, had the upper hand, especially when it came to distributing largesse to their districts. The Senate came under the domination of Lyndon Johnson, a moderately liberal Texan who fancied himself a protégé of Rayburn. Johnson, too, played the southern game of pork barrel politics. San Antonio, near Johnson's home, got four air force bases. Cutting deals with Eisenhower to pass bills, Johnson developed the reputation as the most effective leader in the Senate's history. His biggest triumph was to get the Senate in 1957 to pass the first civil rights act since the 1860s. This law sent a strong signal that Johnson intended to seek the presidency in 1960.

The 1956 election was never in doubt, assuming that the popular Eisenhower was alive and well enough to run again. (He had had a serious heart attack in 1955.) Almost everyone agreed that the president would win a new term, despite the Democrats' control of Congress. Adlai Stevenson defeated Estes Kefauver in the Democratic primaries and thereby proved his own primacy in the party. Stevenson had told Senator Hubert Humphrey that the liberal Minnesotan was his personal choice for the vice presidency. However, it made little sense for the Democrats to nominate two midwesterners, and Humphrey's name was anathema to southern Democrats because of his strong civil rights views.

On the issue of the vice presidency, Stevenson found himself under pressure from two different directions. Kefauver had a bloc of delegates at the convention, and since he had been deprived of the presidency twice, prudence suggested that Stevenson pick the runner-up in the primaries as his running mate. However, Stevenson personally disliked Kefauver ("I don't like the son of a bitch"). In addition, Stevenson was under pressure from others to pick John Kennedy, the young, telegenic Massachusetts senator who some argued would bring Catholics who had voted for Ike in 1952 back to the Democrats. Kennedy's top aide, Theodore Sorensen, had prepared a memo making this argument by citing the large percentage of Catholic voters in fourteen states. In order to avoid a direct association with Kennedy, the document had been given to John Bailey, the Connecticut Democratic state chair, who leaked it to key Democrats at the convention. Deception was always a weapon in the Kennedy arsenal. The "Bailey memo" was the first effort to present Kennedy's Catholicism as a political asset. Since Al Smith's disastrous defeat in 1928 the Democrats had avoided Catholic candidates.[6]

Adlai Stevenson asked the convention, in democratic fashion, to pick his running mate. Stevenson's attempt to put some excitement into the otherwise dull convention was perceived as further evidence of indecisiveness and revealed his limitations as a leader. Wishing not to displease any faction in the party, he managed to annoy everyone. Humphrey, left with the empty promise that he was Stevenson's personal choice for the vice presidency, lost respect for Stevenson. Kefauver, with a large bloc of delegates, was cheated out of the honor of being asked to be vice president, and he had to make deals to get the delegates for a nomination that he felt, as the runner-up, should have been offered automatically. Kennedy was perhaps the most irritated. Had he been given advance notice of Stevenson's intentions, he would have been in an excellent position to argue that a Catholic would be useful for the ticket. Now he had to twist arms with little time for persuasive argument. Stevenson's action struck Kennedy as demeaning to all the potential vice presidential nominees.

The balloting proved both strained and strange. Given less than twenty-four hours, Kennedy mounted a major effort for the vice presidential nomination. Some were surprised at how quickly the Kennedy forces, led by Robert Kennedy, organized. The Kennedys were always good at organizing. The argument that a Catholic could sell the ticket to Catholics who had drifted to Eisenhower in 1952 played well among delegates from large industrial states. Although older party bosses with painful memories of 1928 were leery, Mayor Richard Daley of Chicago gave strong support on the grounds that Kennedy would help in Illinois. Kennedy's address to the convention had impressed other delegates. So had his narration of a party film at the convention. Labor, however, preferred the more liberal Kefauver. Walter Reuther of the United Auto Workers later told Kennedy, "Improve your voting record."[7]

Interestingly, many southerners who despised Kefauver as a renegade voted for Kennedy. However, Sam Rayburn opposed Kennedy. The Speaker disliked the young senator's father as a political meddler and regarded the son as a lightweight. "Well, if we have to have a Catholic," Rayburn said, "I hope we don't have to take that little piss-ant Kennedy." On the first ballot Texas went to the populist senator Albert Gore of Tennessee (father of the later vice president). Lyndon Johnson, however, respected Kennedy's political skills, and he persuaded Rayburn that Texas should switch to Kennedy on the second ballot. In a memorable moment, Johnson personally announced, "Texas proudly casts its 56 votes for the fighting sailor who wears the scars of battle."[8]

At the end of the second ballot, with Kennedy about to go over the top, convention chair Rayburn recognized Tennessee. Gore withdrew in favor of Kefauver, who won after a series of switches. Rayburn recognized states that switched to Kefauver while ignoring others that wanted to go to Kennedy. If the Speaker had recognized states in a different order, Kennedy would have won. For a short time, Kennedy was furious. Later, Joe Kennedy counseled his son that losing the nomination was a good thing. Kennedy's Catholicism would not be blamed for Stevenson's inevitable loss to Eisenhower. Having come this close to a nomination, Kennedy decided to run for president in 1960.

In his reelection bid, Eisenhower won nearly 58 percent of the vote and carried forty-one states, losing only six states of the Old Confederacy, plus Missouri. His most impressive showings were in the nation's booming suburbs, but he even won industrial cities like Chicago, Milwaukee, Baltimore, and San Francisco. By 1957 Americans were content with Eisenhower balanced by a Democratic Congress. That fall, for the first time, the administration faced new challenges. One came from the Soviet Union, which in October 1957 shocked the world by launching the first global orbital satellite, Sputnik. Although the original Sputnik was small in size and served only a limited scientific purpose, it did demonstrate that the Soviets could send missiles into space. The fact that the United States did not have this same capacity was proof for many of a Soviet technological and military edge. Eisenhower, the five-star general who presided over both the real physical security and the psychic inner security of Americans, was put on the defensive.

Immediately, Democrats began to lament the nation's defense weaknesses. The main hawk in the late 1950s was Missouri senator Stuart Symington, who had an instinct for innuendo and demagoguery that guaranteed headlines. If he had been half as smart as he was clever, he would indeed have been president. Symington claimed that the United States faced a future in which the Soviets would hold the edge in missile technology. He called this phenomenon the Missile Gap, a phrase the media adopted. Senator John Kennedy found the concept of the Missile Gap enticing, and he too began to lament the technological deficiency.

In 1958 President Eisenhower sent Vice President Nixon on a goodwill trip to Latin America. (National Park Service, Dwight D. Eisenhower Library)

In the hands of a plodder like Symington, the issue garnered headlines but did little to get the Missourian either popularity or delegates. In the hands of a more artful politician, however, the concept proved extraordinarily useful. Ever since the Korean War, the Democrats had been perceived as weaker on defense than were the Republicans. The Missile Gap proved to be a wonderful way to demonstrate that a Democrat could be tough on defense.

Kennedy warned against the Missile Gap without attacking the popular Eisenhower. The argument was subtle, powerful, and effective. Kennedy conceded that the nation's present security was acceptable, thus avoiding any direct challenge to the beloved president. Rather, he lamented that the administration's policies were insufficiently concerned with future security. The alleged Missile Gap would take place after Eisenhower left office. Thus, it was precisely because of concern about who would be the next president that Kennedy worried about the Missile Gap. The issue had one other dimension, which also aided the senator. Kennedy's most important claim was that the country needed action—needed to get moving again. Every Kennedy speech in the late fifties included a line to that effect. Much of that rhetoric evoked a psychological sense that the Eisenhower years had involved too much stasis, an idea that appealed to Democrats, and the "moving again" theme also gently reinforced the Missile Gap claim.

Eisenhower was furious about the Missile Gap charge. He knew from intelligence sources that the charge was total nonsense. Although it was true that the Soviets had built powerful rockets capable of hurling small payloads into space, Soviet missile capacity was not robust. The Soviets had poor guidance systems, which mattered little for thrusting a rocket into space but mattered enormously for trying to aim a guided missile to a specific military target on earth. More important, the Soviets had put Sputnik into orbit largely for propaganda purposes, in order to hide the inadequacies in their missile program. Eisenhower knew how many missiles the Soviets had, and he also knew how fast they were capable of building them. Due to constraints inside the faltering Soviet economy, the capacity was nowhere near the rate projected by the media's hysterical but inaccurate estimates. He also knew at what rate the United States would be acquiring its own missiles in the next decade. There simply was no Missile Gap.[9]

What enraged Eisenhower was that he knew the truth but could not talk about it except with a very select group of intelligence insiders.

Because the Soviets did not realize how much the United States knew, Eisenhower could not talk about the nonexistence of the Missile Gap without revealing to the Soviets how effective American intelligence capabilities had become, through the use of the top secret U-2 spy airplanes. If the Soviets learned the potency of the U-2 planes, they would quickly invent technology to prevent overflights. Thus, the president had to remain silent, even as irresponsible critics who lacked correct information hurled wild charges. This whole episode was one of the main reasons that Eisenhower, on his way out of office, denounced the military-industrial complex. He saw a pack of scheming wastrels (including politicians) who preyed upon public fears in the nuclear age in order to line their own pockets with fat profits from worthless expenditures made in the guise of defense.

Eisenhower was more vulnerable to criticism on civil rights. Somewhat discomfited by the U.S. Supreme Court's *Brown* decision declaring segregation illegal in 1954, he had expressed irritation at the massive changes in race relations that it dictated. Despite misgivings, Eisenhower had ordered desegregation of the public schools in the District of Columbia in order to set an example for the southern states. He had called for calm, and many Republicans were quick to point out that they were the party of Lincoln, and that it was southern Democrats, not Republicans, who invariably blocked civil rights bills with filibusters in the Senate. But when Martin Luther King Jr. had launched the Montgomery, Alabama, bus boycott to protest segregated buses in December 1955, the administration had steered clear of that local crisis. As King's nonviolent movement in Montgomery gained publicity and a certain amount of support, especially from African Americans, during 1956, the Eisenhower administration continued its silence. Perhaps the administration was focused on gaining as many southern white votes as possible in 1956. Indeed, Eisenhower, elected by an even larger landslide than in 1952, carried Virginia, Tennessee, Florida, and Texas a second time and added Louisiana, a state that had not voted Republican since Reconstruction ended. All of these states were conservative, although carrying Texas and Louisiana was mostly about the administration's position on tidelands oil.

In 1957 the federal courts ordered desegregation at Central High School in Little Rock, Arkansas. Democratic governor Orval Faubus, an opportunist, saw a chance to shore up his sagging political career. He called out the Arkansas National Guard to bar the nine black students from entry to the school. President Eisenhower could hardly ignore the challenge. Either federal court orders would be obeyed, or the federal government might as well revert to a policy of allowing the white South to rule its own affairs. Eisenhower federalized the Arkansas Guard and ordered the same guardsmen the next day to escort the nine students into the school. The president also sent thousands of federal troops into the area. To many white southerners, the sending of federal troops by a Republican president into the South to enforce racial rules smacked of the return of Reconstruction. Attempts to build a Republican Party in the South stalled with Little Rock.

At the same time, African Americans had begun to vote Republican in large numbers. In 1956 Ike received 39 percent of the black vote. He carried the black vote in fourteen of twenty-one southern cities, including Atlanta, Montgomery, and Richmond. Blacks began to consider whether their future might not lie with the Republican Party, the party of Lincoln, rather than with the Democratic Party, with its improbable New Deal coalition of northern blacks and southern whites. In 1958, in New York, Nelson Rockefeller gained significant African American support when he ran for and won the governorship. Nationally, the Republican Party faced the difficult question: Was it better to go after southern white votes and build the party in the South, or was it better to go after northern black votes in order to hold Republican strength in the North? Eisenhower, disinterested in party building, never asked the question. In 1960 Richard Nixon, the heir, straddled the issue. In the end, he got fewer southern white votes than he wanted, and he did not gain many northern black votes either. John Kennedy cleverly went after northern black votes and sent his running mate, Lyndon Johnson, after southern white votes.

In 1958 the country suffered a severe recession, the worst since the end of World War II. Unemployment peaked at 7.5 percent and was especially high in manufacturing areas in the Midwest. Furthermore, this was not just the usual cyclical inventory recession. Many experts believed that automation was destroying high-paying factory jobs and that when the recession was over, manufacturers would recover and produce more goods than ever, but no doubt with fewer workers. Unions gave strong support to the Democrats in 1958, especially in six states where conservatives put antilabor right-to-work measures on the ballot. Democrats voted in droves; Republicans did not. At the same time, Republican candidates in 1958 faced voters without having coattails from the popular president, who was not on the ballot.

The Democrats made sweeping gains in the 1958 congressional elections, winning 56 percent of the House vote, the highest since 1936. The party gained forty-nine House seats, for a 283-to-153 edge, and the traditional bipartisan conservative coalition that had run the House since 1938 was temporarily a minority. Of course, Eisenhower would veto any liberal bills the House passed, even if they did get through the Senate. The Senate, too, was ripe for turnover. In 1946 a good many mediocre Republicans had been elected, and in Eisenhower's 1952 landslide, they had been reelected. But after 1954 they were not committee chairs, since the Democrats controlled the Senate, and William Knowland's ineffective leadership made them vulnerable to the charge that they had done little for their states. In 1958 the Democrats elected fifteen new senators, including two from the new state of Alaska, for a 64-to-34 majority. In the Senate, labor-backed Democrats defeated eight Republicans and picked up one open Republican seat.

For Sam Rayburn and Lyndon Johnson, the new Congress posed a serious challenge. Both leaders' power came from an inner core of southern Democrats from safe districts or states. Johnson had carefully pointed out to the dozen or so Mountain West Democrats that their influence inside the Senate required an alliance with the South. Because the Mountain West was rural and included oil and gas, its interests were more congruent with the South than with the big industrial states. If Johnson could unite the Mountain West Democrats with the twenty southern Democrats (Tennessee's Gore and Kefauver had to be discounted), then he could normally hold a majority inside the Democratic caucus. However, with sixty-four Democrats, many of them new northern liberals, this was going to be increasingly difficult. "I hope that Lyndon will be able to manage that crowd," Barry Goldwater wrote Harry Byrd, "but frankly, I have my doubts." The huge majority risked the southerners losing control of Congress.[10]

The Democratic landslide of 1958 was interpreted differently in different quarters. Although it clearly signaled that the Republican Party was in bad shape, it did not necessarily predict a bright future for the Democrats, because they were internally divided between liberals and conservatives. In New York, Nelson Rockefeller had won a Republican landslide as governor by adopting liberal views. Perhaps this was a suggestion that liberalism was on the rise and that either party might become the liberal bastion. In 1958 both parties contained liberals and conservatives. Liberal Democrat Hubert Humphrey and liberal Republican

Nelson Rockefeller shared many views, and so did conservative Democrat Harry Byrd and conservative Republican Barry Goldwater. Liberals certainly chose to interpret the 1958 results as signifying an emerging liberal upsurge. They saw themselves as one presidential election away from a new liberal age that might rival Franklin Roosevelt's.

Other observers were more skeptical. The recession had a lot to do with the Democrats' success. A party that had to count on a recession to win a resounding victory was not in a very enviable position. The country did seem ready for some sort of change, but an attempt to establish an all-out liberal government might produce a tremendous backlash, especially when the higher taxes needed to pay for the extra services began to bite. Also, the Democratic majority in Congress was both too lopsided and too philosophically incompatible to produce any coherent policy. It did not make sense for the liberal Humphrey and the conservative Byrd to be in the same political party. They agreed on almost no public policy. Once the party majority became so large, it was bound to cause internal friction, and given the wide range of opinions inside the Democratic Party, the real question after the 1958 election was the party's future orientation. Here was one way in which the 1960 presidential election would prove significant: It would go a long way toward solving the question of whether the Democrats would be liberal or conservative. The Republicans, as the weaker party, would then have to define themselves in relationship to the Democrats.

As Americans entered the 1960s, they enjoyed peace abroad and unprecedented prosperity at home. From 1945 to 1960, per capita income had risen by 50 percent, which was a large increase for half a generation. It was all the more impressive because adults had painful memories of the Great Depression. Furthermore, this new wealth was shared widely throughout the society. Both whites and African Americans were abandoning southern rural poverty to take high-paying factory jobs in northern cities. Industrial employment was high and unionized workers were well paid, but the shift to a white-collar, service-oriented economy that depended upon a college-educated workforce was already under way. In an important sign of rising aspirations, blue-collar workers increasingly expected their children to go to college and move into white-collar careers.

The growing economy was accompanied by earlier marriages and by the birth of many children, as prosperous parents decided to have more children than they had originally planned. The baby boomers caused explosive growth in the sale of clothes, furniture, and toys, and schools were built at an unprecedented rate. In 1960 Americans were rapidly buying suburban dream houses, and a quarter of the population lived in homes that had been built within the past decade. Ownership of automobiles had grown so much that the two-car family was the new middle-class norm, and mass-produced washers, dryers, and air conditioners added to the quality of life. Television brought nightly entertainment directly into the home, even in remote areas, while TV advertising celebrated middle-class consumption and established a homogenized national taste. Popular culture was upbeat, and it stressed possibilities for future dynamic change—free nuclear-generated electricity, miracle cures for disease, supersonic air travel, and even the colonization of Mars. This was the heady atmosphere within which the 1960 election took place.

By 1960 Eisenhower had to take seriously the issue of his successor. He continued to hold a strikingly ambiguous attitude toward his own vice president. Of course, Dewey, not Ike, had picked Nixon initially—for practical reasons—and the president complained privately that Nixon was "not presidential timber." What most troubled Eisenhower was the vice president's cold personality. The president constantly said, "I can't understand how a man can . . . not have any friends." The vice president did have one friend: Bebe Rebozo, a Miami businessman. Much of their odd friendship consisted of the two men sitting together in a room for hours without either saying a word. Eisenhower and Nixon had an uncomfortable relationship. Although Ike always consulted Nixon about Republican Party matters, a topic about which the president knew that the vice president had special knowledge, Eisenhower was less likely to consult Nixon about matters of policy or governance, and Ike never treated Nixon as a friend.[11]

In 1960 Eisenhower had two off-the-record conversations with *New York Times* columnist Arthur Krock about possible presidential candidates that year. Ike was surprisingly blunt. Of all the candidates, the president felt that the vice president, his fellow Republican, best expressed his own moderate political views, and Nixon's nearly eight years in the number two post was superb preparation for the presidency. The "experience" theme would be the major one in Nixon's 1960 campaign. Whatever private reservations Eisenhower had about Nixon were not going to be shared with the press. Turning to the Democrats, Ike told Krock that Kennedy was "immature," an "inexperienced boy" unfit to be president. Humphrey, Symington, and Stevenson were dismissed as unqualified, too, although Eisenhower showed slightly more respect for Stevenson, perhaps because he was older and seemed more serious in demeanor. Eisenhower's comments to Krock about Johnson, however, were quite different. Johnson, he thought, could neither be nominated nor elected because he was from Texas, which was a southern state. Eisenhower seemed to regret this prejudice against southerners, and he certainly did not call Johnson immature, inexperienced, incapable, or too liberal. On the other hand, the president confided to a friend that Johnson was "superficial and opportunistic." Thus, Eisenhower entered the 1960 election season with little confidence in any of his possible successors.[12]

2

THE DEMOCRATIC PRIMARIES

At the end of 1959, as the important primary season loomed, the Democratic contenders for the 1960 presidential election were in place. As we shall see in this chapter, each candidate pursued a different preconvention strategy appropriate to that candidate's particular circumstances. First to announce was Senator Hubert Horatio Humphrey of Minnesota, before national television cameras on December 30 in the ornate Senate Caucus Room. Humphrey was the first to enter the contest because he needed to win primaries in order to have any chance of success. Three days later, Senator John Fitzgerald Kennedy of Massachusetts announced his candidacy in the same room to great media acclaim. He, too, needed to run in the primaries. The senator had made a striking impression at the 1956 convention and had campaigned across the country ever since. He was already a favorite and Humphrey was an underdog; but the Minnesotan boldly intended to use the primaries to knock Kennedy out of the race. Contested primaries in Wisconsin and West Virginia would decide whether Kennedy or Humphrey survived to the convention.

The other candidates held back. Senator Stuart Symington of Missouri, who had campaigned across the country during most of 1959, did not announce until March. Lacking both popularity and money, he skipped the primaries. Senator Lyndon Baines Johnson of Texas, the Democratic leader in the Senate, insisted that he was not a candidate. Johnson did not formally enter the race until a few days before the Democratic National Convention opened in July 1960. Finally, former nominee Adlai

E. Stevenson also declined to announce, although he remained popular. To varying degrees, Symington, Johnson, and Stevenson gambled on being a compromise choice if the convention deadlocked. In March, as the primaries began, the Gallup poll reported Democrats' preferences: Kennedy, 34 percent; Stevenson, 23 percent; Johnson, 15 percent; Symington, 6 percent; and Humphrey, 5 percent.[1]

To understand the Humphrey-Kennedy primary contests, background about each candidate is in order. Hubert Horatio Humphrey was born in the apartment over his father's drugstore in Wallace, South Dakota, in 1911. The family soon moved to nearby Doland, a town of about 500 people, where Hubert grew up. He was very close to his father, whose drugstore was the local community center. His father was also intensely interested in Populist-Progressive politics and served as a Democrat in the South Dakota legislature. Hubert's mother was a Norwegian immigrant, and he grew up speaking Norwegian at home, which had utility in the region's ethnic politics—as long as the Swedes did not discover this fact. Raised as a liberal Methodist, Humphrey retained a lifelong empathy for farmers, for the "little people," and for the elderly and sick.

In 1929 Humphrey entered the University of Minnesota in Minneapolis, but his father soon recalled him to South Dakota to try to salvage the drugstore from bankruptcy. Hubert became a pharmacist. Better than most politicians, he knew from painful personal experience that good people who worked hard could be destroyed by circumstances beyond their control. In 1936 Hubert married Muriel Buck, and a year later, with Muriel's help, he returned to the university to study political science. After graduation, he decided to obtain a Ph.D. to become a professor. In 1939 and 1940 Humphrey attended Louisiana State University, earning a master's degree. Living in Baton Rouge gave Hubert and Muriel their first exposure to southern segregation, and both were appalled. Much of Humphrey's early commitment to civil rights can be dated to this experience. Humphrey returned to Minnesota to work on his Ph.D., but he soon dropped out. Working for various New Deal programs involving the unemployed and adult education, he demonstrated an unusual capacity for a quick, thorough understanding of a problem and a talent for administration.

At the time, politics swirled crazily in Minnesota in a unique way. The Twin Cities' business elite, mostly of Yankee ancestry, had long controlled the state with a conservative Republican Party that depended heavily upon rural Scandinavian Lutheran votes. Irish Catholics in St.

Paul and assorted Catholics in timber and mining areas often affiliated with a weak, conservative Democratic Party. When the Great Depression hit, there had been a stampede to the Farmer Labor Party, a coalition of two distinct strands. One was composed of poorly educated, financially strapped, and culturally conservative Scandinavian Lutheran farmers, most of whom had previously voted Republican. They had been organized politically for the Farmer Labor Party through farm cooperatives. The other wing was a mixture of organized labor in the Twin Cities, union miners from northern Minnesota's Iron Range, and assorted radicals, including Communists. Rural voters provided the numbers that gave the party power, and urban members supplied money and leaders. At an early date, the astute Humphrey saw that the Farmer Labor Party and the Democrats could be merged into a liberal majority party. Humphrey believed that politics should be based on programs, not on ethnicity. He also felt that unions had an important role to play in politics.

It was in this unusual environment that Humphrey launched his political career. Deferred from the military during World War II by a double hernia, for which he wore a truss, he ran in 1943 for mayor of Minneapolis, partly at the request of local American Federation of Labor union leaders and partly because he was personally offended by the massive corruption of the city's thuggish Republican administration. Although Humphrey lost, he became determined to absorb the larger Farmer Labor Party into the Democratic Party. Humphrey intended to provide imaginative liberal leadership to the Democrats, and ties to Franklin Roosevelt's administration would give the Democratic Party a stature that the Farmer Labor Party could never have. The merger occurred in 1944, and when Humphrey ran for mayor in 1945, he won. He fired the corrupt police chief, installed an honest professional, and drove mob-oriented racketeers out of the city. People were impressed. Here was a politician who actually delivered the reforms that he promised. The black population in Minneapolis had grown during World War II, and when African Americans told Humphrey about widespread discrimination in housing and jobs, he took action through both mediation and council legislation. Humphrey also addressed the problem of anti-Semitism, and in the process he cemented the city's small Jewish business community as part of his liberal coalition. Jews would be major donors in his later political races.

By 1948 Humphrey was convinced that America had a liberal future. Through Americans for Democratic Action, a liberal, anti-Communist organization that Humphrey had helped found, the Minnesotan met other young postwar liberals like Arthur Schlesinger Jr. and Franklin Roosevelt Jr. As mayor, Humphrey had already learned that cities had limited resources and that rural conservatives dominated state legislatures. Humphrey and his junior political partner, Orville Freeman, wanted Minnesota to be a laboratory to show how a liberal Democratic Party purged of both leftist elements and patronage-ridden hacks could be popular, but to achieve success he knew that the federal government was necessary for large-scale liberal action. Furthermore, discrimination, Humphrey knew, was an issue ripe for national attention.

As a delegate to the 1948 Democratic National Convention, Humphrey decided to raise the civil rights issue. Older party leaders warned that southern delegates might walk out and that the convention was unlikely to adopt a liberal civil rights platform plank. Democrats could not win the election without the South, and the Truman administration proposed a weak civil rights plank. Humphrey, as a matter of conscience, took the matter to the convention floor. In a memorable speech, he urged, "The time has arrived for the Democratic Party to get out of the shadow of states' rights and walk forthrightly into the bright sunshine of human rights." Ignoring Truman, big city bosses recognized the large and growing black vote and swung behind Humphrey's plank, which narrowly passed. Humphrey's father, a delegate, persuaded the South Dakota delegation to vote yes as a personal favor. Having become famous, or in the eyes of some southerners, infamous, at the convention, Humphrey then launched his bid for the U.S. Senate. When he won in November, he was the first Democrat ever elected to the Senate from Minnesota. Truman also won the state, largely on Humphrey's coattails.[2]

In 1949 Humphrey entered the southern-controlled Senate, endured ostracism, and soon came to the attention of Lyndon Johnson. To succeed in the Senate, Johnson advised Humphrey, "From your orange juice at breakfast to your bourbon nightcap, it's all politics or no politics. The Senate is not a part-time job." By the time Johnson became Democratic leader in 1953, he had singled out Humphrey as a northern liberal with whom business could be conducted. More than anyone else, Humphrey became Johnson's go-between with the Senate's other northern liberal Democrats. As a senator, Humphrey showed imagination. In 1957 he introduced the concept of the Peace Corps on the Senate floor. He was one of the first senators to recognize the perils of atmospheric nuclear testing, and in the mid-fifties he proposed what became the Nuclear Test Ban Treaty (1963).[3]

One key moment in crystallizing Humphrey's decision to run for president took place in December 1958, when the senator met Soviet leader Nikita Khrushchev. Humphrey had, like other presidential aspirants in the fifties, made a series of overseas fact-finding trips. On such trips, senators always hoped for interviews with top foreign leaders. After Humphrey arrived in Moscow, he was surprised to be summoned to a late afternoon meeting with Chairman Khrushchev. Instead of a short courtesy call, Humphrey spent an unprecedented eight and a half hours with the world's top Communist. No other American had enjoyed such access. In one day, Humphrey had talked more with Khrushchev than had the U.S. ambassador in his entire tour. Humphrey wrote his account of the meeting for *Life* magazine and gained new stature as a global political figure worthy of the presidency. Eleanor Roosevelt publicly declared that Humphrey had the "spark of greatness." In a small group, Republican journalist Clare Boothe Luce privately said that no senator was "smarter" or "abler" than Humphrey.[4]

Traditionally, the easiest way to run for president was to be governor of a populous state. But the postwar years had changed the rules. The Cold War, not domestic issues, dominated the headlines. Governors had little credibility on global issues. Furthermore, few governors were well known outside their own states. In the 1950s, television, that new magical communications medium, gave senators, who lived in Washington, the chance for national sound bites. In the late fifties, Humphrey decided to run for president in 1960. There were several reasons for his decision. He was not shopworn like the twice-defeated Adlai Stevenson. Humphrey had served longer in the Senate than had either John Kennedy or Stuart Symington, and his role in the Senate had been more consequential. Although Lyndon Johnson had an even more impressive Senate record, few Democrats believed that the party would nominate a Texan in 1960.

The 1958 election suggested a liberal Democratic trend, and Humphrey presented himself as being in the liberal vanguard. "The Democrats must be a liberal party," he said. "If this is going to be a Tweedledum and Tweedledee affair, we are going to be Tweedledeed right out of a victory we richly deserve." Humphrey calculated the odds of being nominated as only one in ten, but he resolved to force the party to adopt a liberal

Adlai Stevenson helped Hubert Humphrey inspect poultry on a visit to Minnesota. (Minnesota Historical Society, St. Paul)

platform. He also believed that the election was likely to be decided in the Midwest, which had a large farm vote and a Republican edge. Humphrey was an expert on agricultural policy, and his ability to win farm votes could not be doubted—Kennedy's could. Also, Republicans had made inroads into the black vote in 1956. More than any other candidate, Humphrey could bring African Americans back to the Democrats. Finally, although many southerners distrusted Humphrey, his agricultural views played well in the South, and the areas that disliked him the most were also the least likely to vote for the probable Republican nominee, Richard Nixon.[5]

This analysis ignored certain harsh truths. Humphrey was a poor man. He had no money. Of the Democratic candidates, he was the only one who was not a millionaire. Furthermore, neither Minnesota nor the Twin Cities had many people. His home state was unlikely to generate the large funds needed to win the nomination. Also, his liberal message did not attract fat cat donors. Both he and his staff were hopelessly naive about how much money it took to win a nomination. The role of money in politics was changing. More than in the past, huge sums would be needed. Then, too, Humphrey would go to the convention with only a modest number of delegate votes from his small home state, and his presumptive ability to carry Minnesota's 11 electoral votes in November counted for little. The party was likely to nominate someone from a larger state or someone who enjoyed strong regional support. Humphrey had little popularity beyond Minnesota, except in lightly populated South Dakota.

Nor was the Midwest the best region from which to launch a candidacy. When midwestern politicians talked about agriculture, eyes glazed over in the urban East. Easterners considered midwesterners stodgy, and Humphrey's long-winded speeches, which were in the Minnesota tradition, did not play well elsewhere. Adlai Stevenson lamented, "Poor Hubert, he does have a quality of total utterance." One eastern boss asked, "Why should Humphrey be president? He's from Minnesota, where's that?" Finally, Humphrey underestimated the degree to which his advocacy of civil rights in 1948 had permanently injured him in the South.[6]

Humphrey's innate optimism led him to downplay the negative considerations. He understood that running in the primaries was the only route that could bring him the nomination. If he could win decisively all the primaries that he entered, the party bosses might let him have the nomination, especially if other northern liberals believed that he was the best hope for a liberal nominee. Perhaps Johnson, recognizing that he himself could not be nominated, would then help persuade southerners to accept his candidacy. Given the friendship of these two self-made poor boys from the hinterlands, a Humphrey-Johnson ticket was a distinct possibility. This ticket could win by sweeping the Midwest, while taking Texas, much of the South, and a good part of the West. Because money was limited, Humphrey targeted only a few primaries. Tentatively, he picked neighboring Wisconsin; the District of Columbia, which had a large black vote; West Virginia, where the Humphrey-friendly United Mine Workers union was powerful; and Oregon, a reform-minded state whose law required all candidates to run. He skipped New Hampshire, the first primary, because New England was John Kennedy's home turf.

Humphrey made Wisconsin his first contest. The rural western third of the state, heavily Scandinavian, watched Twin Cities television, so Humphrey was well known there. With a strong labor record, he expected energetic help from local unions in Milwaukee, Racine, and other industrial cities. His Americans for Democratic Action ties would help in Madison, where Stevenson, who had declared that he was not a candidate, was a local hero. Humphrey could staff Wisconsin by using Minnesota volunteers to work the state on weekends. The senator could easily visit Wisconsin on trips from Washington to Minnesota. Finally, Humphrey planned to put virtually all his money into radio and television advertising in Wisconsin. If he won, he would be able to raise more money. If he lost, his chances of gaining the nomination were poor in any case. Only one inconvenient fact stood between Humphrey and success in Wisconsin, and that fact was the candidacy of John Kennedy.

John Fitzgerald Kennedy's background was about as different from Hubert Humphrey's as could be imagined. Both of Kennedy's grandfathers had been old-style Boston Irish politicians, and his maternal grandfather, John "Honey Fitz" Fitzgerald, had been a legendary Boston mayor. The family patriarch was Jack's fabulously wealthy father, Joseph P. Kennedy, who had shown striking upward mobility by graduating from Harvard College in 1912 at a time when few Irish Catholics were admitted to that elite institution. A brilliant entrepreneur, Kennedy invested in taxis, rental cars (Hertz), Hollywood "B" movies (creating RKO), stocks, liquor (after Prohibition), and real estate. He owned the huge Merchandise Mart in Chicago, and as the city's largest property tax payer, he enjoyed easy access to that city's politicians. After World War II, he invested in oil. By the late fifties, Joe Kennedy was thought to be worth at least $200 million, which made him one of the twenty or so wealthiest Americans. He had already bestowed $10 million trusts on each of his children.

Family was everything to Joe Kennedy. In 1914 he had married Rose Fitzgerald. The devout Rose attended daily mass, counted rosary beads under the hair dryer, and eventually produced nine children. Paying little attention to the five daughters, Joe focused on his four sons, whom he coaxed, encouraged, and browbeat to excel in academics and sports. A tremendous competitor himself, Joe Kennedy could not stand seeing any Kennedy come in second in any contest. The four sons were sent to Harvard College. The oldest, Joe Jr., was strong, aggressive, athletic, and smart but unlikable. Slated for politics, he served as a delegate to the 1940 Democratic National Convention. The sickly second son, John, was born in 1917. A bit shy, quiet, and a reader, he was targeted for a writing career, perhaps as a journalist or professor. (While he was president, John Kennedy told *New York Post* publisher Dorothy Schiff that he would like to buy the paper after he finished his presidency.)

Joe Kennedy was obsessed with the presidency. Long fancying himself the first Irish Catholic president, he had backed Franklin Roosevelt in 1932. After the election, Kennedy was named to chair the Securities and Exchange Commission; he reformed the stock market and resigned in boredom. In 1938 Roosevelt picked Kennedy as U.S. ambassador to Great Britain. Getting the politically meddlesome Kennedy out of the United States appealed to the president, who shared Kennedy's pleasure in the fact that the appointment of an Irishman to the Court of St. James was also a way to snub the British government. However, Kennedy's enthusiasm for the British policy of appeasing Hitler put the ambassador on a collision course with Roosevelt, who opposed Hitler vehemently.

In late 1940 Kennedy returned to the United States and found his appointment terminated. Recognizing that his own political career was over, Joe Kennedy focused his presidential ambitions on his oldest son, Joseph P. Kennedy Jr. John was naturally jealous. The two brothers were strong rivals, and Jack got the upper hand when he published, with his father's help, his Harvard College senior thesis, *Why England Slept* (1940), on British apathy toward Hitler before World War II. Surprisingly, the book became a best seller, and John Kennedy used his royalties to buy a flashy Buick to attract women.

World War II was deadly for the Kennedys. In 1943 the Japanese sank John Kennedy's U.S. Navy PT boat in the South Pacific. Kennedy miraculously survived, swimming with his crew to an uninhabited island and then rescuing them by scrawling a message on a coconut that a friendly native carried to American forces. But it was almost a full year before he recovered from the additional injury to his already troubled back. While Joe was ambassador, daughter Kathleen had fallen in love with Billy Hartington, the oldest son of the Duke of Devonshire, one of the wealthiest and most powerful families in Britain. (One cousin was Harold Macmillan, who would be prime minister during Kennedy's presidency.) Over Rose's religious objections, the couple married. Both Hartington and Joe Jr. died in the war in 1944.

After the war, Jack was diagnosed with Addison's disease, which was then considered fatal, and Kathleen was killed in an airplane crash. Joe Kennedy quickly transferred his attempt to make Joe Jr. president to Jack. When Jack complained to his navy friend Red Fay about his father's pressure on him to pursue a political career, Red suggested that Jack simply decline. It was not easy to do so. "I can feel Pappy's eyes on the back of my neck," said Jack. Not long after, in 1946, Jack was elected to the U.S. House from a safe seat in Boston. One of sixty-nine veterans elected that year, Kennedy emphasized the issues important to his generation: housing and jobs. The House seniority system, however, gave newcomers like Kennedy little say. Bored by the House and hampered by chronic ill health, the restless Kennedy preferred chasing beautiful women to congressional work. His reputation as a playboy and a dilettante lasted well into the fifties.[7]

Joe Kennedy was determined to advance his son's career, and the next logical step was to be governor or senator. A governor served only a short time, made enemies over patronage decisions, and usually lacked national visibility. A senator could develop expertise, be independent, and bide his time to run for president. Kennedy prepared to run against incumbent Republican senator Henry Cabot Lodge in 1952. Kennedy mounted a major campaign effort, led by his brother Robert, who turned out to be a gifted political manager. Jack had charm; Bobby was an excellent organizer. Many observers considered a race against Lodge to be political suicide, since 1952 looked like a Republican year, with the popular Eisenhower heading the ticket. Indeed, Lodge had worked hard to get Ike nominated, but in the process Lodge had alienated conservative Taft Republicans, many of whom were supporters of the anti-Communist Republican senator Joseph R. McCarthy of Wisconsin. Joe Kennedy, a staunch anti-Communist, made a contribution to McCarthy, who had dated two of the Kennedy daughters, and in return for this help, Mc-Carthy agreed not to campaign in Massachusetts. (In 1950 Joe Kennedy also aided Nixon out of hatred for the leftist Helen Gahagan Douglas.)

The numerous Kennedy women, including matriarch Rose Kennedy, who was a brilliant campaigner, held teas across the entire state. As a shrewd practitioner of the family's art of political manipulation, Rose was perfectly dressed for each occasion. When going from a society event at a fancy hotel in Cambridge to a working-class gathering in adjacent Somerville, she carefully removed her pearls and covered the elegant designer chemise that she had bought in Paris with a simple cotton sweater while traveling in the back of the car. Joe Kennedy also loaned $500,000 to the financially strapped *Boston Post*, to get its editor to endorse Kennedy. Practicing the politics of inclusion, the Kennedys also organized thousands of volunteers to stimulate votes. Lodge campaigned too little and too late, and, in a major upset, Kennedy narrowly won. The only other Democrats to defeat incumbent Republican senators in 1952 were Stuart Symington of Missouri and Henry Jackson of Washington.

As a senator, Kennedy presented himself as a moderate liberal with strong anti-Communist credentials. His political views were a matter of calculation rather than ideology. When he had been invited to join the liberal Americans for Democratic Action in the forties, he had declined, because he suspected that membership would make advancement to high national office more difficult, even though he agreed with most of the organization's goals. Kennedy favored most liberal programs, including federal aid to education, but he made enemies out of the Catholic hierarchy by opposing aid to parochial schools. He knew that any Catholic who advocated such aid could not be nominated for president. Like organized labor, he had opposed the Taft-Hartley Act in 1947; he had generally supported labor's bills, but he demonstrated his moderate liberalism in the fifties by pushing a labor reform bill to end control of unions by the mob or by crooked union leaders like the Teamsters' Jimmy Hoffa. While Senator Kennedy served on the Senate Labor Committee, his brother Robert became the committee's leading staff member. By being prolabor but opposing union excesses, Kennedy could hope to gain labor support for the presidency without frightening the public.

Another example of Kennedy's moderate liberalism concerned his votes on civil rights. Like other Massachusetts politicians, he favored legislation, but on minor issues he voted for amendments that southerners offered to the 1957 Civil Rights Act. In particular, he voted that persons charged with violations of civil rights under the new law would have to be tried in federal court in a jury trial. At the time, white southerners believed that southern juries would invariably deny that any rights violation had occurred. In other words, the law would be nullified in practice. Most liberals strongly opposed the jury trial amendment, but Kennedy knew that without the amendment the Senate would be unable to break the southern filibuster and pass the bill. Kennedy's vote for the southern-backed jury trial amendment also sent a signal to white southerners that should he be president he would show some sympathy for their political position.

On foreign policy, Kennedy's anti-Communism was more pronounced than that of most liberals. In the early fifties he had not objected to the excesses of Senator Joseph R. McCarthy. "How could I demand that Joe McCarthy be censured for things he did," Kennedy later asked, "when my own brother was on his staff?" The Wisconsin senator was a family friend, and both Kennedy and McCarthy were staunch anti-Communists with hostility deeply rooted in Catholicism. Because of his religion, it was difficult to attack Kennedy as soft on Communism. The Senate censured McCarthy when Kennedy was in the hospital recovering from serious back surgery, and he was the only Senate Democrat who did not vote against McCarthy. Liberals like Eleanor Roosevelt were appalled. They saw Kennedy caving in to McCarthy's considerable popularity among Irish Catholics, especially in Massachusetts. Kennedy's refusal to acknowledge any error during the remainder of the decade only exacerbated the issue.[8]

Throughout the fifties, Kennedy was deeply concerned about Communism in the emerging Third World. In 1954, Kennedy visited Vietnam, just as the French were abandoning their colony. Three years later, the senator gave a speech favoring Algerian independence. This anticolonial speech insulted the government of France, an important ally; and Truman's former secretary of state, Dean Acheson, publicly attacked Kennedy. Not wishing to gain the powerful Acheson's permanent enmity, Kennedy beat a hasty retreat. To be elected in 1960, Kennedy knew that he needed the support of hard-liners like Acheson as well as softliners like Adlai Stevenson. The tension within the Democratic Party explains why so many of Kennedy's foreign policy statements during his presidential campaign employed Cold War rhetoric while avoiding specific details.

Joe Kennedy also demanded that his son marry a proper upper-class Catholic. In the early fifties, John Kennedy met Jacqueline Bouvier, a Washington journalist from a prominent Catholic family. Jackie's mother, Janet Lee Bouvier, had dumped Jackie's father to marry Hugh D. Auchincloss, an heir to the Standard Oil Company fortune. The Auchinclosses maintained two houses, Merrywood, the Virginia home that overlooked the Potomac River across from Washington, and Hammersmith Farm, at Newport, Rhode Island. Janet Auchincloss employed twenty-five live-in servants to maintain the summer place. Because Jackie was not heir to any Auchincloss money, she had to marry well, and Janet Auchincloss found Joe Kennedy's fortune adequate. Of Jack, Jackie said, "Of course, I don't like politics and he's a lot older than I am, but life will always be interesting with him, and then there's the money." In 1953 Jacqueline married Senator John Kennedy in a society wedding at Newport's small Catholic church. *Life* magazine covered the story.[9]

Kennedy had decided to run for president after the 1956 Democratic National Convention. Robert Kennedy had traveled with the Stevenson campaign to learn how to run a national operation, but Stevenson's ineptness had so disgusted Bobby that he voted for Eisenhower. After Stevenson's loss in November, the Kennedys began to make more serious plans. The day after Thanksgiving, Kennedy told his friend Dave Powers, "You know, if we work like hell the next four years, we will pick up all the marbles." Because party leaders resisted Kennedy's candidacy, his nomination depended upon his ability to generate personal popularity. The ambassador saw the issue as one of marketing. "We're going to sell Jack like soap flakes," he announced. Of the Kennedys, Gore Vidal observed, "They create illusions and call them facts." The key to this new kind of politics was image making, which Joe Kennedy had learned about in Hollywood and in promoting goods at the Merchandise Mart. Travel, personal contacts, speeches, media, and polls all mattered. Although Kennedy was not the first to hire a pollster, he used Louis Harris with unprecedented intensity and benefited from Harris's subtle, in-depth analyses of the public mood. In the past, candidates had bargained wholesale with state bosses; Kennedy cultivated individual delegates at retail. This new method required both a lot of money and a large, vigorous organization.[10]

For Kennedy, 1957 was a banner year. He was named to the Senate Foreign Relations Committee, won a Pulitzer Prize for *Profiles in*

Courage, and made the cover of *Time* magazine for the first time. Joe Kennedy used journalist Arthur Krock to boost his son for the Pulitzer and was said to have paid *Time* $75,000 for its cover. Connections and money could be artfully used to turn Kennedy into a celebrity, to groom him as if he were a film star. The buildup made him more exciting and appealing to Democrats he met and cultivated. All year, the senator, his aide Ted Sorensen, and youngest brother Ted Kennedy traveled around the country to meet local Democratic Party leaders. Kennedy kept all the details in his head. He had a "remarkable computer of a mind," recalled Walt Rostow. Occasionally, Jackie went along on these trips. Whenever she accompanied Jack, crowds doubled. Meanwhile, Joe Kennedy quietly cultivated Chicago mayor Richard Daley and the Bronx boss, Charles Buckley.[11]

Building an organization was a main task. In West Virginia, Kennedy met and recruited Bob McDonough, who later played a key role in that state's primary, and in Wyoming the senator signed up Teno Roncalio, whose delegates would put Kennedy over the top at the 1960 convention. In 1958 Kennedy hired Jerry Bruno, a brilliant advance man. For the next two years, he arranged Kennedy's public appearances and drummed up crowds. A bit later, Joe Kennedy decided to hire a top photographer. The still photographs would be used in campaign literature and for television commercials. Jacques Lowe of *Paris-Match,* then the world's best-designed magazine, joined the campaign. The journalist Hugh Sidey believed that Kennedy had assembled a far higher quality staff than had any other candidate. The purpose of all this effort was to allow the senator to meet as many influential Democrats as possible, as well as to showcase the senator, to promote his name, and to flood the public consciousness with his image.

One reason that it took a large team to promote Jack Kennedy was that the senator was complicated and even paradoxical. Lacking any coherent ideology, Kennedy tried to project an image calculated to appeal to different kinds of people. Like many politicians, he could be inscrutable, dodging a question with a question or a joke in order to avoid an answer. "He always had an escape hatch," noted the columnist Walter Lippmann. Even his staff often could not predict how he would vote in the Senate. The restlessness and easy boredom were readily apparent. "He was," said Pamela Turnure, "always in motion really." At times, Jackie Kennedy found it hard to keep up. "It was," she said later, "like being married to a whirlwind." Finding a staff able to organize and harness this human cyclone for a presidential campaign was no easy task.[12]

Senator Kennedy concluded that he could be nominated only by winning primaries. Although winning the dozen or so open primaries would gain some delegates, it would still not be enough to get the nomination. The purpose of running in the primaries, then, was not so much to gain delegates as to demonstrate electability. Kennedy had to prove to the party bosses who would control the convention that he would be able to run the best race of any Democrat. Many older bosses thought Kennedy, who would turn forty-three in 1960, too young and too inexperienced. Winning primaries would tend to neutralize those assessments. Also, older Democrats recalled Al Smith's painful humiliation in 1928. These party leaders, including many Catholic bosses, worried that a Catholic candidate would produce a horrendous backlash in the Bible Belt. Kennedy had to demonstrate in the primaries that he could both get Protestant votes and energize Catholics. Even if there was some loss of Protestant votes, he wanted to show that a big pro-Kennedy Catholic vote might tip several states into the Democratic column. "The only issue," Joe Kennedy had declared, "is whether a Catholic can be elected president." The primaries could prove the claims made in the Bailey memo at the 1956 convention.[13]

For a while, Kennedy's quiet campaign did not get much attention from rivals. However, in late 1958, party activist and Johnson confidante India Edwards warned Humphrey's friend Eugenie Anderson, "I hear on good authority that Kennedy has people on the road, already lining up delegates. So Humphrey ought to get busy." She added, "It is frightening what they are doing. Unlimited wealth can be mighty ugly, as you know." Kennedy's television appearances at the 1956 Democratic National Convention were remembered, and he easily brought out the party faithful to fund-raisers, where he met past and future delegates. In 1959 he received more than 10,000 speaking invitations, twice the number Humphrey did. One major challenge was to book the senator into states where he could build support and get maximum positive publicity. In June 1959 Ohio governor Michael DiSalle privately pledged to Kennedy. DiSalle had little choice, after Kennedy, citing a private poll, threatened to oppose and demolish the governor if DiSalle ran in the Ohio presidential primary. When Humphrey later asked DiSalle for support, the governor said that he was already committed. Humphrey told DiSalle,

"I'll be back to see you after I beat Kennedy in Wisconsin and West Virginia."[14]

Family money eased the way to the nomination in so many ways. In 1959 Joe Kennedy arranged for the family to buy the senator a $385,000 jet turboprop Convair, to avoid the bumpy roads that were hard on his back and to reach destinations quickly. The plane, reconfigured from forty-four seats to eighteen seats, plus a private cabin for Kennedy, was eventually named the *Caroline*, in honor of Kennedy's daughter. As Kennedy continued to travel, he kept a data bank of information on the political situation in every state inside his own head. At an important staff meeting in October 1959, he spent several hours running down the precise situation in each state without using a single note. Despite his successful travels, Kennedy's candidacy had little support on Capitol Hill. Speaker Sam Rayburn, contemptuous of Kennedy as a rich playboy and fearful of an anti-Catholic backlash, was vehemently opposed, and as of April 1960, only two senators, Henry Jackson and Edmund Muskie, had endorsed Kennedy.

Although Kennedy spent a lot of time cultivating Democrats in California, the reception was mixed. The senator puzzled over the state's weak party structure, lack of patronage, and extreme factionalism as well as the presence of the California Democratic Clubs. These clubs of liberal volunteers ran campaigns in the absence of a strong party organization. Tension existed between the clubs and elected officials, especially Assembly Speaker Jesse Unruh. Unruh's early enthusiasm for Kennedy made it harder for Kennedy to appeal to club members, whose hearts still throbbed for Adlai Stevenson. The Kennedys asked Governor Pat Brown to organize a pro-Kennedy slate of delegates formally pledged to Brown so that Kennedy could skip a competitive California primary. In late summer 1959, Brown, pressured just as DiSalle had been, privately agreed to this plan, but he lacked the power to name only Kennedy supporters to the delegation.

In early 1960, banker Bart Lytton, a Democratic fund-raiser who was not privy to Kennedy's deal with Brown, asked Kennedy if he had enough money to enter the California primary. Kennedy replied that money was no problem. Lytton said, "Don't you ever say that again if you want to win an election." Kennedy was puzzled, and Lytton added, "The very thing that stands in your way, if you want to make it, is the feeling that you can buy the election. You must *never* have enough money." Lytton pointed out that a person could influence a candidate only with votes or with money. Lytton concluded, "You can't win the nomination if the belief is you have enough money to win by yourself because you have foreclosed a large part of the leadership from feeling they have any access to you. They must feel that they've at least bought your ear." Kennedy quickly grasped the point.[15]

Kennedy's campaign in Wisconsin in the spring of 1960 resembled Allied saturation bombing in World War II. Perhaps the resemblance was due to the fact that so many veterans were involved in the campaign. Organization was superb, and nothing was left to chance. Every possibility was examined and then handled in a way to advance the effort. Kennedy regarded Wisconsin as crucial. It was the first contested primary, and national media attention was intense. If Kennedy won decisively in a state next to Humphrey's own Minnesota, it would force Humphrey to quit. Conversely, if Kennedy lost, he might be dismissed as strictly a New England candidate. No effort was to be spared, since knocking Humphrey out early would free the candidate and resources for the nonprimary states. It was important to keep local unions from helping Humphrey. Many union leaders favored Humphrey, but they found it hard to oppose members who wanted Kennedy.

Because Kennedy had to visit other states, he limited his own campaigning in Wisconsin and instead used many surrogates. As an example of thorough organization, a member of the Kennedy family visited every place in Wisconsin that had at least 300 people. And so they came, brothers Robert and Ted, sisters Eunice, Patricia, and Jean, as well as Joe and Rose, Jackie, and in-laws Sargent Shriver and Peter Lawford, the Hollywood star who was married to Pat. Humphrey said, "I feel like an independent merchant competing against a chain store." But Kennedy as a campaigner should not be underestimated. Thriving on long hours and little sleep, he enjoyed meeting new people. After shaking hands before dawn at a factory when it was 15 degrees below zero, Kennedy had a scratched and swollen hand. He drank coffee out of a paper cup in a cheap café and cheerfully told his friend Dave Powers, "You know, Dave, they have pretty good coffee here, don't they?"[16]

The two campaigns contrasted painfully. While Humphrey slowly bumped around the state in a bus with a broken heater, which annoyed reporters accompanying the candidate, Kennedy quickly glided aloft in his plane. The press was served hot meals, while Kennedy, subject to a sensitive stomach, ate his favorite tomato soup. In addition, Kennedy set up headquarters in eight of the state's ten congressional districts.

John Kennedy campaigned one-on-one in Wisconsin.
(Wisconsin Historical Society, Madison, Image ID 27843)

Humphrey had only a dysfunctional headquarters in Milwaukee, a volunteer office in Madison, and Minnesota volunteers who operated in the districts closest to Minnesota. Kennedy had paid professional staff; Humphrey's press aide was his nineteen-year-old son-in-law. Kennedy's staff kept the press happy by not losing their luggage, by serving cold martinis at the end of the day, and by handing out well-crafted press releases; reporters had to puzzle through Humphrey's clumsy handouts. Kennedy's staff members were coldly rational; Humphrey's were idealistic, liberal, and mediocre.

Kennedy may have spent more on office rent and brochures alone than Humphrey spent on his entire Wisconsin campaign. Finally, Kennedy bought a lot of TV and radio time. Altogether, Humphrey spent $150,000 in Wisconsin; Kennedy spent about twice that much. More important than the amount was the savvy way in which the Kennedys used money. They flooded the press with stories that stressed Kennedy's glamour and ignored his mediocre Senate record. To neutralize the agricultural issue, which was Humphrey's greatest advantage, Kennedy announced a bold, new agricultural initiative, and Humphrey faced reporters asking about Kennedy's new program and ignoring Humphrey's distinguished record in the field. All the Kennedy propaganda contained the same underlying message: "Kennedy can win, Humphrey can't." Building excitement and a glamorous image, routine work for a budding film star, was a major part of the Kennedy effort. An exasperated Humphrey said, "We're not in American politics to select a lead star for Hollywood drama." In a more irritable moment, Hubert announced, "Mink never wore so well."[17]

Humphrey could scarcely believe how the Kennedys manipulated the press. Annoyed by a newspaper story that ignored Humphrey, the Minnesotan wrote, "This Kennedy has the damnedest public relations I have ever seen in my life. Does he own all the newspapers or does he have something on every publisher?" In fact, the ties between the Kennedy family and the media were thick and deep. Ever since Joe Kennedy's days as a film producer, he had cultivated publishers in order to get good reviews of his films in their papers. In the 1930s, Kennedy had helped William Randolph Hearst avoid bankruptcy, and the Hearsts had remained sympathetic to their fellow Catholics in a mostly Protestant upper-class world. Jack Kennedy worked as a Hearst reporter covering the founding of the United Nations in San Francisco in 1945, and a year later, when Kennedy ran for Congress, Hearst's *Boston American* refused to cover his opponents or accept their paid advertising. Although Henry Luce, the publisher of *Time* and *Life*, was a Republican, he was also friendly with Joe Kennedy, whose liquor advertising had helped keep the magazines afloat in the lean thirties. Joe Kennedy aided favorite reporters and columnists, too. Arthur Krock, a family friend, received lavish gifts, paid vacations, and, on at least one occasion, $25,000, considerably more than his annual *New York Times* salary, to tout the family in his syndicated column.[18]

Because Jack Kennedy had worked as a reporter, he knew the needs of the press. Personal friends included Phil Graham, publisher of the *Washington Post* and companion in chasing women; Ben Bradlee, a *Newsweek* editor and Georgetown neighbor; Charlie Bartlett, Washington correspondent for the *Chattanooga Times* and wealthy socialite neighbor of the Kennedys in Palm Beach; and Joe Alsop, influential syndicated columnist. The *New York Times* gave major play to Kennedy's National Press Club speech but did not report on Humphrey's. The negligent reporter was James Reston, whom Humphrey accused of "obvious favoritism." The *Times* often slighted Humphrey in its coverage, providing only bare wire service copy. The Kennedys had many informal ties to the *Times*, including the fact that future publisher Arthur Ochs Sulzberger had been John Kennedy's classmate.[19]

Considering the disparity in resources, the results in Wisconsin disappointed Kennedy. Winning 56 percent of the overall vote, 474,024 to 366,753, he carried only six of the ten congressional districts. The victor calmly said, "It means that we have to do it all over again." Kennedy had a huge margin in Milwaukee's two districts and in two districts in the Fox River Valley, Joe McCarthy's old stronghold near Green Bay. All four districts were strongly Catholic. Careful inspection of the returns suggested that thousands of Catholic Republicans in these areas had voted for Kennedy. (Wisconsin had an open primary, and Nixon was unopposed on the Republican side of the ballot; Nixon won fewer votes than Humphrey.) Whether Catholic Republicans would stick with Kennedy in the fall was unclear.[20]

At the same time, the Minnesotan had easily carried three rural western areas whose residents were predominantly Scandinavian Lutheran. And Humphrey beat Kennedy two-to-one in three black wards in Milwaukee. Although Kennedy was disappointed, he was much better off than Humphrey. The Minnesotan should have realized that losing his neighboring state marked the end of his presidential bid. Without solid support from the Midwest, his candidacy was doomed. Furthermore, the two-to-one drubbing that union enthusiast Humphrey took in Milwaukee's solidly blue-collar Polish Catholic fourth congressional district showed a strong working-class preference for Kennedy that the Democratic Party could not ignore.

On election night, Humphrey was tired and angry. "Poor Hubert never knew what hit him," observed Senator Barry Goldwater. Resentful of Kennedy's money and campaign organization, Humphrey chose to see hope in the returns. Carrying four districts, with a narrow loss in a fifth, was not a bad performance. In addition, Humphrey felt that Kennedy had played dirty with the religious issue. Protestants were told that they were bigots if they voted for Humphrey, and Catholics were told that they could elect a Catholic president. Humphrey could scarcely imagine anyone using religion in a political campaign, but anti-Catholic leaflets suddenly had appeared in Wisconsin, a state where that sort of thing had seldom if ever been employed. There was suspicion in Humphrey's camp that the Kennedys were responsible for mailing these materials to Catholic voters, in order to drive up the vote for Kennedy. In fact, later, a Kennedy volunteer from Massachusetts was found to have mailed some of the offensive items. He quickly disappeared from the campaign, and it was never determined whether he had acted on his own or on orders.[21]

It was largely because of the way the religious issue had been played that Humphrey decided, against the advice of most of his staff, to continue into the West Virginia primary. Very well, he thought, if the Kennedys want to play religious politics by beating me with cheap political tricks designed to gain Catholic votes in a heavily Catholic state like Wisconsin, we will go on to West Virginia, where the United Mine Workers will be with us, and where there are so few Catholics that Kennedy's gutter politics will fail spectacularly. Never has a tired candidate so completely outfoxed himself.

The Kennedys, master deceivers and manipulators, had prepared a wonderful trap for Humphrey in West Virginia. It was true that the state had many Protestants, and if the Kennedys had been certain that West Virginians were bigots who would never vote for a Catholic, they would have avoided the state like the plague. But Al Smith, a Catholic, had won the state's Democratic primary in 1928, and the Kennedys knew a lot more about West Virginia than Hubert Humphrey did. They knew more because for two years they had made it their business to learn all about this state. Again, organization made a difference. The most important fact about religion in West Virginia was that a majority of its residents had no religion. Although Baptist and Methodist ministers might stir up their congregations, anti-Catholicism was not too likely among the nonreligious majority.[22]

Furthermore, primary elections depend upon intensity, and West Virginia's small Catholic population, generally estimated at about 5 percent, might be useful to the Kennedy campaign. Kennedy's effective state organizer, Bob McDonough, was a Catholic businessman, a nonunion printer who had been drawn to the campaign by the candidate's religion, as were a good many other Kennedy volunteers. Those who had no religion were also less likely to be registered to vote: Catholics might have made up 7 percent of the electorate. Close to 40 percent of the state's voters were Republicans, whose ancestors had almost all been unionists in the Civil War. Catholics had mostly been post–Civil War immigrants, often Irish immigrants drawn to the coal mines. Thus, few Catholics in West Virginia in 1960 were Republicans. Unlike Wisconsin, West Virginia had a closed primary, and Catholics might have made up as many as 11 percent of registered Democrats. In the primary, Catholics felt a strong urge to vote for Kennedy; Protestants, especially conservatives who did not like either Kennedy or Humphrey, simply did not vote. Catholics might have been more than 15 percent of the primary vote. Three-fourths of Kennedy's margin of victory may have come from Catholic votes. There is no way to tell, because no exit polling analysis was undertaken.[23]

On the surface, the West Virginia campaign was almost entirely about religion. Early on, Kennedy found that residents wanted him to talk about the issue, and he did so, over objections of many on his staff. Protestant ministers denounced Kennedy, and anti-Catholic hate propaganda was widely distributed. Unlike in Wisconsin, this time there was no suspicion that Kennedy was behind the literature. "I am not the Catholic candidate for president," Kennedy declared. West Virginians admired his decision to fight back, and Kennedy's pointing out that no one had asked his brother Joe his religion in World War II did much to undercut the bigotry. The senator argued that the locals could show that they opposed bigotry by voting for him.[24]

Humphrey, like Richard Nixon in the fall, found the religious issue paralyzing. An exasperated Humphrey wrote *Washington Post* reporter Chalmers Roberts, "Apparently it is perfectly okay for every person of the Catholic faith to vote for Kennedy, but if a Protestant votes for me then he is a bigot." Roberts later conceded that reporters, including Roberts, had parroted the Kennedy line, which was another example of Kennedy's successful manipulation of the press. In his memoir, the reporter cited Kennedy's charm. Any comment Humphrey made lost votes, and the national media's incessant focus on religion prevented the Minnesotan from discussing the economic issues that were at the core of his campaign. Humphrey was heartsick. This was not the campaign he wanted to run. In fact, almost nothing went right. The labor help that he expected did not materialize. West Virginia union leaders told Humphrey of pressure from national offices in Washington to remain neutral. Labor wanted to win in November, and Kennedy looked like a winner. Humphrey did not. Even if Humphrey won West Virginia, he would still not be the nominee. It would merely eliminate Kennedy and lead to the nomination of either Symington or Johnson. Union leaders lacked enthusiasm for Symington and were afraid of Johnson.[25]

Humphrey discovered in West Virginia that his New York donors would give no more money. One of them, Bill Benton, explained why. The Kennedys had made it clear that any further contributions to Humphrey would be considered an act of war, and such an act would mean that after the Kennedys won the presidency, the donor would be treated as a permanent enemy. The Kennedys saturated the state with radio and TV ads, staffed local offices with volunteers who mailed campaign literature, and delivered suitcases of cash to county bosses in return for getting out the vote for Kennedy on Election Day. Humphrey had spent all his money in Wisconsin and could not compete. At the end of the campaign, a TV station demanded cash in advance from the strapped senator before he could go on the air for a paid broadcast, and when told by a staffer that there was no money to pay for the ad, Humphrey wrote a personal check for $750 to cover the cost. Muriel was aghast because the money was needed for their daughter's wedding, which was to take place the next week.

In addition to Kennedy's limitless money and superb organization, Humphrey faced Kennedy's dirt. The cruelest and most despicable trick played upon Humphrey in West Virginia came at the hands of his old Americans for Democratic Action friend, Franklin Roosevelt Jr. Ever since the 1930s, the Roosevelt name had had special magic in West Virginia. In many primitive cabins and mining shacks there could be found just two cheap magazine or newspaper pictures hung on the wall: John L. Lewis, founder of the United Mine Workers, and Franklin Roosevelt.

Bob McDonough had told the Kennedy organization about the special appeal of the Roosevelt name, and the Kennedys brought Franklin Roosevelt Jr. into the state to campaign with the senator. This joint campaigning helped dampen the anti-Catholic issue, and the crowds were larger whenever young Frank Roosevelt accompanied John Kennedy. Humphrey was disappointed that he did not enjoy Frank's support, but he could take solace in the fact that he enjoyed the enthusiastic backing of Frank's important and powerful mother, Eleanor Roosevelt.

Then the Kennedys played their trick on both Frank and Hubert. Young Roosevelt was handed a speech that charged, in effect, that Humphrey had been a draft dodger in World War II. Roosevelt balked, refusing to say anything so mean, nasty, and untrue about his good friend Hubert Humphrey. Robert Kennedy put heavy pressure on Frank Roosevelt to make the charge, and Roosevelt, rumored to be financially strapped, finally agreed to make the false charge. He did so not once but several times, ignoring Humphrey's back-channel pleas to stop, not out of the callousness that Humphrey felt but caught in the Kennedys' determination to use the draft-dodging charge to destroy Humphrey in proud and patriotic West Virginia. After the damage had been done, John Kennedy sanctimoniously disavowed Roosevelt's slur. The ploy worked, but Roosevelt's role ruined his political future, and Humphrey, who eventually learned the whole story, permanently avoided political dealings with the Kennedys.[26]

Both Humphrey and Kennedy knew that in certain counties in West Virginia, especially in the coal mining counties south of Charleston, it was traditional to pay county bosses for presidential candidates to be put on the boss's slate on primary Election Day. The standard rate had been two or three dollars per vote, and the bosses justified the charges because many voters lacked cars and had to be driven to the polls. The boss also had to pay the poll workers who made sure that the voters actually voted. Some voters expected to be paid in cash or in whiskey. Humphrey had bought one county, but a couple of days before the election he had his money returned to him in a satchel in a men's room because the Kennedys had offered more money. In another county, the price was rumored to have reached ten dollars per vote.

Humphrey spent no more than $30,000 in the state. West Virginia television was cheap: Humphrey paid $2,000 and Kennedy paid $34,000. Overall, the Kennedys spent much, much more than Humphrey. Official estimates for the Kennedy campaign ranged from $200,000 to

$400,000, but one private estimate ran as high as $4 million, which included the value of unpaid time for all the volunteers. Perhaps a more realistic estimate would be $1.5 to 2.5 million. About $150,000 went to Charleston, which was won narrowly; $100,000 was spent in Huntington, which was lost. About $100,000 went to Logan County, considered to be among the most corrupt. The campaign thus spent $350,000 for just three counties, and the state had fifty-five counties. One Kennedy operative who managed only part of one county recalled years later that he received $60,000 in cash from a courier from Boston. Another minor operative wanted $3,500, asked for "35," and got $35,000. In addition to slating, much of the money was used to make contributions to Protestant churches, especially black churches. Unlike in Wisconsin, Kennedy won the small African American vote in West Virginia. Joe Kennedy and Cardinal Cushing in Boston jointly decided which preachers would get $500 and which $1,000. Cushing gave Joe Kennedy $950,000 cash from the diocese's Sunday collection plates, and in return Kennedy wrote a tax deductible check to the church for $1 million.[27]

The Kennedys were able to keep stories about the vast sums of money and West Virginia's corruption out of the media. Money, it appeared, could buy votes and manipulate the press into silence. One enterprising reporter for the *Baltimore Sun* wrote an excellent account of the vote buying that he had personally witnessed. He assumed that the story would run on page one but was surprised to find only a watered-down version in the paper. The independent, family-owned, and undercapitalized *Sun* could not afford to take on the powerful Kennedys. At the time, Baltimore had a pair of competing newspapers owned by the wealthy and privately held Hearst Corporation. There had long been ties between the Hearsts and the Kennedys, and the *Sun* could not at that time risk a newspaper war. Publishers had to be alert. Years later, the Republican *Boston Herald Traveler* was involved in a television license scandal. The publisher suspected that the paper's corporate counsel had set it up. It was ruined financially and closed, and the Kennedy-oriented *Boston Globe* became dominant.

After the Hearst gossip columnist Igor Cassini irritated the Kennedys, Cassini was indicted on an unrelated matter and had his column killed. "You never crossed the Kennedys twice," he observed. The *Washington Post* sent a pro-Kennedy reporter to West Virginia who found no evidence of any vote buying. When an infuriated Humphrey saw the story, he denounced it as a "whitewash." In a later oral history interview, the reporter who had written the story declared that Kennedy was "the most brilliant president of all time." Among the few stories to make it into print was one in the *Pittsburgh Post-Gazette*, but the national press was not interested in circulating it. In his memoir, journalist David Brinkley denied that there was any vote buying, but in an interview that he later did for a documentary film on the 1960 election he claimed that he had personally witnessed money being exchanged for votes.[28]

The irony is that Kennedy might have won, although with a smaller margin, even without these huge expenditures and without the Franklin Roosevelt draft-dodging smear. Organizational superiority mattered. Kennedy had eight headquarters with fifty high-level volunteers; Humphrey had one headquarters with ten volunteers. Copying the 1952 Senate campaign, Kennedy promoted inclusiveness by using college and navy friends to organize local residents. On Election Day, 9,000 volunteers worked for Kennedy. The large numbers suggested popularity and predicted victory, creating a bandwagon effect. The Massachusetts senator also exuded confidence and charm. One miner asked Kennedy, "Is it true that you've never done a day's work with your hands all your life?" The candidate admitted it was so. Far from being jealous, the miner declared, "You haven't missed a thing." Unlike Humphrey, Kennedy went into deep coal mines several times, and his serious questions convinced the miners that he was truly interested in their industry and its problems.[29]

Most important, Kennedy was brilliant on his frequent West Virginia TV appearances. In the one joint debate staged in Charleston shortly before the primary and carried live on a statewide hookup, Kennedy was crisp and to the point, lamenting West Virginia poverty, which seemed to have touched him personally. He pledged that if he won the White House he would try to reverse the state's downward economic slide. To dramatize the problem, Kennedy brought to the studio some stage props—small amounts of food, which he placed in front of himself in the camera's eye. These items, he said, represented the amount of food aid that a poor family could expect in one month under existing federal programs. He promised to provide more food. Privately, Humphrey marveled, "This guy thinks of *everything*." In contrast, the garrulous Humphrey unleashed a torrent of words, but it all seemed muddled and ineffective. One station in Washington carried the debate, and those who saw it in the nation's capital agreed that Kennedy had struck a knockout blow.[30]

On election night, Kennedy won, 236,510 to 152,187. Humphrey withdrew from the presidential contest, but he did not endorse his rival. After Jack Kennedy gave a victory speech in Charleston, Robert Kennedy visited Hubert Humphrey at his headquarters. Both Hubert and Muriel went icy as the organizer of the draft-dodging slur crossed the room. Bobby shook hands with Hubert and, to show friendliness, kissed Muriel on the cheek. Muriel fled into another room in tears, later telling her husband that it was all she could do not to sock the insolent Bobby. Robert Kennedy had a knack for doing exactly the wrong thing where other people's feelings were concerned. Joe Kennedy boasted, "Bobby's hard as nails." Hubert agreed to accompany Bobby on a visit to the Kennedy headquarters. It was important for the underlings to see that the Democrats would be united for the fall campaign. Muriel never forgave Bobby, and months later, when overtures were made to Humphrey to run as Kennedy's vice president, Muriel vetoed it. She had no intention of being caught in the Kennedy spiderweb ever again.[31]

Kennedy and Humphrey had competed in the primaries because they had no choice. Only by winning such elections did either have a chance of being nominated, but most politicians in 1960 did not consider the primary route as a plausible way to a nomination. Theodore Roosevelt, a former president, had lost the nomination after winning all except one of the Republican primaries in 1912. Estes Kefauver had been passed over after winning most of the Democratic primaries in 1952. Conventional wisdom was that winning primaries did not guarantee a nomination, but losing just one primary might knock a candidate out of the competition. And primaries posed other problems. If more than one candidate ran, a primary was inordinately expensive. Since few candidates had the money to run in more than one or two contested races, and since one or two victories would mean little in the overall pattern of delegate selection leading up to the national convention, there was not much to be gained by entering such a contest.

One candidate who had skipped the primaries was Missouri senator Stuart Symington, whose candidacy was rooted in the fact that he had steered a cautious political path that made him agreeable to all party factions. From a prominent Maryland family, he retained ties there and in the Northeast. Born in 1901, he was an Episcopalian, had graduated from Yale College, and had married Eve Wadsworth, whose family had significant money. A St. Louis businessman and World War II defense contractor, Symington in 1947 became Truman's first secretary of the

U.S. Air Force, a post that led him to become a fan of big bombers. In 1952 he was elected to the Senate from Missouri. Overwhelmingly reelected in 1958, he ran for president in 1960 with Truman's encouragement. His main issue was the Missile Gap, and he promised a tough foreign policy.

Symington's candidacy faced problems. About one-fifth of Democratic county chairs supported him on the grounds that all factions could accept him, but polls consistently found that only 5 to 7 percent of Democratic voters favored him. No matter how hard he campaigned, he was unable to rise in the polls, even though he did generate news coverage. Journalist Robert Novak wrote that his campaign had a "somnambulistic air." Long before the primary season was over, many reporters had written Symington off as a blowhard and a single-issue candidate, that of the Missile Gap, whose tall stature, good looks, excellent grooming, and expensive tailored suits constituted a facade behind which was nothing of consequence. Both Joe and Stewart Alsop found him too shallow to be president. To Ben Bradlee, Symington wanted "to be all things to all men." William White thought the senator "evasive," judged his work "not in the first rank," and detected a "less than average willingness to get hurt." Kyle Palmer, the political reporter for the Republican *Los Angeles Times*, wrote both accurately and cruelly that Symington's candidacy was like "an airplane buzzing up and down a runway, but never getting up enough power to leave the ground."[32]

Another "reluctant" presidential contender in 1960 was Lyndon Baines Johnson, who also declined to enter any primaries. Born in 1908, Johnson had grown up amid rural poverty in a dry area west of Austin. Raised in the Disciples of Christ church, he had been influenced by his father, a Populist dreamer and sometime Democratic state legislator. At Southwest Texas State Teachers College, Johnson talked his way into a part-time job as the president's assistant. All his life, Lyndon rose by cultivating powerful people. For a time he taught school in the Rio Grande Valley on the Mexican border, where most children were very poor. His lifelong interest in poverty and education and awareness of racism dated from that stint. In 1937 he won a House seat in a special election. A New Dealer, he emphasized building dams and developing rural electric power. After narrowly losing a special election to the U.S. Senate in 1941, Johnson served briefly during World War II as a U.S. Navy reservist. In 1948 he won a Senate seat by a controversial 87 votes.

*Stuart Symington and Harry Truman met fans in Missouri in
1959. (Harry S. Truman Library, Independence, Missouri)*

In 1953, with strong support from the shrewd Georgia senator Richard Russell, Johnson became the Democratic leader, and after the Democrats regained control of the Senate in 1955, he became the majority leader. In the fifties, Lyndon Johnson dominated politics, and Lady Bird Johnson, a formidable politician in her own right, cultivated senators' wives. Johnson's relationship with House Speaker Sam Rayburn mattered, as did the tie to Senator Richard Russell, the leader of nearly twenty southern Democrats, many of them powerful chairs with decades of seniority. Almost every weekend, Russell, a bachelor, dined with the Johnsons. The Senate's internal politics also favored Johnson. To control the Democratic caucus, southerners routinely traded votes with about a dozen senators from the Mountain West. Both regions were rural and conservative. The westerners wanted dams, and the southerners needed to protect anti–civil rights filibusters. Because these lightly populated western states had few African Americans, their senators were free to make the trade. As a Texan, Johnson pivoted between the two blocs, sometimes emphasizing the southern aspect and sometimes the western.

Oil and gas bound Johnson to both regions. Louisiana, Texas, Oklahoma, Mississippi, New Mexico, Colorado, Wyoming, and Montana had oil and gas. In all of these states, there was pressure to keep the oil depletion allowance, which allowed anyone connected to oil to pay substantially lower income taxes. After being elected to the Senate in 1948, Johnson drew close to the oil industry, which was essential to his remaining in the Senate. Oil money fueled political campaigns not only in the oil states. For Democrats, political funds were always a problem. Southern Democrats who had seniority rarely had opposition, but outside the South, Democrats had trouble raising campaign funds. Most local businessmen were Republicans, and unions gave money only in states where they were strong. To compete, Democrats had to find out-of-state money. Democrats' money came from New York liberals, Hollywood, or the oil patch, which had its share of Democratic millionaires. Johnson's management of the Senate was designed to keep oil money flowing to Democrats outside the South, who often faced expensive, tough races.

Lyndon Johnson made deals with President Eisenhower and became the foremost legislator in the country. An activist by temperament, Johnson believed deeply that the purpose of government was to pass legislation to solve problems. But Johnson suffered a massive heart attack in 1955, and his recovery was slow. The heart attack as well as the inevitability of Ike's reelection left Johnson disinterested in running for president in 1956. Johnson's influence inside the Senate was enormous. He understood the political forces that operated on each senator better than many of these senators themselves did, his timing in bringing up bills was impeccable, and his ability to be persuasive one-on-one was unsurpassed. Johnson was famous for his physical approach to persuasion, which was known as the Treatment. Senator Frank Church recalled, "He would pick you up and wrap his arms around you and just squeeze all the air out." Johnson was more liberal than most people realized. Among the few to know the truth were Humphrey and Humphrey's friend Mary Lasker. When Lasker told Eleanor Roosevelt that Johnson was a "secret liberal," Mrs. Roosevelt said, "You're crazy."[33]

No one doubted Johnson's desire to be president. By 1959 his long-time friend and fellow Texan, House Speaker Sam Rayburn, was urging Johnson to run in 1960. Rayburn worried that a northern liberal Democrat would lose to Nixon. Both Rayburn and Johnson felt confident that Johnson could beat Nixon. The problem was that there was no clear route to Johnson's nomination. In 1960 Texas was still considered to be a southern state, and no southerner had been nominated for president since the Civil War. To overcome the southern problem, Johnson throughout the fifties presented himself as a westerner, by giving ten-gallon hats to friends and by constantly talking about his ranch. Visits to the LBJ Ranch were memorable. The senator gave tours to visitors by driving a Lincoln convertible across the property at speeds up to ninety miles an hour. One journalist whispered to another, "This will be a great story but we won't be alive to write it." During deer season, a guest was expected to hunt with Johnson. When Bobby Kennedy's rifle recoiled hard and knocked him to the ground, Johnson said, "Son, you've got to learn how to handle a gun like a man."[34]

Although Johnson could go to the convention with solid support from the South's nearly 30 percent of the total delegates, such support would be his only support unless he could show strength in other parts of the nation. As a Texan, he had been forced to support the Taft-Hartley Act in 1947, and labor vehemently opposed his candidacy. He could get no support from any state where unions were strong. To compete, Johnson needed the 128 delegate votes from the Mountain West. These eight states did not have primaries, and Johnson hoped to corral their delegates using his friendships with the Democratic senators from those states. Such support would enable Johnson to call himself a western candidate, and when those votes were added to his southern base, he might go into the convention with about the same number of votes that Kennedy had. Johnson could then prod party bosses to pick a Johnson-Kennedy ticket. All during 1959 Sam Rayburn urged Johnson to signal to supporters that he planned to run, but Johnson declined.

When Jim Rowe, Johnson's friend since the 1930s, a political confidant, and one of the wisest political operatives in Washington, asked to be allowed to put together an organization on behalf of Johnson's candidacy, the Texan refused. Subsequently, Rowe asked Johnson for permission to work for Hubert Humphrey, Rowe's second choice for the nomination. Johnson said yes. Others saw another motive at work. "The Humphrey camp is just a front for Johnson," concluded an irritated Kennedy. "All over the country," conceded liberal Humphrey supporter Joe Rauh, "the Kennedy boys are saying Hubert is too close to Johnson." The majority leader knew that Humphrey's liberalism and strong civil rights views meant that he would never be nominated by a party that needed to carry southern states. So if Humphrey beat Kennedy in the primaries, Johnson would be the beneficiary, and if Kennedy forced Humphrey out, then Rowe could return to work for Johnson. In resisting an open candidacy, Johnson may have had more than one motive. In any case, Johnson's inaction annoyed Rayburn, who declared, "He ought to shit or get off the pot."[35]

Finally, in the spring of 1960, Johnson decided that he had to take a more active role. He spoke with Boston congressman Tip O'Neill, who was not part of the Kennedy faction in Massachusetts politics. Recognizing that O'Neill had to back Kennedy on the first ballot, Johnson asked for support on the second ballot. O'Neill said that Kennedy would win on the first ballot. Johnson insisted, "You *know* the boy can't win." Claiming there would be no second ballot, O'Neill explained, "You don't know the strength they have. You don't know how quickly they can move. And you have never seen money work the way the Kennedys know how to work it. They don't get into fights they can't win." Johnson replied, "Come on, Tip, you know better than that. That boy is going to die on the vine." Far too late, Johnson began to make calls, give speeches, and visit states where he might get support, but the effort was underfinanced and poorly organized.[36]

Everywhere that Johnson went in the Mountain West he found that the Kennedys had been there first. Wyoming party chair Teno Roncalio, who favored Kennedy, lined up some delegates after Sorensen visited in 1958. Ted Kennedy visited the state seven times in 1960, when ten delegate votes were locked up. Had Johnson visited the state earlier and simply ridden on a horse, he might have rallied Wyoming's powerful ranching and oil interests behind his own candidacy. Colorado's former Democratic senator Edwin Johnson supported Johnson, but Byron White, a young Denver attorney and lifelong Kennedy personal friend, had organized a citizens' movement that resulted in 10 of 21 votes for Kennedy. (At the convention Kennedy got 13.5.) In New Mexico, Johnson had assumed that Senator Clinton Anderson, plus the importance of ranching and oil, would give Johnson all that state's delegates. But Kennedy was popular with the state's Catholics, he attended the state convention, and the delegate count split—Johnson received 13, and Kennedy got 4.

In Arizona, young congressman Stewart Udall quietly packed the county conventions and state convention with Kennedy enthusiasts and stole the delegation from former senator Ernest McFarland, who favored Johnson, before McFarland noticed what was happening. Udall then imposed the unit rule to give Kennedy all 17 votes. In Montana, Ted Kennedy won votes by staying on a bronco for five seconds. He also won a half vote in Utah by personally visiting the delegate, who lived in a remote spot. The local airport was fogged in, and Ted landed his small plane in the middle of a road. Because of Kennedy's early start and superior organization, Kennedy won 79 delegate votes from the Mountain West, even though the region was intrinsically far more oriented to Johnson than to Kennedy. Johnson ended up with only 29 votes. At the Democratic National Convention, Idaho's Frank Church shocked Johnson by announcing for Kennedy, whom he considered most able to win in November. Johnson privately complained to some Idaho delegates, "Who does that little pipsqueak think he is? After all, I made him and now he's biting the hand that fed him."[37]

Adlai Stevenson, born in 1900, had mixed feelings about running for president a third time. Having been the party's sacrificial lamb against Eisenhower twice, he confidently believed that he could defeat Nixon. "Yes," he admitted to a friend, "I confess 'I do have a taste a little in my mouth.' But I also have distasteful memories in my head!" The ambivalence was genuine. Already a global superstar, Stevenson had easy access to persons of wealth and power, frequent opportunity to offer public comments, and no responsibilities. In 1959 he summered in England, and the first few days of his trip exemplify Stevenson's comfortable upperclass lifestyle. After spending the night at the country estate of a duke and duchess, he lunched with his good friend, novelist John Steinbeck, toured Stonehenge, and dined with actress Lauren Bacall. The next day he lunched with the Duchess of Kent, the Queen's aunt, at Kensington Palace and then watched tennis from the royal box at Wimbledon. Is it surprising that Stevenson was reluctant to run for president? If the presidency came calling, fine, but otherwise he was content with life.[38]

A realist, Stevenson doubted that party leaders would turn to him a third time. Still, if the convention deadlocked, he was available. "If the party wants me," he said, "they can have me." (Longtime supporter George Ball said, "He's waiting to be raped.") Like Symington, the Illinoisan was acceptable to various party factions. More important, Stevenson enjoyed popularity that Symington lacked. Polls showed that he ran second only to Kennedy among Democrats and retained the keen support of intellectuals. "He is still the thinking man's candidate," wrote journalist Mary McGrory. He enjoyed excellent relations with a host of major party donors, including Agnes Meyer of the *Washington Post* and Alicia Patterson of *Newsday*.[39]

In February, as the primary season began, Stevenson made a month-long fact-finding trip to South America. The trip highlighted Stevenson's keen interest in foreign affairs and generated a lot of news. His decency and the affection with which he was greeted contrasted sharply with the riots that Richard Nixon had faced on a trip to the region in 1958. "Beautiful women!" Stevenson noted in his travel diary. He called his trip "this South American primary." By the time he returned, Stevenson was under pressure from supporters to pursue a more active candidacy, and he did so by delivering a major foreign policy speech in Charlottesville, Virginia, in April 1960. The nationally televised speech triggered media speculation about Stevenson's potential candidacy.[40]

Senator A. S. Mike Monroney of Oklahoma, one of Stevenson's staunchest supporters, put together a small national staff, largely funded by Agnes Meyer, to push Stevenson's nomination. "Of course, you know NOTHING," Mrs. Meyer wrote Stevenson about this behind-the-scenes effort to create an organization. Although Monroney had personal affection for Stevenson, his support was not altruistic. Monroney believed that anti-Catholicism would prevent Kennedy from carrying Oklahoma and other conservative Democratic Bible Belt states. Around the same time, Stevenson met privately with Lyndon Johnson, who denounced Kennedy as "the boy" and asked for Stevenson's support. "We'll teach that little prick a thing or two," vowed Johnson. Stevenson indicated that he shared Johnson's views about Kennedy but explained that the party's titular leader had to remain neutral. If the convention deadlocked, someone had to be available to lead the party. Johnson, who probably calculated that the kind of stalemate that Stevenson envisioned was unlikely, humored Stevenson by not challenging this assessment.[41]

Neither Johnson nor Stevenson could be nominated unless both blocked Kennedy on early ballots. They needed each other. Both Johnson and Stevenson claimed that, after themselves, they favored each other for the nomination. If Stevenson stopped Kennedy, and Johnson won the nomination and the election, a grateful Johnson could make Stevenson secretary of state, since Johnson had little interest in foreign policy. Kennedy, however, had warned Stevenson, "Lyndon is a chronic liar. . . . He has been making all sorts of assurances to me for years and has lived up to none of them. . . . That fucking bastard can only understand power." Privately, Kennedy observed, "I don't think Adlai realizes that Lyndon Johnson thinks he's a fruit." In fact, Johnson did not feel comfortable with Stevenson, whom he privately described as "the kind of man who squats when he pees."[42]

After Kennedy won the Oregon primary, he flew back to Massachusetts by way of Chicago in order to meet with Stevenson at his farm in nearby Libertyville, Illinois. Kennedy drove to the farm with Bill Blair and Newton Minow, two young liberal attorneys from Stevenson's law firm who had helped Stevenson in the past but had now joined the Kennedy campaign on the grounds that he was a winner. En route, Kennedy shocked Minow by saying that if he failed to be nominated, he favored Johnson as the nominee. Minow and Blair also quickly realized that Kennedy might pick Johnson for vice president. (Sorensen later said that he believed at the time that if Kennedy lost the nominee would be Symington, but he and Kennedy constantly cited Johnson to scare liberals.) Then, referring to Stevenson, Kennedy asked, "Do you think I should suggest the possibility of secretary of state to him?" Silence. Then Minow replied, "No, I wouldn't." Kennedy asked, "Why?" Minow answered, "He'll be offended[,] and on top of this you shouldn't put yourself in the position of being committed." The private meeting between Kennedy and Stevenson did not go well. When the senator asked for the governor's support, Stevenson declined, citing his need to remain neutral as the party's titular leader. The Illinoisan made the "dire mistake" of mentioning Johnson's name. "Obviously," Stevenson told Arthur Schlesinger, "the feeling between the two of them is savage."[43]

Kennedy was furious. He later told his friend Charlie Bartlett, "If he couldn't come up with a better one than that, he certainly wouldn't make a very good secretary of state." The senator told his aide Kenny O'Donnell, "The same old double-talk. He's got to be playing with Johnson." Schlesinger drew the same conclusion after Stevenson ruefully said that he could not "double-cross Johnson." Stevenson had made a deal with Johnson to stop Kennedy, but Kennedy was certain that the ultimate consequence would be Johnson's nomination, not Stevenson's. At the meeting with Stevenson, Kennedy had exploded. "We are sorry," he warned, "we are going to have to shit all over you." The blunt vulgarity enraged the refined Stevenson, who told his friend George Ball, "I should have told the son-of-a-bitch off[,] but, frankly, I was shocked and confused by that Irish gutter talk." Kennedy decided that Stevenson was actually a candidate but lacked the guts to admit it to Kennedy's face. Stevenson's repressed anger, missed by Kennedy, was interpreted as coyness and indecision. Kennedy complained, "God, why won't he be satisfied with secretary of state?"[44]

Stevenson wanted Kennedy to wait his turn for a presidential nomination in four or eight years. The Illinoisan asked, "Why can't he wait? What's the rush?" Had Stevenson known about Kennedy's poor health, he might have better understood Kennedy's impatience. A few days later, journalist Arthur Krock told Kennedy that Adlai was running. Kennedy replied, "And how!" Stevenson said of Kennedy, "How could I ever go to work for such an arrogant young man?" Jack Kennedy, according to Jackie, could scarcely stand being in the same room with Adlai. Stevenson later said, "That young man! He never says 'please' and he never says 'I'm sorry.'" In April 1960 Kennedy privately told the journalist William White, "Like hell will Adlai be *my* secretary of state—though of course I'll have to give him *something*. He's a goddam weeper." Kennedy meant that Stevenson was soft on foreign policy. Joe Alsop called Kennedy, "A Stevenson with balls." The incompatibility with Kennedy explains why Stevenson had made the deal with Johnson. Stevenson wore a mask of indecision, but he was actually one of the most guileful of politicians. He even misled the usually shrewd Senator Clinton Anderson, who declared, "Stevenson was just too pure to be in politics." Stevenson's supporter John Sharon observed that, far from being indecisive, Stevenson was a "stubborn bastard."[45]

As the primary season ended in early June, Kennedy's march to the nomination stalled. According to the press, he had a big lead, having accumulated about 600 of the 761 delegate votes necessary to win; but the last 160 or so proved much harder to get. The primary season had allowed Kennedy to use campaign money to translate his popularity with Democratic Party voters into delegates, even though local party leaders often remained unenthusiastic. After the primaries, Kennedy's popularity with voters mattered less than did the opinions of party professionals. Party leaders who had earlier discounted Kennedy now had to take seriously the likelihood of his nomination or the difficulty that would occur should he be denied the nomination. Precisely because he was so close to victory, the professionals wanted to be certain that his nomination was in the party's best interest.

Meanwhile, the other candidates acted to stop delegates from announcing for Kennedy, to encourage support for Johnson, Symington, and Stevenson, and to keep favorite sons in the race through the first ballot. After the first ballot, Kennedy would lose some delegates in Indiana and Maryland that had been committed to him in primaries only for the first ballot. If his overall vote started to decline on a second or third ballot, he would not be nominated. The inability to gain more votes exasperated Kennedy. When an airplane stalls out, it stops flying and comes down to earth. As the Democratic National Convention opened in Los Angeles, many observers thought that Kennedy's plane seemed barely airborne.

3

THE DEMOCRATIC CONVENTION

In the weeks before the Democratic National Convention met in Los Angeles in July, John Kennedy was a strong front-runner, but it was uncertain that he would prevail. This chapter tells the story of how Kennedy narrowly won the nomination and of the emergence of the Kennedy-Johnson ticket. May and June 1960 frustrated Kennedy. He had demonstrated his appeal with voters both in the polls and in the primaries, winning all ten primaries that he entered. No one could doubt that he was more popular than other possible Democratic nominees. Kennedy had also cultivated party leaders in nonprimary states, even in the South; and in states outside the South where leaders did not favor him, he had set up his own organizations to get supporters selected as delegates to the convention. Despite his efforts, he did not yet have enough delegates to claim the prize. Outside the Northeast, party leaders who might have embraced his candidacy hesitated to endorse him. They were not certain that he ought to be the nominee because they were afraid that he would lose the election.

Kennedy was badly hurt when the U-2 spy incident exploded in the news on May 5. On May 1 the CIA had sent its top-secret, high-flying spy plane, the U-2, over the Soviet Union to photograph military targets. The Russians had shot the plane down and captured the pilot, Francis Gary Powers, who, after a few days, had been exhibited to the world. The spy mission, which President Eisenhower had authorized, seemed inept because it had been launched on the eve of a peace summit between Eisenhower and Khrushchev in Paris. On May 16, an angry Khrushchev went to Paris, denounced Eisenhower to his face, demanded an apology, and broke up the summit in a huff.

Khrushchev's childish bullying helped Nixon, a fervent anti-Communist seen as tough enough to stand up to the Soviet leader. Nixon's poll standings rose in matchups against the various Democratic candidates. According to Gallup, Nixon led Kennedy 51 percent to 49 percent, the reverse of a short time before. The incident hurt Kennedy by reminding voters about his youth and inexperience. Financier Eliot Janeway privately asked, "Can you imagine Kennedy up against Khrushchev?" Kennedy then stumbled by saying that it might have been possible for Eisenhower to "apologize" to the Soviet Union. Nixon called Kennedy's remark "naive." Lyndon Johnson pointedly said, "*I'm* not prepared to apologize to Mr. Khrushchev—*are you?*" Kennedy's slip led other Democratic contenders, as well as party leaders, to question whether the young senator was ready for the presidency.[1]

Suddenly, Democrats showed renewed interest in Adlai Stevenson, whose calm maturity and deliberation contrasted with Kennedy's clumsy remark. Governor Pat Brown of California declared, "The world situation is changing every day and the world travels of Adlai Stevenson could make him a more potent candidate." In the end, however, Stevenson could not capitalize on Kennedy's mistake. About the U-2 flight and the summit Stevenson said, "We handed Khrushchev the crowbar and the sledgehammer to wreck this meeting." Lamenting the Eisenhower administration's "incredible blunders," Stevenson blamed the administration for the summit failure and thereby produced a backlash. The Republican National Committee called the speech "reckless," and Nixon said he was "greatly shocked." Jim Farley, who was backing Johnson, denounced Stevenson as the "Apostle of Appeasement." Still, among the Democrats, Stevenson was the main beneficiary of the U-2 debacle. By late June there were Draft Stevenson clubs in forty-two states, and an advertisement appealing for funds in the New York newspapers brought in $42,000. The strategy was to use volunteers to stampede the convention.[2]

Stevenson's rise coincided with Kennedy's private and public cultivation of liberals. To stop Stevenson, Kennedy worked hard to get liberal support. He told Arthur Schlesinger Jr.: "I want to be nominated by the liberals. I don't want to go screwing around with all those southern bastards." In reality, Kennedy had little choice, since the South was Lyndon Johnson's turf. On June 9 Kennedy faced a further challenge when a group of intellectuals, including Reinhold Niebuhr, Archibald MacLeish, John Hersey, Carl Sandburg, and John Steinbeck, endorsed Stevenson. The reply was swift. Eight days later, Kennedy received backing in an advertisement in the *New York Times* from sixteen prominent liberals, including Schlesinger, Kenneth Galbraith, Allan Nevins, James M. Burns, Henry S. Commager, Joe Rauh, and Arthur Goldberg. All had once been prominent boosters of Stevenson. There was a lack of sincerity in Kennedy's pursuit of liberals, and not long after he complained to Schlesinger, "The trouble with the northern liberals is that they want their arses kissed all the time." However, the prospect of Kennedy's nomination with liberal support caused indigestion in the more conservative wing of the party, especially among southerners.[3]

During June, Kennedy retained his lead, but the Kennedys were nervous. Key party bosses in populous states, notably Mayor Richard Daley of Chicago and Governor David Lawrence of Pennsylvania, held large blocs of publicly uncommitted delegates that Kennedy needed. As early as mid-1959, Daley had privately pledged support to Joe Kennedy, but Daley did not want to announce his backing until the national convention. Illinois had 69 delegate votes, most of which Daley controlled. Daley's private pledge did not help create the bandwagon effect that Kennedy needed. Governor Lawrence favored Adlai Stevenson, but a majority of Pennsylvania's delegates supported Kennedy, so Lawrence kept his 81 delegate votes uncommitted. With a party boss like Lawrence, there was an excellent chance the delegation would be delivered to Lawrence's candidate rather than to the delegates' choice. New York was a cauldron of warring bosses and factions. Although the party bosses were a problem, they could be counted on to pay attention to polls that showed that Kennedy would run stronger than other Democrats in Illinois, Pennsylvania, and New York.

As the convention neared, Kennedy's position remained delicate. On July 2, former President Harry Truman, who was backing Symington but was also sympathetic to Johnson, told a nationally televised press conference that the Los Angeles convention was "rigged" for Kennedy. When pressed as to why the youthful senator was unacceptable, Truman said that Kennedy lacked "maturity and experience." The former president asked, "Senator, are you certain that you're quite ready for the country or the country is ready for you?" (Kennedy replied, "It is time for a new generation of leadership. . . .") The Kennedys were furious that Truman gave arguments to the Republicans to use in the fall campaign. And

Truman tried to sidestep the religious issue by expressing his opposition in a more palatable framework. "I'm not against the Pope," Truman told the press, "I'm against the Pop," a reference to Joe Kennedy's money, hunger for power, and manipulations behind the scenes in behalf of his son's candidacy.[4]

The stop-Kennedy movement was in high gear. Two days after Truman's outburst, India Edwards, Johnson's close friend, held a televised press conference to charge that Kennedy suffered from Addison's disease, which was then generally considered fatal. The Kennedys recognized that this claim, if not instantly refuted, might cause Kennedy's candidacy to unravel. Both brothers, John and Robert, denied that John Kennedy had Addison's disease or was being treated with cortisone. "I do not have it," Kennedy told Arthur Schlesinger, "and I have never had it." To bolster the statement, two Kennedy physicians, including Janet Travell, held a press conference to confirm the denial. This brazen lie is a wonderful example of Kennedy deceit and manipulation (in his diary, Schlesinger called Kennedy "devious"). As Doctor Travell revealed in her oral history opened more than thirty years later, Kennedy did have Addison's and was being treated for the disease with cortisone derivatives. Believing the denials, the mesmerized press showed little interest in the story, which most reporters saw as an attempt by Johnson to use wild charges to steal the nomination from Kennedy.[5]

In part, the Addison's disease charge failed to stick because India Edwards was too obscure a person to make the charge. Then, too, classic Addison's disease, a form of adrenal insufficiency, caused its victims to waste away with lethargy. All during 1960 Kennedy had proved himself to be a tireless campaigner, and it was difficult to believe that anyone who had Kennedy's high energy level could have this disease. There are two explanations for this apparent contradiction. First, Kennedy's Addison's had been under control since 1947 with treatments of cortisone and, during the fifties, a milder cortisone-derivative pill that had fewer side effects. (One side effect of both treatments was increased sexual drive.) In effect, Kennedy showed no signs of Addison's and had normal or near-normal adrenal function as long as he continued to take the pills, along with Travell's occasional booster shots. Second, Kennedy's particular form of Addison's was unusual. Although he had low adrenal function, he lacked the disease's usual symptoms of swollen lymph glands, blotched tongue, and deteriorating general health leading to early death. Although a physician would have classified Kennedy's disease as a form of Addison's under the medical terminology in use in 1960, it was true that the senator did not have the common form of that disease.

The day after the Addison's charge was made, Lyndon Johnson announced his candidacy. One explanation for the near-simultaneous announcements was that Johnson was setting in motion a plan to become vice president. If Kennedy was perceived to have a potentially life-threatening medical problem, the vice presidency would have to be taken seriously. Although Johnson privately called Kennedy "that spavined hunchback," he made a point in his announcement of declaring that Kennedy's successful campaigning had proved that Kennedy's health was fine. Outraged by the Addison's charge, Bobby Kennedy at the convention told Bobby Baker, Johnson's operative, "You Johnson people are running a stinking damned campaign, and you're gonna get yours when the time comes." When Kennedy spoke, his fists were clenched and his face was red. Baker tried to calm Bobby Kennedy, but he stalked off.[6]

By the time that the Democratic National Convention opened in Los Angeles on Monday, July 11, Kennedy was back in the driver's seat, with the polls propelling his candidacy. In the final Gallup poll released on the eve of the convention, Democratic voters gave Kennedy 41 percent; Stevenson, 25 percent; Johnson, 16 percent; and Symington, 7 percent. For the party to ignore the polls would be an act of folly. In the liberal and heavily Catholic Northeast, Kennedy was a strong favorite among Democratic voters. He also ran first in the Midwest, although his dominance was less strong there. In the West, Kennedy ran a close second to Stevenson; and in the South, Kennedy ran a weak second to Johnson. Johnson had a commanding position in the South, but he ran a poor third or even lower in the other regions. Stevenson's overall support was second only to Kennedy's, and it was more evenly distributed. Stevenson's problem was that by skipping the primaries he retained the image of a two-time loser, which killed his candidacy with the crucial big state bosses. Symington was below 10 percent in all regions except the Midwest, and he was only barely above that number in his home region.[7]

Democratic national chairman Paul Butler had planned a spectacular, innovative convention in Los Angeles. Of necessity, the event had to be held in a truly large city, since there were 4,509 delegates and alternates, 4,750 reporters, and thousands of candidates' workers, party officials, and family members, for a total of about 45,000 people. Most delegates had only a half vote, which greatly increased the number of attendees and led to shortages of hotel rooms. The most expensive party meeting in history, it cost $749,000, of which $400,000 came from local Democrats. The price exceeded that of the Republican convention and was more than double the amount that the Democrats spent in 1956. The choice of the host city had not been an accident. Butler wanted to avoid older cities, which were dominated by traditional Democratic Party political machines that were both in decline and in increasing disrepute, especially among suburban, small-town, and rural voters who were seen as crucial to victory in the fall.

Butler understood the advantage of the intangibles in the age of television. Los Angeles was a boomtown, and much of it had been built after World War II. When network reporters arrived from the East, they found dazzling modern architecture, a massive freeway system, sprawling suburbs that filled much of Los Angeles County, and poolside life. Los Angeles, more than any other city in the United States in 1960, was about possibility, about reaching for success. And the most important industry was Hollywood. During convention week, film stars were encouraged to attend the Democrats' social events, and studios sponsored special tours for delegates and their families. Furthermore, the entertainers had money, and they were an increasing source of funds for the Democrats, who had traditionally depended upon New York and Texas money. On Sunday night, Kennedy, Johnson, Symington, and Stevenson spoke to a $100 per plate fund-raising dinner; Stevenson drew the most applause. Frank Sinatra, Kennedy's personal friend, mingled with Johnson, Stevenson, and Symington, and Kennedy sat with Judy Garland.

The television industry used the convention to demonstrate new technology. Videotape had only recently been invented, and now the networks could rebroadcast East Coast shows on the West Coast three hours later, the difference between the time zones. The convention showed a new use for videotape—instant replay. For the first time, viewers saw split screens that projected two different camera shots side by side. This convention was also the first to use teleprompters at the podium. The speaker's face was projected onto the world's first 10-x-16-foot big screen television behind the podium. The entire convention was programmed around television, much to the annoyance of print reporters. At prior conventions, crucial decisions had been announced to meet the deadlines for the morning newspapers. Now key moments were played live on national television during prime time. The challenge was to get the

John Kennedy spoke at a fund-raiser in Los Angeles on the eve of the Democratic National Convention. Judy Garland stood next to Kennedy. (Ollie Atkins Photo Collection, Special Collections and Archives, George Mason University Libraries, Fairfax, Virginia)

delegates into the Los Angeles Sports Arena early enough so that memorable moments did not take place after the eleven o'clock news on the East Coast.

On the Saturday before the convention opened, 3,500 supporters greeted Kennedy at the airport, and the candidate was mobbed like a matinee idol when he checked into his suite at the Biltmore Hotel in downtown Los Angeles. That same afternoon, 5,000 to 6,000 fans, including Henry Fonda, Vincent Price, and Lee Remick, showed up at the airport to meet the locally popular Stevenson. On Sunday, the crowds grew. David Lilienthal encountered "handsome bronzed California-type gals with startled looks and Kennedy hats." One Johnson volunteer said, "Have a kiss?" as she handed out candy kisses. Symington arrived at the Biltmore and, according to Lilienthal, looked "irrelevant." On Sunday there was talk of an early Kennedy victory. At least twenty Kennedys, Shrivers, Sargents, and Lawfords were in Los Angeles for the convention. "They seem to be everywhere," concluded the *New York Times* reporter. The only member of the family who was not seen was the controversial Joe Kennedy, who carefully kept out of sight during convention week. Asked if he had seen Old Joe, Speaker Sam Rayburn replied, "I haven't seen him, but he's in the bushes around here."[8]

When the Illinois delegation met on Sunday, Mayor Daley recommended Kennedy, and the caucus gave Kennedy 59.5 votes, Symington 6.5, Stevenson 2, and uncommitted 1. Without support in his home state, a Stevenson candidacy looked ludicrous. On Monday, Governor Lawrence of Pennsylvania capitulated to his own delegates and came out for Kennedy. At the caucus, Kennedy won 64 votes, Stevenson 8, and other candidates 9. That same day, New York announced 102 of 114 votes for Kennedy. Kennedy's bandwagon was now rolling in the vote-rich big states, even if 1,000 Stevenson supporters were marching outside the Sports Arena. The Illinois, Pennsylvania, and New York results put Kennedy over 700 votes. Victory required 761 votes.

The Kennedys pushed for a first-ballot victory. Robert Kennedy knew that in Indiana and Maryland, two primary states that Kennedy had won without serious opposition, the right to delegate votes expired at the end of the first ballot and that both state delegations, controlled by anti-Kennedy forces, would desert Kennedy as early as the second ballot. Although these losses might be offset by gains from New Jersey and a few other states, the danger was that Kennedy would fall short on the first ballot and that a second ballot would show support ebbing. Once a leading candidate began to slip, he was doomed. Squeezing out delegate votes became an obsession to the manipulative Kennedys. That was why Kennedy could not talk honestly about the vice presidency, a carrot that was dangled deceitfully before many politicians. Senators Stuart Symington of Missouri, Henry Jackson of Washington, Hubert Humphrey of Minnesota, and Governors Orville Freeman of Minnesota, Herschel Loveless of Iowa, George Docking of Kansas, and Robert Meyner of New Jersey were all left with the impression of being under consideration. Lyndon Johnson joked, "You know there's a certain colleague of mine who's already got 11 vice presidents!"[9]

One issue that dogged the Democrats in 1960 was civil rights, the leading domestic issue. In the spring, Paul Butler had appointed the liberal, pro-Kennedy Chester Bowles to head the Platform Committee at the convention. A former governor of Connecticut, Truman's ambassador to India, and a member of the House elected in 1958, Bowles had a keen interest in both the Third World and civil rights. His appointment to draft the platform and his ties to the Kennedy campaign signaled that the committee would favor civil rights and that Kennedy supported this idea. Kennedy could afford to promote civil rights because he had few southern delegates, and the southerners could not walk out because they needed to stay to work for Johnson's nomination. The Kennedy camp believed that a strong civil rights stand might gain an added 10 percent of the African American vote, or up to 1 percent of the total vote in several key, close northern states. They also felt that segregationist Democrats in the South were more likely to stay home than vote for Nixon and that the Democratic Party in the southern states was so strong that Kennedy could still carry most of Dixie, although with a reduced margin.

Bowles and the Platform Committee staff used the weekend before the convention to draft an extreme plank on civil rights. Bowles calculated that the South would publicly denounce the platform while privately seeking compromise. He intended the compromise that resulted to be as pro–civil rights as possible. Fearful that Kennedy might capitulate on the issue, Bowles wanted his platform to force Kennedy to endorse civil rights. Much to Bowles's surprise, after the platform was finished, Robert Kennedy indicated that the Kennedys would accept the document in toto. The report, which was presented to the Platform Committee itself on Monday, gave African American lobbyists all that they wanted, including an endorsement of recent sit-ins in the South. The platform also backed all the legislation that unions were seeking. Filled with new spending proposals for Medicare, education aid, and slum clearance, the platform was generally seen as the most liberal ever adopted by a major American political party. Although privately annoyed by the document, which would complicate the fall effort, Kennedy believed that the platform was not relevant to the campaign. What mattered between the convention and Election Day was what the candidate said. Political considerations, not ideology, would drive Kennedy's agenda.

Sunday and Monday had been about Kennedy's "inevitability." Tuesday belonged to Adlai Stevenson. In the afternoon, during a lull in the convention proceedings, the former governor entered the Sports Arena to take his seat among his fellow Illinois delegates. Stevenson's arrival was neither casual nor unplanned. A spontaneous demonstration broke out on the floor, even as Illinois delegates chanted, "We want Kennedy." But the more calculated part of the surging emotion came from the balcony, which had been filled with thousands of Stevenson backers provided by local California Democratic Clubs. In addition, sitting strategically in the front of the balcony was Stevenson's main supporter, the formidable Eleanor Roosevelt. Visible to many people in the balcony and to everyone on the floor, she led the noisy, frenzied cheering. A certain amount of electricity spilled over from the balcony onto the floor, where the demonstration continued for fourteen minutes.[10]

Was it possible that all of Kennedy's primary victories and hard commitments from delegates could be swept away in a tide of Stevenson fever? Were the delegates "madly for Adlai"? Anyone who had been around politics could not entirely discount the possibility. Kennedy aide Dave Powers called Kenny O'Donnell on the convention floor on a private line to ask, "Kenny, what the hell is going on?" O'Donnell replied, "Tell Jack that Adlai has everything going for him but the delegates." Asked what the demonstration signified, Mayor Daley said, "Nothing." Daley reported that the balcony demonstration appeared to be real and widespread but that most Kennedy and Johnson delegates were either quiet or only mildly applauding. To Daley, the evidence was clear that, despite the enthusiasm in the balcony, there would be no Stevenson stampede. New York's former governor, Averell Harriman, found the balcony demonstration "a ridiculous performance," too preposterous to work.[11]

The sentimental Stevenson was moved by the expression of affection. He loved adulation as much as any politician, except perhaps Lyndon Johnson, who once said to an aide about an ecstatic crowd, "Oh, boy! Listen to that! It even beats screwing." Stevenson went to the podium to speak to his supporters. En route, he must have wondered what he could say to escape from an awkward situation—a supporter on the floor observed that Stevenson's face showed "sheer terror." At the rostrum Stevenson enjoyed one last moment in the national limelight as the titular head of his party, basking in it briefly. Then he said, "I've decided I know the one you are going to nominate. It will be the last survivor." The lame joke totally deflated the situation. Stevenson's friend and supporter Agnes Meyer said, "He could have swept that convention. I could have murdered him." His supporters were surprised, hurt, and angry. They wanted him to express his affection for them and to announce his candidacy. He had done neither. His pride in standing in front of his supporters and depriving them of the leadership they craved was further evidence of his unfitness for high office. Robert Kennedy later said that Stevenson had acted like "an old woman."[12]

The Kennedys attempted to pressure both Adlai Stevenson and Hubert Humphrey to endorse Kennedy, but these manipulations failed. Artless arm-twisting did not work on major political figures who believed their own talents to be superior to those of Jack Kennedy. Stevenson declined to endorse Kennedy because he had promised both Johnson and Symington that he would remain neutral in the presidential contest. A furious Kennedy told Kenny O'Donnell, "Neutral for Johnson?" The anti-Kennedy movement was still alive, although it was nearing its end. Johnson's aide John Connally told Stevenson's supporter John Sharon, "Well, what are you all going to do? You going to cave in? It looks pretty bad. I don't think we can win it." Sharon replied, "Well, I recall that your boss told mine that if he [Johnson] couldn't make it he'd throw his support to him [Stevenson]." So Stevenson and Johnson held tight. On Tuesday, Robert Kennedy jabbed a finger into Humphrey's chest and said, "Hubert, we want your announcement and the pledge of the Minnesota delegation today—or else." An angry Humphrey jabbed Kennedy back and replied, "Bobby, go to hell." On Wednesday morning, the Kennedys were even more exasperated when Humphrey suddenly announced for Stevenson. For days, the press, caught up in its own Kennedy euphoria, had speculated that Humphrey was about to endorse Kennedy.[13]

Balloting was to take place on national television on Wednesday night. Each morning of convention week, in a model of disciplined organization, Robert Kennedy held a staff meeting at which the thirty-two Kennedy state coordinators reported on the exact number of delegate votes for Kennedy in the states that they covered. A few coordinators were assigned to two small states, but most covered a single delegation. They followed the delegates around, ate meals with them, and spent time at the hotel where the delegation stayed. Once an hour, they were to telephone headquarters on their walkie-talkies with the latest delegate count. If there was any change, they were to phone immediately, so that remedial action might be taken with a potential loss or massaging might begin with a potential gain. When a delegate on the floor needed bolstering or upbraiding, Robert Kennedy and a half dozen or more Kennedy operatives surrounded the victim. While Bobby flattered, persuaded, cajoled, and threatened, the other staffers formed a circle to make sure that the press could not eavesdrop on the conversation.

On Wednesday morning, Bobby was able to inform the staff that the nomination could be won on the first ballot, now that Illinois, Pennsylvania, and New York were on board, if all the votes were cast just as they had been committed. There was, however, little margin for error, and any change, no matter how trivial, had to be reported immediately to headquarters. Although Kennedy had only about 740 hard votes, he could exceed the necessary 761 with switches at the end of the first ballot. Among the private pledges from those seeking to curry favor from a winner, Tennessee's governor was committed to switching his state as soon as Kennedy reached 650 votes, and Alabama's governor held back a few votes that could be shifted to begin a stampede. Because Alabama voted first, Kennedy did not want the voting to start with the impression that he was depending upon southern votes for the nomination. This masterful orchestration of the vote showed effective organization, artful manipulation, and a keen sense of how to maximize television drama. Robert Kennedy added, "If we don't win this evening, we're gone."[14]

All day Wednesday the Kennedys worked hard to keep the nomination on track. New votes were hard to find. Attempts to bully Stevenson into nominating Kennedy continued to fail. Although Governor George Docking of Kansas had endorsed Kennedy, he was unable to deliver his delegation. Governor Robert Meyner of New Jersey refused to give up being a favorite son, even though many of his delegates wanted to vote for Kennedy. California was shaky. Governor Pat Brown resented Robert Kennedy's pressure and called Bobby a "punk kid." Brown publicly endorsed Kennedy, but the delegation caucus gave Stevenson 31.5 votes to Kennedy's 30.5. The Kennedys had irritated the California Democratic Club Democrats, and Eleanor Roosevelt had personally worked the delegation for Stevenson. On Wednesday, Brown was heard saying ominously that he favored Kennedy only on the first ballot.[15]

Minnesota was in turmoil. Governor Orville Freeman, who faced a tough reelection bid after raising taxes, backed Kennedy with the hope of an appointment if Kennedy won the election and Freeman lost. Hubert Humphrey feared losing reelection to the Senate if the Stevenson-Kennedy split within Minnesota's Democrats continued into the fall campaign. He endorsed Stevenson but took no further action. The longtime Humphrey-Freeman partnership permanently ruptured. To complicate matters, Minnesota senator Eugene McCarthy had been publicly announced for Johnson. McCarthy hoped to be Johnson's Catholic running mate. Frankly jealous of Kennedy, McCarthy in 1959 touted his own nomination by telling many reporters, "I'm twice as liberal as *Humphrey*, twice as Catholic as *Kennedy*, and twice as smart as *Symington*." Because of Kennedy's playboy reputation, the straitlaced McCarthy, a onetime seminarian, considered Kennedy to be a "bad" Catholic.[16]

The nominating and seconding speeches on Wednesday night were not memorable, with the exception of McCarthy's call for Stevenson. On short notice, the Johnson campaign had given permission for the speech, proof that Johnson and Stevenson had continued to maintain an anti-Kennedy alliance. "Do not reject this man who made us all proud to be Democrats," said McCarthy. "Do not, I say, leave this prophet without honor in his own party." It was a striking speech, the best of McCarthy's career, and it was seen on national television. The speech set off a frenzied thirty-minute demonstration, the largest and most emotional at the convention. The Sports Arena police chief told Symington's son, "Here comes the long haired boys and the short haired girls." And it was true. The Stevenson fans had an eight-foot papier-mâché ball to bounce around the convention floor. It looked good on television, but no one wanted to be bumped by it, and it was quickly sidelined. The bitterly divided Minnesota delegation cast no votes.[17]

For insiders, the balloting on Wednesday night had little drama. Kennedy won near the end of the first ballot when Wyoming's 15 votes gave him 765 votes, 4 more than the necessary 761 votes. The District of Columbia, Puerto Rico, and the Virgin Islands added another 20 votes. (Had Kennedy remained below the magic 761, he would not have received all 9 of the District of Columbia's votes.) In an anticlimactic moment, Kansas, which had passed, then reported 21 votes for Kennedy. The final tally at the end of the roll call was Kennedy, 806; Johnson,

409; Symington, 86; Stevenson, 79.5. Favorite sons, scattered votes, and absences amounted to 140.5 (see Appendix C). By the time of the roll call, most of the media had come to realize that Kennedy did have a lock on the nomination. Talking with Kennedy delegates all week, reporters, many of whom favored the senator, found that Kennedy supporters were determined and decided. Delegates who wanted other candidates were far more reticent.

The Kennedy organization had overwhelmed the party by leading in the polls, by sweeping the primaries, by cultivating key party leaders, by impressing the bosses, and by organizing grassroots efforts to elect delegates in nonprimary states where party leaders opposed Kennedy. They had followed this impressive early campaign to elect delegates with an equally dazzling effort at the convention. The key, again, was organization, and much of the vigorous effort involved spending freely. They published a daily newspaper; they shepherded delegates to Las Vegas for amusement; they provided free transportation in a city maddeningly short of taxis; they wined, dined, cajoled, and flattered the delegates; and they paraded a bevy of Hollywood stars, many arranged through Frank Sinatra and Kennedy's brother-in-law Peter Lawford, into parties that welcomed the delegates. Kennedy's own off-the-record meetings with various state delegations were extraordinary. The candidate charmed the delegates. Not using notes, he often demonstrated an astonishing knowledge of local political problems and realities, which sometimes exceeded what the delegates themselves knew about their own states. When delegates from different states compared notes, they discovered to their amazement that he knew every state inside out.

The opposition was stunned. Even before Kennedy arrived on Wednesday night at the Sports Arena to give the delegates a brief personal thank-you, Eleanor Roosevelt quietly slipped away to the airport in anger and nearly in tears. Journalist Stewart Alsop overheard a prominent Democrat ask, "How in Hell did he do it?" Norman Mailer observed that the professional politicians were depressed because they recognized that Kennedy was "a great box-office actor" with skills that they could not fully comprehend. Senator George Aiken understood Kennedy's public relations capabilities only too well—his Senate office was adjacent to Kennedy's. "I've been tripping over his TV and radio cables for five years," the Vermont Republican noted. The Kennedy staff felt that the victory represented the triumph of the World War II generation, which had organized itself more effectively and more creatively than had earlier generations.

They had used discipline, cold logic, and postwar tools of self-promotion to overwhelm and transform an older political system based on local bosses, parochial loyalties, and old-fashioned horse-trading.[18]

Unlike previous nominees, Kennedy had not traded offices for delegate votes. Instead, his political currency was media-generated mass enthusiasm. Of Kennedy, the columnist James Reston observed, "He is the symbol of all the new young men who are toppling the old." Kennedy's victory marked the triumph of the junior officers of World War II. In another column, Reston described what had happened as the "story of the old bulls and the young bulls." Truman, Acheson, Harriman, Rayburn, and Eleanor Roosevelt no longer mattered. The most astute bosses, Mayor Daley of Chicago and Governor Lawrence of Pennsylvania, understood their own future interest and went to Kennedy. The dean of journalists, Walter Lippmann, declared that "1960 marks the passing of the old political generation and the appearance of the new." Before 1960, politicians had used conventions to fight for nominations, but Kennedy had used the 1960 convention to ratify a decision that public opinion had already made. After 1960, candidates quickly learned that the new Kennedy method was necessary for victory. Polls, primaries, jet travel, vast sums of money, and arduous travel for years before an election were now required to gain a major party nomination. Money, organization, and television were the new realities.[19]

The Kennedys studied the electoral college math. By cultivating African Americans and labor, Kennedy intended to surge in America's large cities. He expected to win suburbs in the Northeast and Midwest that had large middle-class Catholic populations. On the negative side, Kennedy represented one of the most urban states, and he had consistently opposed farm subsidies in Senate votes. He would lose rural areas, and his liberalism, although muted, hurt in traditionally conservative small towns, especially in Republican areas outside the South. On the other hand, the Republicans were neither trusted nor well organized in the South, and Kennedy had a better chance in that region than some people thought. He did not need to repudiate the liberal platform, but he did need to make a gesture to the white South to indicate empathy.

The election was apt to turn on seven populous states that together had 205 electoral votes—whoever carried a majority of those states was likely to win. Kennedy calculated that New York (45) and Pennsylvania (32) could be won with big votes in New York City, Philadelphia, and Pittsburgh, plus an impressive showing in their suburbs. The United

Auto Workers could deliver Michigan (20). Kennedy would try to carry California (32), Illinois (27), and Ohio (25), but each was doubtful. Nixon had to be favored in his home state, and both Illinois and Ohio had formidable Republican parties. The loss of California would be offset with Pennsylvania, and New York's electoral votes were almost equal to Illinois plus Ohio. In addition to Michigan, the key to victory was to take Texas (24): In the seven big states, Kennedy would lead 121 to 84, a net plus of 37. Without Texas, Nixon would lead in the large states 108 to 97, a net deficit of 11 for Kennedy. Because Kennedy was weak in lightly populated, rural states, he had to get a majority of the electoral votes from the largest states in order to have a chance to win. Specifically, he needed Texas.

Thus, electoral math quickly suggested the advantage of picking Lyndon Johnson for the vice presidency. Stuart Symington could bring Missouri's 13 electoral votes, but Kennedy was convinced that he could carry Missouri, which had voted for Stevenson in 1956, without Symington. Senator Henry Jackson would nail down Washington State's 9 votes, but these votes might be won anyway, and they were, in any case, probably not enough to matter. Governor Orville Freeman could possibly bring Minnesota's 11 votes, but he was unpopular in his home state and might not help at all. Furthermore, Johnson was a far bigger name on the national stage. As demonstrated by his support at the convention, he enjoyed popularity throughout the South. An effective Johnson campaign rallying local Democratic officials might win most of the South, and Johnson's Senate friendships mattered. He might be able to persuade James Eastland of Mississippi, Harry Byrd of Virginia, and Richard Russell of Georgia to endorse the ticket. Each of these endorsements would go a long way toward carrying those states.

There were hints that Johnson was available. After the Texan had announced his candidacy for the presidency, he had been asked whether he would accept the vice presidency. Unlike Kennedy, Johnson did not entirely rule out the possibility. As a senator from a former Confederate state, Johnson knew that no such person had been nominated for president since the Civil War. Johnson's only route to the presidency was to serve as vice president and, like Nixon, become the heir. Other important figures suggested Johnson's name for vice president, including the publisher William Randolph Hearst. Columnist Joe Alsop and *Washington Post* publisher Phil Graham, both of whom thought of themselves as friends of both Kennedy and Johnson, had jointly proposed the idea to

Kennedy on Monday at the convention. Kennedy's subdued reaction suggested that he had already given the idea deep consideration. Alsop left the conversation convinced that Johnson would be picked, and Graham promoted the idea on the front page of the *Post*.

The oil interests also weighed in. Johnson was a strong supporter of the oil depletion allowance—a tax write-off that liberals generally fought—and oilmen feared that a liberal Kennedy presidency might seek to pay for new social programs by ending the depletion allowance. Through an intermediary, billionaire H. L. Hunt indicated that he would back the ticket financially if Johnson were on the ticket. Hunt's support was important for carrying Texas. Ed Pauley, a California oilman and major party contributor in that state, made a similar pledge. Joe Kennedy, another oil investor, urged Johnson's selection as well. There was also the matter of the August session of Congress that Johnson had arranged. With Johnson on the ticket, the session would go well. Otherwise, Kennedy might face trouble. Bobby Baker had told Arthur Krock, "If Kennedy gets the nomination, watch what we'll do to him in the special session."[20]

A final signal from Johnson that he was willing, perhaps even eager, to play the role came just after Kennedy won the nomination. Johnson issued a public statement larded with sweetness and flattery. Kennedy was both startled and moved when he read the telegram. The wire almost certainly led Kennedy to realize that Johnson would accept the vice presidency if it were offered. Kennedy and Johnson agreed on many policies and had worked well together in the Senate. Both were moderate liberals. (Kennedy's conservative Americans for Constitutional Action rating was 11 percent; Johnson's was 10.) If anything, Johnson was the more liberal of the two, especially on civil rights, as would become clear in later years.

So very early on Thursday morning Kennedy placed a surprise phone call to the Johnson suite and invited himself over for a visit. The conversation between the two men was private and brief. Kennedy made an offer, contingent upon approvals from key party leaders, which he was confident would be forthcoming, and Johnson accepted, contingent upon House Speaker Sam Rayburn's approval. Throughout Johnson's career, he had made no political move without consulting the sagacious Speaker, who was a surrogate father figure in Johnson's long career. Rayburn had first met Johnson as a boy, when Rayburn and Johnson's father served together in the Texas legislature. In the present case, however, the insistence upon Rayburn's approval must be viewed mostly as a face-saving device in case opposition forced Kennedy to withdraw the offer. Johnson could then claim that Rayburn had requested that he not leave the Senate.

As events unfolded on Thursday, Sam Rayburn played a key role, but to describe this role accurately is a challenge. The best politicians are consummate actors who hide true motives behind facades that usually project whatever the person they are talking to wants to hear and see. Master politicians explain little, and subsequent explanations are often mere vignettes for self-promotion and deception that today are called "spin." No politician would ever be surprised by another practitioner's use of subterfuge or manipulation. The brilliant, cunning Rayburn, the longest-serving House Speaker in history, played a curious role in Johnson's selection.

According to one credible story, Rayburn realized shortly before the convention that Kennedy had the nomination locked up. At a meeting at Rayburn's hideaway office in the Capitol, Rayburn, Johnson, Senator Richard Russell, Senator Robert Kerr, and Senator Everett Dirksen (a Republican), all fast friends, discussed this turn of events. All detested Richard Nixon and feared that Nixon would defeat Kennedy. In addition, Kennedy's candidacy threatened to destabilize the Democratic Party. Johnson agreed to run for president, even though his chances were nil, in order to force Kennedy to pick Johnson for the vice presidency. Only a Kennedy-Johnson ticket could both defeat Nixon and restore harmony to the Democrats. However, Johnson's goal of the vice presidency had to be kept secret, since success depended upon Johnson first making a strong presidential bid.[21]

The liaisons in these secret negotiations between the Rayburn-Johnson forces and the Kennedys were House Majority Leader John McCormack, Representative Tip O'Neill, and Representative Hale Boggs. During the convention, contacts were maintained—for example, O'Neill had told Kennedy privately outside Chasen's restaurant on Monday night that Johnson might be available. Because of raw feelings among Johnson's supporters following Kennedy's victory, Rayburn at first had to pretend to oppose Johnson being given the vice presidency. By making Kennedy beg Johnson to take the post, Johnson could also get better terms: control of half of Texas patronage, membership on the National Security Council, and the promise of a meaningful role for the vice president in the administration. Rayburn also knew that liberals and labor leaders would be unhappy, which were added reasons for a stealth campaign for the vice presidency.

In the short conversation early on Thursday morning between Kennedy and Johnson, the crystallizing moment had occurred near the beginning, when Kennedy first made his tentative offer. Johnson, perhaps suspecting that the offer was merely a flattering pro forma offer to a runner-up not intended to be accepted, said, "Well, now I don't know about this. I think I'd rather be majority leader." Kennedy shot back, "Well, how do you know that you will be majority leader?" Large numbers of liberal Democratic senators wanted to replace Johnson, and they might soon, perhaps as early as January 1961, make such a move. In addition, the remark could be viewed as a threat. If Kennedy won without Johnson on the ticket, the new president would pick his own majority leader, and it would not be the person who had rejected the vice presidency. And even if Johnson somehow managed to retain the post, he would merely be carrying out the new president's orders. The political power that he had enjoyed under Eisenhower would be gone.[22]

Shifting tactics, Kennedy said, "Now, Lyndon, you're going to be needed on this ticket. If you don't go on, I'll lose, the party will lose, and you'll be to blame, and I'll say so." If Kennedy lost with Johnson having refused the vice presidency, Johnson would be blamed for Kennedy's defeat, and Kennedy might join the liberals to remove him from his post. This possibility would be especially likely if Kennedy carried much of the North and only lost the election because the South deserted the Democratic Party. The Texan had no choice but to be Kennedy's running mate. In explaining his acceptance to Senator Russell, Johnson said, "Hell, the man asked me." Furthermore, he had to do everything in his power to make sure the Democrats carried Texas and the rest of the South. If the party won in the South, and if the southern states turned out to be crucial to a national victory, northern pressure on the South would diminish; and if the party won the South but lost the election in the North, then Johnson would have an excellent chance to be the party nominee in 1964.[23]

The decision to put Johnson on the ticket proved difficult to implement, as opposition emerged in a number of quarters. Many southern politicians were aghast. Still gagging on the platform, they were inclined to let the arrogant young Bostonian fall flat on his face to prove that the party could not ignore the South. Johnson's presence on the ticket, as Kennedy astutely realized, would make this sort of petulant response on the part of southern party leaders impossible. They had too much respect for Johnson, who would be their link to the new president, and they had no link to Richard Nixon. Southerners were divided during the morning hours as the proposal circulated among the governors, senators, and other high party leaders. Although Senators George Smathers of Florida and Herman Talmadge of Georgia opposed a Kennedy-Johnson ticket because they wanted to keep Johnson as majority leader, Representative Hale Boggs of New Orleans loved the idea. A Catholic, he had worried about the backlash against Kennedy in the northern Baptist portion of Louisiana, but with Johnson to balance Kennedy, Boggs was certain that the ticket would carry the state.

There was some playacting as the deal unfolded. One "hostile" response came from Senator Robert Kerr of Oklahoma, who cornered Johnson's aide Bobby Baker in a bathroom. Kerr slapped Baker hard and yelled, "Bobby, you betrayed me!" Baker finally "persuaded" Kerr that Johnson had to accept the offer. Like a good bit of politics, this was probably a sham, in this case performed for the benefit of staff members who were within earshot. The most important "convert" was Sam Rayburn, who had been brokering the deal secretly all week. Publicly opposed on Wednesday night, Rayburn "reversed" himself on Thursday morning by declaring, "I'm a damnsight smarter than I was last night." His public position changed after a crucial late night phone call signaling the desires of H. L. Hunt, a breakfast with Ed Pauley, and a crucial personal meeting with Kennedy in which the deal was sealed. Truly sorry to lose Johnson as majority leader, Rayburn had looked deep into Kennedy's eyes and said, "I can see that you need him more."[24]

Thus the southerners quickly fell into line, but many northern liberals had a difficult time swallowing the idea of Johnson as vice president. The problem began with Kennedy's staff. Early on Thursday morning, when Robert Kennedy presented the idea to Pierre Salinger and Kenny O'Donnell, it stunned both men. Sounding unhinged, O'Donnell protested, "Do you realize this is a fucking disaster? Nixon will love this. Now Nixon can say Kennedy is just another phony politician who will do anything to get elected." O'Donnell's strong reaction led Bobby to agree that both would go to Jack about the decision. O'Donnell rarely challenged Jack Kennedy directly, but he did so now, bluntly telling the nominee, "This is the worst mistake you have ever made." A bit shaken, Jack Kennedy replied, "Wait a minute. I've offered it to him, but he hasn't accepted it yet and maybe he won't." The nominee knew that he had to soften the blow by suggesting that the idea was not yet a hard fact.[25]

When Robert Kennedy and O'Donnell told a few key liberals about the plan to make Johnson vice president, the northerners exploded, and some of them threatened a floor fight. One Michigan delegate spat in rage at what he called Kennedy's betrayal. "The quickest doublecross we ever got," said a Steelworkers Union official. Alex Rose, head of New York's important Liberal Party, indicated that his group might not endorse a Kennedy-Johnson ticket. Without the votes from Rose's group, it would be difficult to carry the Empire State or win the election. (As it turned out, Nixon got more votes as a Republican in New York than Kennedy did as a Democrat; the Liberal Party votes did matter.) Meanwhile, other prominent northern politicians had calmly signed off on the idea: Governor Lawrence, Mayor Daley, Governor Michael DiSalle, Governor Abraham Ribicoff, and Connecticut's boss, John Bailey.[26]

Late on Thursday morning, Jack Kennedy met with a large group of labor leaders in his suite to solicit vice presidential names, without revealing his deal with Johnson. As the meeting ended, Kennedy asked Arthur Goldberg to stay behind. Goldberg said, "You've picked Johnson, haven't you?" Kennedy responded, "Yes." Goldberg asked, "Why?" Kennedy explained, "Look, every poll says I've got to have Texas to win. Without Johnson, I can't win." Goldberg was unhappy but accepted the fact. Labor disliked Nixon more than they did Johnson. To calm the angry unionists, Arthur Goldberg was sent to talk to George Meany, head of the AFL-CIO, who had great influence over other labor leaders. For a short time Meany could not be found, which brought a sense of panic. When Averell Harriman later told Meany, "It's a great ticket," the unionist replied dourly, "I'm glad you think so." Meany, however, was a political realist and did nothing to block the choice.[27]

Telephone systems were primitive in those days, and jammed lines often stopped messages. Sometimes the most important information was the number of a rarely used private line. Phil Graham had acquired Kennedy's private line phone number, which proved important. During Thursday morning, operatives reported back to Kennedy that there was some opposition among southern conservatives, and Kennedy himself had seen the lack of enthusiasm among other southern conservatives that he had consulted in person. Although this lack of approval was far from universal, it did cause Kennedy to wonder if the idea of putting Johnson on the ticket truly would work—perhaps much of the South was lost in any case. Disturbed by O'Donnell's reaction, Kennedy's growing ambivalence toward offering the vice presidency to Johnson was heightened when Bobby Kennedy returned to Kennedy's suite to report the anger of Joe Rauh and Governor Soapy Williams of Michigan.

Rauh was a key figure in the liberal Americans for Democratic Action and a former Humphrey supporter who had recently joined the Kennedy campaign. If Johnson was on the ticket, Rauh threatened to have the organization withhold its endorsement. Governor Williams, who had close ties to Walter Reuther, the United Auto Workers, and African Americans in Michigan, warned that labor, still seething over Johnson's vote for the Taft-Hartley Act in 1947, would not work for the ticket, and blacks, seeing Johnson as the southerner he no doubt was, would vote Republican. The Kennedys had not yet heard back from Meany and some other key players, but what they had heard so far gave them sufficient pause that in the early afternoon Bobby was sent to Johnson's suite to warn that the idea of Johnson as vice president was generating so much hostility that it might be better to drop it.

It is difficult to know at what point Robert Kennedy and Lyndon Johnson first detested each other. "In every conversation I have with him," Bobby later said of Lyndon, "he lies." The Kennedys were not the only practitioners of political deceit, although Johnson was far smoother in his manipulations. Johnson almost certainly held Bobby in contempt for having worked for Senator Joseph McCarthy, a man Johnson loathed. Although Johnson might have admired Bobby's later Senate committee work as a staff member investigating corrupt union leaders, it was easy to read Bobby's career as nothing but opportunism advancing either his brother's or his own interests. Bobby no doubt resented the arrogance with which Johnson and the southern barons ran the Senate during the 1950s. As a lowly staff member, Robert Kennedy was mostly ignored, which would not have flattered the brilliant but acerbic Bobby. Johnson called Bobby all sorts of names, most of them unprintable. "He skipped the grades," said Johnson, "where you learn the rules of life." To Johnson, Bobby's arrogance and inhumanity were really due to Joe Kennedy's money, which had constantly insulated Bobby from reality.[28]

Johnson was not the only person to detest Bobby. In fact, one can find few people outside the Kennedy family or its inner circle who were fond of Robert Kennedy. Like many insufferable people, his major sin was that he was usually correct and got the answer right before anyone else realized that there was even a problem. Johnson was not very lovable either, but he did have a sense of humor, which the moralistic Bobby lacked, and Johnson knew better than the brutally frank Bobby how to get others to do his bidding through subtle and often devious means. On Thursday afternoon, Bobby Kennedy arrived in the now-crowded Johnson suite bringing the news that there was too much opposition for Johnson to be offered the vice presidency. Johnson's staff did not allow the two men to be in the same room, and Bobby left.

Bobby later returned for a second visit to make a new offer: Johnson could be the Democratic national chair instead of vice president. When Bobby revealed the proposal to Rayburn, who, as we have seen, had not long before been publicly denouncing the vice presidential plan, the Speaker turned red and shouted, "Shit." The Kennedys were new at exercising power at a high level, and neither of them had realized that you could not dangle the vice presidency in front of Lyndon Johnson, have word of the offer spread throughout the convention, and then yank the offer back. By this point, the offer, for better or worse, had a momentum of its own, but Johnson and his entourage would never forgive Bobby for his intrusive visits with the unwelcome message that Johnson was unloved in many quarters.[29]

As a bewildered Bobby tried to figure out what to do next, Phil Graham arrived in Johnson's suite. Graham was puzzled, because he had just talked to Jack Kennedy on the phone and thought that the Kennedy-Johnson ticket was a done deal. In fact, Graham may have talked to Jack after Bobby had left the Kennedy suite. Between Bobby's departure and Graham's call, a number of people had urged Kennedy to stick with the plan to put Johnson on the ticket. The southerners, after realizing the many advantages of having Johnson as the running mate, had become enthusiastic supporters, and this fact had overcome the early perception that the South did not like the idea. At the same time, Alex Rose dropped his threats, and even Joe Rauh calmed down. George Meany had signed off on the deal, although with little enthusiasm, and Walter Reuther proved to be much less hostile than had Soapy Williams, who now seemed to be the main obstacle. As the revolt sputtered out, Jack Kennedy, once again bolstered by his father's strong insistence on Johnson's nomination and staring always at the electoral tally showing Texas to be crucial, decided to stick with the original plan.

Johnson's nomination might still have been derailed if Bobby's second mission had not been short-circuited by Graham's timely visit to Johnson's suite. Accompanied by Jim Rowe, Graham again called Kennedy on the private line and demanded that Kennedy call Johnson, and Kennedy did so. Over the telephone, Kennedy read an official announcement selecting Johnson that Pierre Salinger had just prepared for delivery to the press. Johnson then asked Kennedy outright, "Do you really want me?" Kennedy replied, "Yes." Bobby, however, was still in the outer part of Johnson's suite trying to withdraw the offer, so Graham called Jack Kennedy a second time. The nominee laughed and said, "Oh, that's all right; Bobby's been out of touch and doesn't know what's been happening." The Kennedy suite had already issued the announcement that the vice presidential choice would be Johnson. When Kennedy told this to Johnson, Lyndon and Lady Bird looked shocked.[30]

Moments later, the outer door to the Johnson suite opened, and Jim Rowe and Phil Graham pushed Lyndon and Lady Bird into the hallway to meet the reporters. The cameras tell all. Never have any two persons looked as emotionally drained and as miserable underneath their put-on political smiles as the two Texans. After Bobby left the suite, Johnson privately denounced "that fucking little piece of shit, that squirt-assed cunt." The Kennedys made sure there was no floor fight. After Johnson's name was put into nomination on Thursday night, the convention voted to close the nominations and elect Johnson by acclamation, thus avoiding any recorded protest votes. The entire process took less than thirty seconds. Approval by acclamation required a two-thirds vote. The ayes and nays did not seem clearly to favor the ayes by two-thirds, which led convention chairman Leroy Collins to hesitate in declaring Johnson the nominee. Speaker Rayburn could be heard and seen shouting at Collins, "Yes, you damn fool." The ayes had it.[31]

On Friday morning, Kennedy and Johnson met with the convention's 100 or so African American delegates, most of whom had backed Kennedy. The nominees pledged full support for the platform's strong civil rights plank. Although the delegates were clearly skeptical, especially about Lyndon Johnson's promise, Johnson went out of his way to embrace civil rights. He said simply, "You will find at the end of the first four years of the incoming Democratic administration that you will have made more progress than in the past one-hundred years." Both candidates set a pro–civil rights tone. Kennedy said, "We can't win without your help. . . . We want your help and advice." Kennedy did not plan to campaign in the North as a supporter of civil rights, while Johnson campaigned in the South as an opponent, as had sometimes been done in the past. Such tricks could no longer work in the age of national television news.[32]

Both Kennedy and Johnson were seasoned politicians who recognized that the future of the country and the party required a single national racial policy and that the only policy that made sense was to embrace civil rights. Johnson was painfully aware that the South's peculiar legal segregation created southern insecurity and barred southerners, both black and white, from full participation in national life. Discrimination was a bond that held Kennedy, Johnson, and African Americans together. The Kennedys had long faced discrimination as Catholics, and part of the reason that John Kennedy ran for president was to prove that a Catholic could win. Johnson had as much resentment against the old upper-class Protestant northeastern establishment as did Kennedy. Being from Texas was perhaps an even greater barrier than being a Catholic. At least Al Smith and John Kennedy had been nominated for president. Thus Kennedy and Johnson could empathize with the plight of African Americans because they had faced forms of discrimination themselves.

In another one of Paul Butler's many innovations, Kennedy accepted the nomination on Friday night in prime time before 80,000 people at the Coliseum, an outdoor football stadium that held 110,000 people. About 35 million people watched the "New Frontier" speech on television. But the Coliseum proved to be a poor venue. The sound of Kennedy's voice evaporated into the cool night air and echoed strangely off of nearby equipment, and the visuals were even worse. No festive balloons could be dropped from the ceiling, the Coliseum was too large to be decorated lavishly at reasonable cost, and Kennedy was too far from the audience to create crowd excitement. Harsh television lights blanched Kennedy white, while the background was a blur of irregular, sinister blacks. Effective crowd shots were impossible, and the lights at the podium attracted thousands of insects whose tiny bodies were brightly lit as they darted around Kennedy. Once or twice an insect darted into the candidate's mouth. Kennedy later said it had been a unique experience that he wished he had never had to endure.

An even larger problem was the speech's content. Influenced by the post-Sputnik space craze, by Kennedy's pledge to get the country moving again, and by the idea of Los Angeles as a new, exciting, postwar urban frontier, the speech urged Americans to embrace new challenges, just as pioneers had tamed the frontier. The ill-considered metaphor proved awkward. In echoing Franklin Roosevelt's "New Deal," Kennedy was suggesting that he was the new Roosevelt, a theme that the Kennedy campaign used all during 1960. But a "Frontier" is not a "Deal," and the "Frontier" idea did not fit well with many of Kennedy's proposals. The space program was indeed a logical frontier, but it was harder to see urban renewal or medical aid for the elderly as part of any frontier. And the "Frontier" concept had a curious history of its own. Henry Wallace had used *New Frontiers* (1934) as the title for a book. Wallace followers remembered the book, and Kennedy's title could be interpreted as a secret appeal to the Wallaceites of 1948, that is, the leftist portion of the New Deal coalition, to back Kennedy.

Kennedy's "New Frontier" speech laid out a liberal program for the sixties. Of the liberal platform, the nominee declared, "This is a platform on which I can run with enthusiasm and conviction." He promised health insurance for senior citizens, generous federal aid to public schools, and a federal program to distribute food to the poor. Kennedy also backed high federal subsidies for farmers, pledged to clear urban slums, and vowed to oppose racial discrimination. Noting the rise of Communist influence in the Third World, he declared that a more robust foreign policy was necessary. Most attention focused on his conclusion. Kennedy said, "We stand today on the edge of a new frontier." Then he added, "But the new frontier of which I speak is not a set of promises—it is a set of challenges. It sums up not what I intend to offer the American people, but what I intend to ask of them. . . . it holds out the promise of more sacrifice instead of more security." This was a somewhat odd ending, perhaps designed to offset the long list of promises.[33]

The domestic parts of the speech played well with the party's liberal base, and Kennedy thereby stimulated party workers to get out the vote in November. The tough rhetoric on the Cold War undercut any attempt by Nixon to charge that Kennedy was soft on Communism. In 1960, domestic liberals did not necessarily see defense spending and domestic spending as competition for the same dollars. There was a sense in the country that Americans could have it all. After the convention, there was a bounce in the polls for Kennedy, but it was not very large. Although the speech worked with the base, it made middle-of-the-road voters uneasy and it enraged conservatives. Noting the expensive new programs, Senator Everett Dirksen of Illinois declared that the new frontier was "out where the waste begins." Pouncing on the curious conclusion to the speech, the *Wall Street Journal* observed, "Sacrifice without purpose is not noble; it is a form of masochism." In 1960 the Democratic Party included many conservatives, and one was Ronald Reagan, who wrote in a letter to Richard Nixon, "Underneath the tousled boyish hair cut it is still old Karl Marx—first launched a century ago. There is nothing new in the idea of a government being Big Brother to us all."[34]

Always a quick study, Kennedy immediately realized the problems posed by his "New Frontier" speech. Although the media picked up the phrase and used it widely, Kennedy backed away both from the phrase and from the speech's liberal emphasis. Liberals liked the speech, but it did not reassure independents, moderates, or conservatives that the youthful, inexperienced Kennedy could be trusted with the presidency. The challenges for the fall campaign were formidable. And, despite this speech, Kennedy had not yet won the trust of the party's liberals and especially of the disappointed Stevenson enthusiasts. Arthur Schlesinger felt that Kennedy was a liberal due to "a sense of history" rather than by "inner conviction." Only intense campaigning by Stevenson could bring liberals to the kind of energetic devotion that was going to be needed to win on Election Day. Shortly after the convention, Kennedy met with Stevenson, and they planned a full campaign season for Stevenson, mostly in New York and California, his two areas of greatest influence. By November, Stevenson had given more than 100 speeches for Kennedy.[35]

Kennedy also had to reassure moderate and conservative Democrats, as well as independents, that he was not a wild liberal. He chose to do so by downplaying domestic issues in the campaign, particularly in more conservative parts of the country. Instead, he crusaded as a cold warrior, which made him seem more conservative. Polls, however, showed that the public preferred the Democrats on domestic issues and the Republicans on foreign policy, so a certain amount of domestic policy discussion rallied Democrats to his cause. And he discussed foreign policy to try to eliminate the Republican edge in that area. Kennedy developed a special strategy for the South. Although Kennedy made some appearances in the South, the plan was to use Johnson to campaign there heavily. In the summer, the polls showed a close election, as they had all year. What the Republicans did, and how the fall campaign developed, would determine the winner.

THE REPUBLICANS

The Republicans found it easy to select a presidential nominee in 1960. Once Nelson Rockefeller declined to run, Richard Nixon had no competition. To win in November, however, Nixon needed to cultivate both the party's liberals and its conservatives, which required a high-wire balancing act. Even in 1959 Nixon had been the clear favorite for the nomination. As the first vice president in the age of television, he had received much publicity. Since Eisenhower assigned Nixon few duties, he traveled widely to meet key Republican leaders and their business allies in every county and state. In 1954, 1956, and 1958 Nixon campaigned to the hilt for Republicans across the nation. Although cold personally, the vice president had learned to impress people. He kept a card file on every Republican whom he had ever met, and he spent hours memorizing the information. Thus, when Nixon stepped off an airplane, he flashed a wide smile, pumped hands of local leaders, and greeted each by first name. He recalled names of spouses and children and inquired about them. This attempt at flattery worked brilliantly. Nixon demonstrated a thorough command of politics in each county and state. Local leaders, who usually became the delegates or who picked the delegates to the Republican National Convention, could not help but be impressed. By October 1959 Nixon had backing from 84 percent of Republican county chairs.[1]

By 1959 Nixon also had overwhelming support for the 1960 presidential nomination among Republican primary voters. In one Gallup poll, he drew 68 percent. Furthermore, in polls matching various Republicans against various Democrats, Nixon outperformed other Republicans. The vice president appeared to be not just the party's strongest candidate but also the only Republican who could win. In most polls in the last half of 1959, Nixon topped all the Democrats, occasionally falling behind the Democrat who ran best, John Kennedy. Other possible Republican nominees lost to every possible Democrat. The reason for Nixon's unique strength was his capacity for getting support outside his own party. There were many more Democrats than Republicans, largely because there were few Republicans in the South, and a Republican could only win by capturing a portion of Democrats and a majority among independents. Polls suggested that Nixon could get about 90 percent support from his own party, as well as 20 percent of Democrats (mostly conservatives), and over 50 percent of independents.[2]

Among Democrats attracted to Nixon were the Kennedys. In 1959 Jack Kennedy told friends that if he lost the Democratic nomination, he would vote for Nixon, and in early 1960 Joe Kennedy ran into Nixon outside a restaurant and said, "Dick, if my boy can't make it, I'm for you." Nixon's singular position was in part about the Republican Party's weakness and its inability in the 1950s to elect new leaders in the major states that normally produced presidents. Of the seven most populous states, only New York and Illinois had Republican governors in 1960. John Kennedy declared Nixon to be the "one egg" in the Republican Party basket. He was largely correct.[3]

Some Republican leaders, however, discounted the polls, because the polls merely showed that the vice president ran better than did less-well-known candidates, a situation that could change drastically by the time of the actual election. As vice president, Nixon had little upside potential. In fact, there was considerable evidence that Nixon was widely hated, and not just by Harry Truman and Sam Rayburn. Nixon's pollster, Claude Robinson, found a hard core of "hate Nixon" voters. Nixon, unlike Eisenhower, would unite Democrats to stop his election. In a fall campaign, the Democratic Party could bring home a good many Democrats who were telling pollsters that they were planning to vote for Nixon, and even independents might be swayed against Nixon. So in 1959 Republican Party leaders resisted giving Nixon the final green light. Nixon was the front-runner, but the nomination was not locked up. Tom Dewey had privately declared that Nixon could not carry more than three states in 1960. Thoughtful Republicans, including Ohio Republican Party chairman Ray Bliss, wondered if another candidate might not be preferable, and some noted that if Nixon lost key primary elections in the spring of 1960, he might be dumped.[4]

The only exception to 1958's Democratic trend among the populous states had been in New York, where Republican challenger Nelson Rockefeller had upset incumbent Democratic governor Averell Harriman in what the press called "The Battle of the Millionaires." The Rockefeller family had strongly supported the New York Republican Party financially for decades, and Rockefeller had easily persuaded the state convention to give him the nomination as a self-financed candidate. Like Kennedy, Rockefeller won with money, organization, and television. Outspending his opponent $1.8 million to $1.1 million, the newcomer had recruited a large, effective staff, had taken numerous polls, and had run powerful television ads. He had also bought a private airplane in order to campaign in all sixty-two counties. Multitudes came to shake hands with a millionaire. At Coney Island, 300,000 showed up. Fluent in Spanish, Rockefeller so wowed a crowd of Puerto Ricans in Spanish Harlem that they carried him away on their shoulders.[5]

Although 44 percent of Republicans in 1959 believed a Democrat would win the presidency in 1960, Dewey and others felt that the New York governor, unlike the vice president, could be nominated and elected. In the previous one hundred years, thirteen New York governors or former governors had been nominated for president; no sitting vice president had been nominated since 1836. Many members of the press were convinced that Rockefeller ultimately would be the nominee. And so throughout 1959 the New Yorker emerged as the one possible serious rival to Nixon. Rockefeller's money, strong campaign skills, large and impressive staff, and control of the New York Republican Party might enable him to carry states in November that Nixon could not win, including New York, which might well prove to be the key to the election.

In 1959 Rockefeller enlarged his staff to include experts on national issues, signaling a possible presidential bid. But, in the first half of 1959, Rockefeller had to expend considerable political capital dealing with New York State issues. Harriman had overspent the budget, leaving a huge deficit. Acting boldly, Rockefeller proposed a massive spending increase well beyond Harriman's, as well as the largest tax increase in state history. "So this rich character gets elected," said a New York taxi driver, "and right away he's got his hand in my pocket." The governor used party patronage to move his proposals through the reluctant rural-controlled legislature. Rockefeller also cut deals with unions that proved that he was prolabor and pushed tough civil rights bills and policies that paid the political debt for the numerous African American votes that he had received. (Rockefeller had campaigned for black votes as a fellow Baptist, speaking frequently in black Baptist churches both before and after the election, and he had pointed with pride to his family's founding after Reconstruction of Spelman College, which was named for his grandmother.) By the time Rockefeller finished his legislative session in mid-1959, he had demonstrated that he was a brilliant political operator who had easily mastered the complexities of New York politics, but he had also enraged conservatives. His approval rating had plummeted, and his capacity to challenge Nixon in conservative states had been diminished.[6]

Rockefeller spent the last half of 1959 probing whether to run against Nixon in 1960. During this period, the governor spent more money than Kennedy or anyone else. He visited sixteen states, and his magic asserted itself wherever he went. Unlike Nixon, Rockefeller's charm was genuine, not calculated, and he impressed almost everyone he met. At a rally in Seattle, he said, "Let's keep close to the people and what their problems are." In a dig at Eisenhower, he added, "Let's not worry about how green the grass is on the golf links." Many delegates, however, had already made hard commitments to Nixon, and they could ditch Nixon only if Rockefeller won the primaries. Conservative delegates were alarmed by the governor's liberal tax-and-spend record. In a *Fortune* magazine poll, business executives split 76 percent for Nixon, 11 percent for Rockefeller.[7]

Rockefeller, however, may have been less liberal than he appeared. If one looked closely, one saw that the governor used polls, hired experts, commissioned reports, and tried to solve problems. He was perhaps less a liberal than a pragmatist. Conservatives, however, noticed that in no sense could he be called a conservative. Still, many Republicans, especially after the debacle of 1958, were keenly worried about losing the 1960 election. They feared a liberal Democratic president who would lead the almost certainly Democratic Congress into adopting policies that would destroy small businesses and small towns, the core constituencies of the Republican Party. Although Rockefeller was too liberal for the party's conservatives, he appealed to some of the party's moderates and a large percentage of the party's liberals as the candidate most likely to win in 1960. John Kennedy shared this view and told confidants that he could not beat Rockefeller, who would carry New York and the election.

Although Rockefeller found some sympathy for his candidacy among party leaders, he also found that Nixon had a huge head start in collecting delegates. Had Rockefeller swept New York's fiscal problems under the rug and spent the first half of 1959 running for president as hard as he did during the last half of the year, he might well have dislodged Nixon from the nomination. After all, Rockefeller, unlike Nixon, had a superb seventy-person staff, nearly ten times the size of Nixon's. The quality was also higher, in part because Rockefeller paid better salaries. When he acquired staff, he often hired people at three times their current salary. If they were no longer needed on his personal staff, they were transferred for life to one of the Rockefeller brothers' many foundations.

Rockefeller was a formidable campaigner, especially in ethnic areas in the East, where he quickly learned how to joke in Yiddish while downing hot dogs from handcarts at Brighton Beach. Nixon was stiff in such situations. Rockefeller could hire top TV advertising talent, as he did in toppling Harriman in 1958. Nixon had no money of his own and depended upon a small number of financial backers who assumed that he could win the election and defend their interests. Such businessmen would not be scared of Rockefeller becoming president. Thus, if Rockefeller were to beat Nixon in a primary or two, Nixon's candidacy might collapse, as Nixon's backers withdrew their support and Rockefeller continued to spend his own money. Still, Rockefeller hesitated to run. Party leaders did not want a contest for the nomination, and Rockefeller's staff was still fairly green and unseasoned.

Rockefeller's greatest problem was the perceived difference in national, high-level experience between himself and Nixon. About two-thirds of the public told the Gallup poll that Nixon had the "experience" to be president. Whatever Nixon's liabilities, the vice president could claim, and constantly did claim, that he had had unique preparation for the presidency through his occupation of the second-highest office. Because Nixon had traveled around the world to represent the United States and had played a role behind the scenes in the administration's policy making, the "experience" argument became Nixon's strongest argument for being nominated and elected. As Kennedy discovered in the fall campaign, there was no easy way to refute Nixon's claim.

In July 1959 Nixon had gone to Moscow to inaugurate the U.S. Exhibition demonstrating American consumer goods to the Soviet citizenry. The vice president had maneuvered Nikita Khrushchev into the kitchen section of the exhibit in front of television cameras to confront the Soviet leader with the superiority of capitalism in producing consumer goods for the masses. A pleased Eisenhower said, "The vice president has acquitted himself splendidly." In American eyes, Nixon had won the debate, which had caused his poll numbers to rise significantly. Once again, Nixon had demonstrated, as he had in the Alger Hiss case, that he was "tough" enough to stand up to the Communists. In this case, Nixon literally jabbed his finger at Khrushchev. The Kitchen Debate probably sealed Nixon's nomination.[8]

On December 26, 1959, Rockefeller surprised the media by announcing that he would not run for president in 1960. He explained that party leaders "stand opposed to any contest for the nomination." In withdrawing, he also indicated that he would not accept the vice presidency, was silent on Nixon's candidacy, and left open the possibility that he might be available for a draft at the convention. An uneasy Claude Robinson warned Nixon that Rockefeller was "still available" and might copy Eisenhower in 1952 by organizing a write-in campaign in the New Hampshire primary. The New Yorker had made his decision after polls showed Nixon leading Rockefeller consistently with much more than a 20 percent margin in all of the primary states. The governor had calculated that a campaign could not close any gap greater than that size. At the time the decision was made, the vice president was riding high in the polls, still basking in the afterglow of his debate with Khrushchev.[9]

Rockefeller's decision disappointed reporters, who liked the fact that the New Yorker always provided good copy. The governor's friends at Dartmouth College, his alma mater, which happened to be located in the key primary state of New Hampshire, were also deflated, because they had already begun to organize a primary campaign in that state. And it is not clear that the state's party leaders would have backed Nixon over Rockefeller. To New Hampshire's many conservatives, neither was an ideal candidate, but the New Yorker's ties to Dartmouth gave him an appeal that Nixon lacked. In jockeying prior to the governor's withdrawal, William Loeb of the important *Manchester Union Leader*, conservative senator Styles Bridges, and, ultimately, moderate governor Wesley Powell backed Nixon, while the state's two congressmen favored Rockefeller.

Elsewhere, Republicans sympathetic to Rockefeller, or those merely hostile to Nixon, suddenly found themselves without a candidate. During the last half of 1959 Rockefeller had discouraged anyone else from taking on Nixon. Realistically, there was room for only one challenger to the exceptionally strong front-runner, and so long as the New Yorker was contemplating running, no one wanted to face Rocky's money or organization. By December 1959 it was too late for anyone else to challenge

Nixon effectively. In a sense, Rockefeller's near-run gave Nixon the nomination with little effort. The withdrawal, however, also posed dangers for the vice president. To prove his own popularity within the party, Nixon might have preferred meeting and defeating Rockefeller openly in a primary or two.

Furthermore, with Rockefeller out of the race, Nixon faced danger on the right. As long as Rockefeller challenged Nixon from the left, the vice president could count on strong conservative support. As soon as Rockefeller bowed out, a few conservatives began to desert Nixon for the more ideologically appealing Senator Barry Goldwater, even though the Arizonan stood at only 1 percent in polls among Republicans in January 1960. To Nixon, holding the party together remained the most difficult problem prior to the convention. Years later, Rockefeller mused that his decision not to challenge Nixon in the primaries in 1960 was the biggest political mistake that he ever made. Had he defeated Nixon in the primaries, Rockefeller might well have won both the nomination and, as Kennedy had said, the election. Never again in his long political career would Rockefeller have as easy a possible path to the White House.

During the spring, the vice president's polls declined in matchups against Democrats, many Republican leaders feared that Nixon would lose in November, and some turned to Rockefeller. Others, like Vermont governor Robert Stafford and West Virginia governor Cecil Underwood, advocated a Nixon-Rockefeller ticket. That combination might be able to carry both California and New York, which would go a long way to winning the election. But conservative Republicans opposed this idea. Although they respected Nixon as a strong anti-Communist, they knew that he was not a true conservative. In April, Nixon confirmed this view by declaring himself a "progressive conservative." Conservatives were willing to embrace the moderate, nonideological Nixon but not the liberal Rockefeller. Conservative journalist Raymond Moley warned Nixon, "The concept of Nixon-Rockefeller has been called a dream ticket, but I am not certain that it might not turn into a nightmare."[10]

Conservatives wanted Nixon to pick a conservative, such as Barry Goldwater, for the vice presidency, but a Nixon-Goldwater ticket was unlikely to win any big states. Nixon also noted that a Californian and an Arizonan was a poor geographical combination. Conservatives argued that millions of conservatives who had not voted since 1932 or 1948 could expand the electorate if Goldwater was on the ticket. One South Carolinian claimed that the senator could carry "the stay-at-home voter who doesn't go for this me-tooism." (This self-serving and ultimately self-delusional argument resurfaced in 1964.) The Right also argued that a Nixon-Goldwater ticket could win the South's conservative Democrats, but the Republican Party was poorly organized in much of the South and probably could not have tapped southern conservative sentiment, even with Goldwater on the ticket.[11]

Because most Republican delegates were already pledged to Nixon, the vice president at first made little effort to win meaningless primaries. In New Hampshire, where Republicans traditionally won by two-to-one, Nixon received 65,204 votes in the Republican primary to Kennedy's 43,372 in the Democratic primary. Neither candidate had campaigned. Careful observers, however, noticed that Kennedy got 2,196 write-in votes among Republicans, while Nixon had only 164 write-in votes among Democrats. In the second primary, in Wisconsin, both Kennedy and Humphrey outpolled Nixon. Although some pundits speculated that the Democrats would win the state easily in November, politicians knew that Wisconsin's open primary system had led Catholic Republicans to vote for Kennedy and Republican farmers to back Humphrey. Many of these Republicans would go to Nixon in November. Also, the absence of a contest on the Republican side meant that many Republicans had stayed home, while the Kennedy-Humphrey race had stimulated Democratic turnout.

Always savvy about the potency of the media, Nixon quickly realized the damage done in the press by the perception that he was a poor vote getter. A week later, Illinois's formidable Republican Party turned out an astonishing 782,849 votes for an unopposed Nixon. In deference to Mayor Daley, no Democrats ran in that party's primary. Two weeks later, in Pennsylvania, Nixon received 968,538 votes with no competition. Again, no Democrats filed. In Nebraska, Kennedy won 80,408 votes as the only candidate on the Democratic ballot. In the Republican primary, Nixon got 74,356 write-in votes, which was more impressive than Kennedy's result because Nixon was not on the ballot. Nixon outpolled Kennedy in Indiana and Oregon, and in California Nixon's 1,517,652 votes in the Republican presidential primary had been considerably more than Pat Brown's 1,354,031 on the Democratic side. Brown had run as a stand-in for Kennedy. All in all, Nixon won almost 4.5 million votes, more than 80 percent of all the votes cast in the 15 Republican primaries. In the 16 Democratic primaries, Kennedy won only 1.8 million votes, which was 32 percent of the total Democratic primary vote (see Appendixes A and B).

Richard Nixon spoke at a mass rally in San Francisco in May 1960. (Ollie Atkins Photo Collection, Special Collections and Archives, George Mason University Libraries, Fairfax, Virginia)

Nixon would probably have sailed straight to the nomination if it had not been for the crisis in May 1960 over the U-2 spy plane incident and Khrushchev's subsequent sabotage of the Paris summit with Eisenhower. Governor Mark Hatfield of Oregon declared, "Khrushchev's tirade shows fear of Nixon." Although the Gallup poll found the public favoring the president's handling of the crisis by a margin of two-to-one, the episode upset Republican campaign plans. The Republicans had planned to run the 1960 campaign on the themes of peace and prosperity, a duality that had worked well for Ike in 1956. The success of the summit would have allowed Nixon to link himself to Ike, diplomacy, and possible future international triumphs. The vice president's earlier Kitchen Debate would keep conservatives who distrusted the Soviets happy, and Nixon could play the peace card in the fall campaign. Khrushchev, by this point, had decided to tilt toward the Democrats in 1960. The Soviet leader knew he could not bully Nixon and felt that more could be gained negotiating with a Democrat. By derailing the summit, Khrushchev hoped to wreck Nixon's chance to be the peace candidate. Nixon would have to run as the "tough" politician prepared by experience to stand up to Khrushchev. The Soviet leader gambled that Americans, if given a choice between the "tough" Nixon and a more flexible Democrat, would choose the Democrat.[12]

Rockefeller seized the moment after the U-2 incident to declare himself available for the Republican nomination. Since Nixon already claimed a majority of delegates and since Nixon's experience argument was enhanced by the summit failure, Rockefeller doubted that he could win the nomination. He told friends that the odds were only one in ten, which was probably optimistic. Indeed, he refused to run openly but, borrowing from the Adlai Stevenson playbook, declared that he was willing to be drafted. This sort of candidacy is very unlikely to lead to a nomination, especially when another candidate already holds a majority of the delegates, and it is quite likely to produce internal party strains. Eisenhower bluntly told Rockefeller that the possibility of his nomination was "remote."[13]

The governor appears to have believed that the undercurrent of anti-Nixon feeling inside the party could be exploited to bring about a sudden change in his own fortune. Fully aware that Nixon spoke only in platitudes in order to hold conservatives, moderates, and liberals together in an uneasy coalition prior to the convention, Rockefeller cited Khrushchev's belligerence and taunted, "What are Dick's plans to meet these problems?" He added, "I think we are facing new circumstances and we need to do new things." An irate Raymond Moley observed that Rockefeller made "exactly" the same complaints as the Democratic candidates did. In particular, Rockefeller proposed increasing the defense budget by $3 billion, plus spending another half billion dollars on civil defense.[14]

Rockefeller's demand that Nixon take specific positions on issues enraged Republican Party professionals who believed that such stands would split the party. Journalist Bill Lawrence wrote, "Rockefeller tactics are difficult to understand." Pushing the defense issue seemed unwise, since it risked angering Eisenhower. When the governor discussed his possible candidacy with the president in early June, Eisenhower said that Rockefeller could not win the nomination without Ike's backing and that the price of that support was for the governor to adopt the president's defense policies. This requirement would have forced Rockefeller to repudiate his own positions, and it effectively foreclosed his nomination. Eisenhower's stipulation can be interpreted as a sign of presidential deviousness. Finding the New Yorker to be an amateur with an inflated sense of self, the pollster Claude Robinson advised Nixon, "About all you can do is to continue to be kind to him." Nixon's top aide, Robert Finch, wrote, "I suspect that we will manage to survive the Rockefeller thing as far as the convention is concerned, but unless it is handled well, it could cost us the election in November." To another correspondent, Finch reported, "Rockefeller's behavior is simply inexplicable—what a tragic waste of a valuable political property!"[15]

Conservatives were riled. Publisher Harry F. Byrd Jr., son of Virginia's senior senator, in an editorial in the *Winchester Evening Star*, declared Rocky's behavior "strange." Barry Goldwater sarcastically suggested that Rockefeller seek the Democratic nomination. There is no doubt that Rockefeller wanted to shake things up. In 1940 Wendell Willkie had ridden just such a current of change all the way to the nomination, but Willkie's surprise choice had taken place against the backdrop of the startling fall of France in World War II. The summit collapse in 1960 was not a parallel with World War II, and Khrushchev's truculence only reinforced Nixon's claim of experience.[16]

By the end of June, Rockefeller knew that he could not win the nomination, but he continued to pretend to be available to see what he could obtain from Nixon. Nixon wanted Rockefeller to be his running mate, but the governor enjoyed his job and saw the vice presidency as a minor post of little consequence. Money was not only a means to acquire power, but having fabulous wealth gave him an inner serenity that shaped his ambition in a certain way. A man less used to vast private means and public scrutiny, Nixon, for example, might have craved the vice presidency as its own reward. Despite its lack of power, it was a good position for someone who wanted to be noticed. But holding high public office for purposes of prestige mattered little to Rockefeller. Whether in or out of office, he would still be a Rockefeller—a celebrity. He wanted high office for only one purpose—to make public policy—and he could not do so as vice president, even if Nixon promised a meaningful role in his administration. Besides, personal chemistry was a problem. About Rockefeller, Henry Kissinger noted, "He loathes Nixon."[17]

Nixon could offer Rockefeller only one other bargaining chip, and it turned out to be what the New Yorker most wanted: influence over the Republican Party platform. Conservatives had always worried that Nixon, like Kennedy, did not appear to have strong convictions. It was difficult to discern any Nixon ideology. Rockefeller shared this concern about Nixon, but from the opposite perspective. The governor's speechwriter, Emmet John Hughes, who had earlier worked for Eisenhower, criticized Nixon for "a chronic personal incapacity for commitment." Nixon, a Quaker, preferred to forestall controversy with silence. He chose to hide his position, Hughes thought, not out of guile but from lack of conviction. "Fiercely vehement" about trivial matters, the vice president "found it exceedingly hard to be explicit" about serious political issues.[18]

Rockefeller was determined to force both Nixon and the Republican Party in a liberal direction. Dewey's liberal New York party had long dominated the national party. New York's control was largely about Wall Street's financing of Republican candidates. Here, too, was another example of money driving politics. Big business interests controlled the Republican Party in many states and often backed the party's liberal wing in the belief that it had better odds of winning elections. If business wanted Nixon to be president—the vice president had cultivated wealthy executives for years—then Rockefeller could not stop Nixon's nomination, since Nixon also enjoyed conservative support. However, Rockefeller's insistence that the platform reflect his own liberal views threatened to split the party and posed the practical problem that those views appeared to be critical of the popular Eisenhower. The conservative magazine *Human Events* declared that Rockefeller's strategy was "to destroy Nixon and usurp the Republican Party." As Nixon's friend Earl

Blaik later wrote, "The selfishness of Rockefeller who wanted the game played on his terms did not help the Republican cause."[19]

The New Yorker was less interested in whether or not Nixon was elected than in positioning the party so that Rockefeller could make a presidential bid in 1964 or 1968. By this point, Rocky's private polling showed that Nixon could not carry New York in November. Without the Empire State, Nixon was unlikely to win the election, which was an added reason why the governor did not want to be on the ticket. Also, northeastern Republicans worried that Kennedy would swamp Nixon in their region and thereby wipe out the local party. New York Republicans feared losing congressional seats and the state senate. But a Nixon victory also bothered Rockefeller. If Nixon won, he might turn the party over to conservatives, since a president would control party machinery. Republican politicians were furious with the New Yorker for exposing the party's internal tensions to public view. Below the surface, the *Wall Street Journal* noted, the party had "fratricidal impulses," and conservatives were talking about "realignment."[20]

Many Republican Party conservatives wanted a southern strategy, and the antidote to this strategy, Rockefeller knew, was a strong civil rights plank in the platform. The governor also strongly believed in civil rights. On July 22, the Friday night before the convention opened, Nixon asked to meet privately with Rockefeller. In reply, the governor demanded that the vice president come to New York to discuss the platform in detail. Nixon went to the meeting, still hoping that he could persuade Rockefeller to take the vice presidency, but Rockefeller had no intention of doing so. The governor wanted to force Nixon to run for president as a moderate liberal, even at the cost of enraging conservative Republicans.

Tightly controlled Republican Party operatives, taking cues both from the Eisenhower administration and from Richard Nixon, had been grinding out planks to put into the platform at sessions in Chicago prior to the Republican National Convention. Although much less publicly visible than Kennedy's organization, Nixon's staff was crucial for many campaign tasks. The platform praised the Eisenhower administration for peace and prosperity, rejected proposals from the party's liberal and conservative wings, and positioned Nixon to run for president as a moderate by pledging to continue, in effect, Eisenhower's policies. Ike was overwhelmingly popular, gathering more than 60 percent approval in the Gallup poll. Because the president was a moderate, the platform had to be moderate, too. At the convention, Ike declared, "We are truly a middle-of-the-road party."[21]

Thus, Platform Committee chairman Charles Percy, a Chicago business leader, and the other drafters had rejected liberal attempts to put an unusually strong civil rights plank into the platform in order to go after the African American vote. Calling for a plank even stronger than the Democratic one, Rockefeller said that sit-ins were "part of our tradition." However, a strong civil rights plank indirectly criticized Eisenhower's moderate policies. Ike had won 39 percent of the black vote in 1956, and party leaders were convinced that Nixon could do almost that well in 1960, especially since recalcitrant southern Democrats, not Republicans, had blocked civil rights legislation in the Senate. The Democrats had already nominated Kennedy and Johnson, and Johnson's presence on the ticket gave the Republicans an excellent opportunity to seek northern black votes. Moderate party leaders also knew that the Democrats' strong civil rights plank played poorly among white southerners, and they hoped to win several southern states by having a plank that was slightly weaker. However, conservative Republicans felt that the moderate civil rights plank foreclosed an effective strategy to win the votes of white southerners.[22]

To offset conservative restlessness, the platform had to offer at least one plank to please conservatives. The drafters chose defense. Nixon knew that the so-called Missile Gap did not exist, and he also recognized that he could not attack the administration of which he was a part for being weak on defense. Since polls showed that the public preferred the Democrats on domestic issues and the Republicans on foreign policy, it was crucial for Nixon to embrace the foreign policy of the administration. On the other hand, Nixon felt that Eisenhower did not take seriously the political damage that had been caused by the Missile Gap charge. (When the Gallup poll asked who was ahead in missiles, 33 percent of Americans said the United States and 47 percent said the Soviet Union.)

Nixon wanted a robust defense policy, perhaps more than Eisenhower did, and he saw the political necessity for advocating a larger defense budget in order to neutralize the Missile Gap charge, which had been helping the Democrats. Although the platform could not criticize the administration, a promise to increase defense spending would enable Nixon to emphasize how strongly he supported defense. Doing so was imperative because Kennedy was working hard to be seen as more of a cold warrior than Nixon. One suspicious conservative was Ronald

Reagan, who wrote Nixon that to the Soviets "co-existence" meant "don't do anything while I steal your horse." In addition, increased defense spending could help California, where 20 percent of defense dollars were spent. Southern California's prosperity depended upon high defense spending, and Nixon's pledge to increase this spending might help him carry the Golden State.[23]

Just as the party's drafting committee in Chicago finished, the members learned to their astonishment and consternation that Nixon was meeting secretly with Rockefeller at the governor's apartment on Fifth Avenue in New York to hammer out a final draft of the platform. Nixon had not even informed his own staff about the meeting, and press secretary Herb Klein had been galled to learn about it from *New York Times* reporter James Reston, who had gotten the story from Rockefeller headquarters. On Saturday morning, when Senator Goldwater heard about the event, he did not believe it, until he got confirmation from Nixon's top aide, Len Hall. Fearful of what a more liberal platform might mean, a furious Hall told Goldwater, "This won't cost Nixon the nomination, but it might cost him the election."[24]

Nixon had wanted to meet in Washington, but Rockefeller had insisted that the vice president come to his residence as a supplicant. The governor also demanded unilateral control of all announcements to the press about the conference. As usual, Rockefeller's staff handled the public relations brilliantly, and the result was to make it clear that Rockefeller had dictated to Nixon. Like Kennedy, Rockefeller was a master at manipulating the media. Nixon, in contrast, usually just cursed his enemies in the press. "They're all against me, anyway" was a frequent refrain. After a warm and gracious dinner, the two men began serious discussions at 10 P.M. The vice president again tried to persuade the governor to be his running mate, and the New Yorker for the last time declined. Nixon later observed, "I was not altogether sorry, because Rockefeller's independent temperament would have made him a much more difficult running mate for me to deal with than Johnson would be for Kennedy."[25]

In an all-night session that lasted until 4:30 A.M., the two hammered out the platform planks that Rockefeller demanded as the price for his cooperation in running a harmonious convention at which his name would not be submitted for nomination. Nixon and other party leaders believed that any floor fight would ruin the chance to win the election. Having agreed to the meeting, Nixon had little choice but to accept Rocky's plans. In fact, Nixon could see great advantages in getting the

New Yorker on board. Rockefeller's enthusiasm for the party and its ticket might go a long way toward carrying New York, and Nixon's reputation as a man who could bridge all factions inside the party would be enhanced. Raising funds would also be easier. The vice president already had conservative support, and here was the chance to gain liberal backing. Dewey praised the deal as helpful to victory in November, and *Washington Post* publisher Phil Graham called it "a bold and potentially dangerous gamble."[26]

As far as Nixon was concerned, the meeting was a win-win situation. It was helpful to Nixon, to Rockefeller, and to Republican Party unity. Like the equally nonideological Kennedy, Nixon did not put much stock in platforms, and he believed that if Rockefeller could be humored with a dose of liberalism in an otherwise mostly moderate platform it would be well worth the small price. The candidate would set the campaign's tone. Nixon intended to run as a moderate, not as a liberal, because in order to win he needed to hold conservatives, moderates, and liberals inside the Republican Party as well as recruit a certain number of conservative and moderate Democrats and independents. Regardless of whatever Nixon might do, liberals who were not Republicans would all go to Kennedy.

Rockefeller was most concerned about two planks, civil rights and defense. On race, the two men quickly agreed on a plank that mirrored the Democrats' liberal plank. "We did not found this Nation upon any manner of racist concept," Rockefeller had declared two months earlier, "but upon a basic belief in the individual—his worth, his dignity, his freedom." Like the Democratic one, the new version of the plank openly endorsed the sit-ins in the South, which Rockefeller insisted had to be included to get black votes. Like many Californians, Nixon had always been liberal on civil rights. The Republican Party had no white southern wing to protest the plank, and Nixon concurred with Rockefeller's plan to make a bid for the black vote. However, when the wording of the plank was dictated by telephone to the Platform Committee drafters in Chicago, there was anger and consternation.[27]

The party's conservatives believed that the moderate civil rights plank written in Chicago already precluded winning much of the South, and by making the plank stronger in such a highly visible way at the last minute, Nixon and Rockefeller were denying the southern strategy that many conservatives favored. In addition, some conservative Republicans agreed with conservative southern Democrats that, according to the Constitution, civil rights was a state rather than a federal issue. In particular, Senator Barry Goldwater of Arizona took this line. Now the conservatives were in a fury, feeling that the party was being manipulated and even betrayed by its more liberal New York wing. Conservatives may have expected this course from Rockefeller, but they were especially angry with Nixon, who appeared to have caved in to the party's eastern establishment. As far as Nixon and Rockefeller were concerned, the professional politicians who ran the party would have to calm the conservatives down. The two leaders had no intention of retreating on this issue. Nixon had to twist arms to get the Platform Committee to adopt the liberal civil rights plank.

Rockefeller had called for a specific increase in defense spending of $3.5 billion per year, or 9 percent, including civil defense, but Nixon could not allow any specific proposal to be put into the platform, because it would look like an attack on the Eisenhower administration. Privately, Eisenhower blamed the governor's "half-baked" advisers for the demand. A specific figure in the platform would enable Democrats to charge that the Republican Party was admitting that the administration had not spent enough on defense. Many Republican leaders resented the fact that Rockefeller's demand helped the Democrats. One concluded, "Rockefeller has destroyed himself in the Republican Party." In addition, Nixon worried that conservatives would ask how the increase would be financed, and the vice president did not want to be forced to propose a tax increase to pay for higher defense spending. Nixon and Rockefeller quickly agreed that defense spending should increase but that the plank did not need to spell out a particular amount. In fact, both men felt that Eisenhower had been spending too little.[28]

When the drafters in Chicago were told in the middle of the night about the new defense plank, they were alarmed. Since they had been in close contact with White House officials, they knew, better than Nixon and Rockefeller, the explosive reaction that would come from Eisenhower. Expressing little interest in the overall platform, the president had given specific input only on the defense plank. In the early morning, when Eisenhower learned what had happened, he was livid. "I have difficulty," said the president, "in restraining my feelings of indignation." He accused Rockefeller of "personal treachery." Through intermediaries, Eisenhower made it clear to Nixon that the new language that the vice president had hammered out with the governor was not acceptable. The president icily observed that he could not be "enthusiastic" for the ticket if the platform did not show "respect" for his administration. Nixon was forced to go back to Rockefeller and insist on a revision. In the end, a face-saving formula was worked out among Nixon's staff, Rockefeller's staff, and Eisenhower's staff. However, the episode strained relations all around.[29]

As the Republican National Convention opened in Chicago on Monday, July 25, the party's liberals felt that Rockefeller had done an excellent job in turning the platform in a more liberal direction. Liberal pleasure was matched by conservative resentment. Of Nixon's visit to Rocky, one angry Republican said, "He didn't fly, he crawled all the way on his hands and knees." Barry Goldwater, already recognized as a leading figure on the Right, gained new prestige by the vigor with which he attacked what he called Nixon's "surrender" to Rockefeller. The media dubbed the event the "Treaty of Fifth Avenue," a line that did not help Nixon's standing with small-town America, and Goldwater took pleasure in stating that Nixon had staged the "Munich of the Republican Party," a reference to Neville Chamberlain's capitulation to Hitler in 1938. The insult stung because the Arizonan was correct that Nixon had conceded nearly all that Rockefeller demanded. Nixon could get away with his deal with Rockefeller because of his own peculiar position within the Republican Party. Regarded as a moderate figure, Nixon knew that the party's conservatives intrinsically trusted him more than did the party's liberals because of his unique role in the Alger Hiss case. Thus, Nixon's leftward tilt with Rockefeller was balanced by his longtime stronger ties to the Right.[30]

Conservative delegates, many from southern states, were angry. Delegations from Texas, Louisiana, and South Carolina were filled with Goldwater supporters. It had been easy for the Right to take over the Republican Party in those states, since an organized party had barely existed. Republicans held no legislative offices in the three states, which meant that none of the delegates had any elective political experience. The only elected federal Republican Party officeholder from the three states was the very conservative representative Bruce Alger of Dallas. Many of these conservatives were, in truth, ideologues drawn to the Republicans out of anger with liberal Democrats and by a belief that the two-party system should be reorganized along conservative-liberal lines. The Right believed that America had a natural conservative majority that had been denied power because a liberal northeastern establishment effectively controlled both parties.

The party's conservatives wanted to purge liberals like Rockefeller in order to create a conservative majority party by recruiting southern Democrats. They were a new element in the Republican Party, and because they were small in numbers and did not come from states that elected Republican officials, party leaders were uncertain how to respond to them. Shrewd politicians understood that a movement was afoot that could produce a successful Republican Party throughout the South and that a Republican South might create a national majority party. But the southern conservatives' idealism, anger, and lack of compromise were too palpable to believe that much could be done with this particular group. Furthermore, their doctrinaire quality made both moderates and liberals, and even some traditional Taftite conservatives, uncomfortable.

Conservatives decided to take a stand at the Republican National Convention in order to repel Rockefeller's attempt to make the Republican Party into a mirror image of the already mostly liberal Democratic Party. Interestingly, conservatives did not challenge any of the platform planks. They agreed with increasing defense spending, and they quickly learned that they could not win any change in the liberal civil rights plank, since Nixon forces controlled the Platform Committee. Organization mattered. Goldwater said that Rockefeller had "mousetrapped" Nixon on civil rights. The South, which was ripe for the picking, would not vote for a Republican candidate running on a strong civil rights plank. Goldwater doubted that Nixon could win the North in any case, and therefore the election, in effect, had been thrown away by abandoning the South. Conservatives might still have taken a stand out of principle had they had more experience, but their newness inside the party meant that they lacked the skills to lobby for their issues. Many of them literally did not know how to make a motion in a committee meeting. The politicians who ran the convention's committees found it easy to sidestep them by use of parliamentary procedures.[31]

To protest Nixon's pact with Rockefeller, conservatives promoted Barry Goldwater for president. The Arizona senator had emerged as a hero on the Right after being reelected in 1958, a year of general Republican defeat. Interestingly, the national media had paid little attention to Goldwater's victory. Party leaders tried to discourage the Goldwater boom by pointing out that Kennedy would be the only beneficiary from any perceived Republican disharmony at the televised convention. Nixon wanted a coronation, not a divided convention. Then, on Wednesday,

July 27, when Nixon met with Rockefeller and the New York delegates, the governor put his arm around the vice president and said, "We are with you all the way." This lovefest galled conservatives, and a few insisted on nominating Goldwater for president that evening.[32]

The South Carolina delegation was already pledged to Goldwater, and, naturally, the senator also had support from Arizona. After the Nixon-Rockefeller deal, which the head of the Texas delegation called "a damn sellout," the Lone Star State had voted to switch from Nixon to Goldwater. Goldwater agreed to allow his name to be placed in nomination so that he could address the convention on national television and withdraw. When he did so, he told conservatives to work hard to elect Nixon. Then he added, "Let's grow up, conservatives. Let's, if we want to, take this party back—and I think we can someday. Let's get to work." Among those inspired by the speech was a young Pat Buchanan, who later said, "I enlisted." The challenge galvanized conservatives and led to Goldwater's nomination in 1964, an ironic consequence of Nixon's overture to liberals. On the roll call, Nixon received 1,321 votes; Goldwater received 10 (Louisiana delegates cast these votes, even though Goldwater had withdrawn).[33]

Nixon's major remaining chore before the fall campaign was to pick a vice presidential running mate. Polls had suggested that Rockefeller might help the ticket by 2 percent, but none of the other possible candidates seemed to make a difference. The most commonly mentioned names were UN Ambassador Henry Cabot Lodge, Senator Thruston Morton of Kentucky, Senator Everett Dirksen of Illinois, Secretary of Labor James Mitchell, Secretary of the Interior Fred Seaton, and Representative Walter Judd of Minnesota. Each posed pluses and minuses. A Nixon-Judd ticket might have carried Minnesota, but the state's 11 electoral votes were probably not enough to matter. Billy Graham favored Judd, a medical doctor, a former missionary, and a conservative anti-Communist.

The mild-mannered and little-known Fred Seaton came from the safely Republican state of Nebraska and brought nothing to the ticket. James Mitchell, a Catholic, was a favorite of the party's northeastern liberals, but neither conservatives nor the business community wanted him. (Had the Democrats rejected Kennedy, however, Mitchell might have given the Republicans a way to appeal to Catholics.) Everett Dirksen, the Senate's minority leader, was a stronger prospect, but he had angered liberals in 1952 with militant support for Taft, and Nixon felt that he could carry Illinois without Dirksen. Thruston Morton, the Kentuckian who also served as the party's national chair, would have enabled Nixon to pursue a southern strategy. Goldwater favored the moderately conservative Morton. If the Democrats had abandoned the South with an all-northern, all-liberal ticket, Morton would have given Nixon strength in the South. Against Kennedy's pick of the formidable Lyndon Johnson as a running mate, however, the selection of Morton seemed pointless.

The finalists appeared to be Morton and Lodge, but Nixon in reality had decided on Lodge and a foreign policy–focused campaign in late spring, and at that time Lodge privately had accepted the tentative offer from Nixon. In June, Nixon had indicated that he wanted Morton to stay on as the Republican national chair during the fall campaign. Immediately after Nixon's nomination late on Wednesday night, the nominee met with thirty-six prominent party leaders to "pick" the vice presidential candidate. Only the unsophisticated were unaware of Nixon's deception, and the sham meeting to "choose" between Lodge and Morton annoyed party leaders. At the meeting, Tom Dewey said that Morton would please the delegates but that Lodge would please the larger public. Although Governor William Stratton of Illinois, who faced a difficult reelection battle, argued that Morton was more useful in the Midwest, two prominent Ohioans, former senator John Bricker and state party chairman Ray Bliss, neutralized this pitch by backing Lodge. Rockefeller and some New York delegates had also told Nixon that Lodge could help carry New York. After the meeting broke up, Nixon formally offered the post to Lodge at 3 A.M. and he accepted.

The ambassador proved to be an unfortunate choice. Goldwater called it "a disastrous blunder." Midwestern delegates felt Lodge was of no use in their region. One Illinois delegate said, "I saw Lodge on television today, and he'll run like a dry creek." Another added that a Nixon-Dirksen ticket would not only have carried Illinois, but its coattails would have reelected Governor Stratton. Nor could Lodge help Nixon in his home state of Massachusetts, where Kennedy had defeated Lodge for reelection to the Senate in 1952. Neither, as it turned out, did the ambassador help in the rest of New England nor in upstate New York.[34]

Television had a lot to do with Lodge's nomination. He was familiar to the nation's TV viewers as UN ambassador throughout the fifties. Eisenhower had urged Nixon to pick Lodge to reinforce a campaign based on foreign policy, the Republicans' strong suit. Lodge's experience also reinforced Nixon's experience, which was another campaign angle. A strong civil rights supporter, Lodge was supposed to help Nixon throughout the Northeast and especially with African Americans. Liberal Republicans found Lodge more acceptable than the other possible nominees, except Mitchell, and conservatives liked Lodge's tough anti-Communism, even though they did not truly like Lodge. The ambassador was a moderate, although he had played a major role in Eisenhower's nomination in 1952, so he had more ties to the party's liberals than did Nixon. The Taftite conservatives disliked Lodge. An Ivy Leaguer, Lodge annoyed conservatives, mostly because he was part of the northeastern upper-crust establishment that had long dominated the party. The haughtiness was palpable. About Lodge's mansion, Kennedy joked, "If Nixon ever tries to visit Lodge at Beverly, they won't let him in the door."[35]

Because the main public memory was of Lodge denouncing Russian perfidy on television at the United Nations, he began the campaign with the highest ratings of any of the four candidates. He was, as Nixon observed, "non-controversial." The *Chicago Tribune* called him "a natural counter-puncher," which proved to be a wildly inaccurate characterization. Lodge's deficiencies became painfully clear during the fall contest. A lethargic campaigner who had not won an election since 1946, he refused to do more than one event per day and rested on weekends. His appearances were often poorly timed for maximum news coverage, and he looked uncomfortable in television spots. On live TV he came across as arrogant. The clipped upper-class accent did not help. He insisted on taking a nap every afternoon, and he dressed in fancy pajamas for the nap, a mannerism that caused comment. Worse, Lodge failed to coordinate his campaign with Nixon's, so that he and Nixon often contradicted each other. Lodge did real damage to the ticket.[36]

Nixon's acceptance speech at the Republican National Convention on Thursday night impressed the delegates and the national television audience. Kennedy's aide Ted Sorensen called it "brilliant." In contrast with Kennedy's somewhat ethereal address, Nixon was less philosophical, more hard-nosed, more down-to-earth, and more specific about what he planned to do in the presidency. Nixon's mind ran to details and rarely to philosophy. He was most comfortable with politics and policy, not with theory. Not surprisingly, the main theme was emphasizing continuity with the popular Eisenhower and suggesting that Nixon's administration would build on what had already been accomplished.[37]

Promising a strong defense, Nixon declared, "America will not tolerate being pushed around by anybody, any place." But he also pledged a willingness to negotiate with the Soviet Union if negotiations were possible. He endorsed "peaceful competition." Softening his image as a militant cold warrior was probably a necessity. He discussed the role of the United States in the world in a sophisticated way, which suggested that the nine overseas trips to fifty-nine nations that he had made in the vice presidential years had influenced his thinking. Like Kennedy, Nixon saw the United States entering into a period of difficulty. "Americans," he said, "are always at their best when the challenge is greatest." This statement expressed Nixon's innate optimism.[38]

Nixon also argued that his "experience" was not a matter of serving time in an office but of intellectual growth and development as he worked to help Eisenhower grapple with the world's most troublesome problems. Although the government had a duty to act to express collective responsibility, Nixon appealed to the nation's psyche by emphasizing that each American also had individual responsibility. "Each American," he declared, "must make a personal and total commitment to the cause of freedom." Domestically, he endorsed civil rights and further federal programs for education, agriculture, scientific research, and health care for the elderly, but these were not the difficult problems that engaged Nixon's considerable intellect. Foreign policy had always been Nixon's main interest. The speech, Nixon later observed, was the "high point of my campaign." The carefully organized convention and Nixon's effective, globally oriented speech gave the vice president a bounce in the polls, and he emerged in August with a small lead over Kennedy. Neither candidate, however, believed that this lead had any meaning. What the candidates did in September and October would decide the outcome.[39]

After his nomination, Nixon announced the staff that would help him win the presidency. Rejecting the idea of an overall campaign manager, the nominee instead placed a troika in charge. Leonard Hall, a Nixon loyalist and a New Yorker who had been the Republican national chairman in the mid-fifties, assumed many duties as general manager. The vice president later said he did not call Hall his campaign manager because Nixon felt that putting the former Republican Party chair in charge would alienate independents and Democrats. Other duties fell to Thruston Morton, the Kentucky senator and current party chair. The third key leader was thirty-four-year-old Robert Finch, called the campaign director, who had impressed Nixon by reviving the Republican Party in Los Angeles. This three-way division of responsibilities offered a contrast with John Kennedy's confident placing of power in the hands of his campaign manager, his brother Robert. Nixon's peculiar organizational structure confused the media, party leaders, and even the staff. Trying to make sense of the situation, Hall put the matter accurately when he told the press, "Dick is his own manager and makes his own decisions." This statement proved to be painfully true. Another key player in the campaign organization was investment banker Clifford Folger, who was in charge of finance. The tight-fisted Folger had a reputation for getting good value for the dollar.[40]

Nixon's decision to be his own manager caused endless confusion and duplication throughout the fall. No one person ever appeared to know who was in charge of various aspects of the campaign. Fearing Nixon's fierce temper, the staff hesitated to make any decision without consulting the candidate, but he was constantly on the road and frequently out of reach. As the junior staff member, Finch felt a need to defer to the older members of the staff, but, paradoxically, he enjoyed greater confidence from Nixon. However, even after the convention, Finch had still not met many Republican senators. As vice president, Nixon had been reluctant to delegate duties to his small staff. In a national campaign, this reluctance produced great strains. When Claude Robinson warned Nixon against micromanagement, the vice president replied that it was necessary because his staff was incompetent. Although Nixon exaggerated, it was true that Nixon's organization lacked the highly paid talent that Kennedy had recruited. The staff respected Nixon's political acumen, called him "The Boss," hardly a term of endearment, and was kept at a distance.

Nixon made poor use both of his staff and of television. He sought no expert advice, ignored Eisenhower until late in the campaign, and turned down help from Ike's television adviser. Nixon's aide, H. R. Haldeman, kept Nixon's media advisers, Carroll Newton and Ted Rogers, from having access to the candidate. Newton and Rogers wanted a television-oriented campaign with many news clips, but Nixon ignored them and plotted his own media strategy. The moody candidate isolated himself and would neither seek nor heed staff recommendations. Disliking controversy, he often preferred to ignore a staff request rather than reject it, which left the staff uncertain as to the candidate's wishes. Hall, in particular, suffered constant humiliation by being ignored, insulted, or overruled. One main duty was to put down staff mutinies against the boss's sometimes puzzling behavior. Nixon treated his staff as if they were all amateurs and he was the lone professional.

For Nixon, the most difficult challenge remained a question of strategy. Should he, as Republican conservatives urged, pursue a southern strategy, or, as Rockefeller demanded, should he look to the traditional Republican homeland in the North? Throughout the campaign, Nixon never fully answered this key geographical question. In the close election of 1948, New York had voted for Dewey, and Nixon believed that he too could win the Empire State. Rockefeller's state organization would make a difference, and so would internal divisions among New York Democrats. The contrast with the Kennedys' careful calculations about electoral votes is striking. Seeking to have it both ways, Nixon wanted to win both southern white votes, which would give him many southern states, and northern black votes, which would enable him to gain many northern states. Nixon's indecision was rooted in the majority Democratic Party's political dominance, in Nixon's own lack of a coherent political philosophy, and in uncertainty about the political significance of a growing racial crisis in the South.

The vice president sensed opportunity in the South, but he also recognized danger. Had the Democrats nominated Stevenson, Johnson, or Symington, Nixon would almost certainly have opted for a northern strategy, but Kennedy's snubbing of the South before and at the Democratic convention had opened the possibility that Nixon could win by making a major pitch for Dixie. Kennedy, however, had complicated the situation by picking Johnson for vice president. The Kennedy-Johnson ticket meant that Nixon could not be confident of carrying Texas, and he had only slightly better hopes in several other southern states. At the time of the Republican convention, Nixon seems to have chosen a northern strategy. Both the deal with Rockefeller and the Lodge vice presidential nomination suggest this conclusion. According to a northern strategy, Nixon's six key battleground states were New York, Pennsylvania, Illinois, Michigan, Ohio, and California, totaling 181 electoral votes. Of these six, New York's 45 electoral votes were the most important. Rockefeller's liberal platform planks had been designed to nail down the Empire State.

Nixon, however, did not fully embrace a northern strategy. He was unwilling to choose between a northern or a southern strategy because he could not see clearly which course offered the best chance of victory. He hesitated to adopt a southern strategy because he correctly foresaw a close election, and in a close election party organization mattered. In such an election, the party that has been dominant historically in a particular locale is likely to win. If Nixon pursued a southern strategy, he would be trying to win states lacking local Republican elected officials, and in a close race Democrats would prevail in the South due to superior party organization. At the same time, a southern strategy meant ignoring parts of the North where Republicans did have party organizations. Losing those areas would hurt the party in areas where it was well established. Should Nixon win the presidency with a southern strategy, he might find it difficult to govern, because the southern states responsible for his election would have elected a solid bloc of racially obsessed conservative Democrats whom he could not control, while the states he lost would probably have elected even more liberal Democrats who would damage his own party in the North. Nixon as president would be a man without a party. Eisenhower had demonstrated that a popular president could govern without a party, but Nixon lacked that kind of popularity.

To placate Republicans who had wanted a southern strategy and to show that he was not Rockefeller's captive, Nixon, in his acceptance speech, said, "I pledge to you that I, personally, will carry this campaign into every one of the fifty states of this nation between now and November 8." In one sense, the promise was unremarkable, because the vice president had made a similar vow as he traveled around the country all spring. Nixon wanted to build a national Republican Party. Also, this reaffirmation of his position tended to calm conservatives, and by promising to appear in all states, he cheered party officials in northern states (for example, Massachusetts) that almost every Republican conceded to Kennedy. And this pledge enabled Nixon to avoid choosing either a northern or a southern strategy.[41]

The highly visible promise, however, proved unwise. Had Nixon merely proposed to campaign in every region, he would have pleased southern conservatives, and party officials in the Northeast would have understood that he did not intend to write off their region either. The fifty-state pledge was further complicated by Nixon's additional caveat that only travels after the convention counted, a promise that inhibited Nixon's freedom of maneuver. Nixon had already visited many safe states during the spring, and he could gain nothing from return visits during the fall. Such trips took time away from the key states that would decide the outcome. Puzzled by Nixon's extravagant pledge, other politicians did not see any reason for a fifty-state campaign. It was only one sign of Nixon's ineptness.

In a national campaign that focused fully on neither the North nor the South, what states might Nixon try to carry to win? He could count on New England's three small Republican states of Maine (5 electoral votes), New Hampshire (4), and Vermont (3), but on little else in the East. He would contest New York (45), Pennsylvania (32), New Jersey (16), Connecticut (8), Maryland (9), and Delaware (3), but all were doubtful. Kennedy had demonstrated unusual popularity throughout the urban Northeast. In the South, Nixon's best chances were states where the Republican Party had some strength, such as Kentucky (10), Tennessee (11), Virginia (12), and Florida (10). Eisenhower had carried all four in 1956. Although Nixon would fight for Texas (24), Johnson's presence on the ticket made it difficult to win. North Carolina (14) and South Carolina (8) would be contested but were uncertain.

In the Midwest, Nixon could count only on Indiana (13) and Iowa (10), but he had excellent chances in Ohio (25), Illinois (27), Wisconsin (12), and possibly Minnesota (11). He had thinner hopes in Michigan (20) and Missouri (13). With a strong agricultural program, he could expect to win the Farm Belt that ran from North Dakota south through Oklahoma (30 total). Nixon was much more confident about the West (53 plus California). He could contrast his own self-made individualism, earthy pragmatism, and western accent with Kennedy's inherited wealth, Harvard-educated intellectuality, and eastern accent. Kennedy could not be certain of a single western state, and Nixon figured to win the vast majority, perhaps even make a clean sweep. The battle for California (32), however, would be ferocious. Still, when one added up all the numbers, it was hard for Nixon to get to the required 269 electoral votes, and it was extremely difficult without New York.

Barring either a disastrous mistake by Kennedy or some sudden world crisis, Nixon may have lost the election either at the moment that Johnson accepted Kennedy's offer of the vice presidency, thereby winning Texas for the Democrats, or at the moment that Rockefeller rejected Nixon's offer of the vice presidency, thereby giving New York to Kennedy. Without Texas and New York, Nixon's electoral math did not look promising. To win the election, Nixon needed a big lucky break or a series of small ones. A sweep or near-sweep of the West and Midwest was not enough. He also needed a breakthrough either in the East, which seemed attached to Kennedy, or in the South, where Johnson had strength and where Republicans lacked party organizations.

As Nixon brooded upon fall strategy, President Eisenhower held a press conference on August 24. The president was in a grumpy mood, and he wanted to end the event as quickly as possible. After he had signaled that the meeting was over and started to leave the room, a reporter asked a question. The question was a complicated one in which the reporter wanted Eisenhower to cite a specific example of a contribution that Nixon had made to the administration over the past seven and a half years. Annoyed by the query and by its rude intrusion at the end of the press conference, Eisenhower snapped, "If you give me a week, I might think of one," and then left the room. Eisenhower had, of course, meant that the reporter should ask the same question at the press conference that was already scheduled for the following week, but the answer suggested instead that Eisenhower would require an entire week to think of something that Nixon had done, implying that Nixon had done nothing important inside the administration and that Nixon's claim of "experience," a major focal point of his campaign, was bogus.[42]

After Ike returned to his office, he grasped the inadequacy of his response and also how the specific wording, especially when taken out of context, suggested that the president could recall no contributions that the vice president had made. Eisenhower felt that he had been trapped into a careless answer. There was little he could do except apologize to Nixon, which he did immediately. The damage, however, had been done, and once again the public could see the strained relationship between Eisenhower and Nixon and perhaps, through a slip, even the president's lack of confidence in the Republican nominee.

Throughout his political career, Nixon was usually the principal architect of his own follies, but sometimes he benefited from others' mistakes. In August 1960 Nixon received a windfall when the Democratic Congress reassembled for an unusual monthlong session. Speaker Rayburn and Majority Leader Johnson had adjourned the Congress during July so that the two political parties could hold their respective conventions. The unprecedented August session was needed to complete action on pending legislation, but its occurrence during a presidential election season guaranteed that nothing could be enacted. About the only significant measure that passed was a bill authorizing the first televised presidential debates. Had the telegenic Kennedy not been the Democratic nominee, the Democratic Congress might well have killed the bill. Indeed, that bill might have been the main reason that the August session was scheduled. Finally, at the end of the month, Congress adjourned, and the presidential campaign began in earnest during its traditional starting point over Labor Day weekend.

5

THE SOUTH

In 1960 the South was in political turmoil, strained by racial upheaval and angry about northern liberal control of the national Democratic Party. As this chapter shows, racist southern Democrats organized a movement for unpledged electors calculated either to bargain over civil rights with the major party candidates or to throw the election into the House of Representatives. However, Lyndon Johnson used his famous arm-twisting to get southern Democratic Party organizations to back the Kennedy-Johnson ticket, while his brilliant campaigning personally persuaded many southerners to back the national team. The local party organizations were crucial, but not everyone bought the argument, and some southern Democrats ignored tradition to vote Republican. The continued weakening of the Democratic Party in the former "Solid South" would be the most important long-term consequence of the 1960 presidential election.

At the Democratic National Convention, Mississippi governor Ross Barnett, a staunch segregationist, opposed Kennedy's nomination and the party's strong civil rights plank in the platform. After returning to Mississippi, the governor vowed revenge upon Kennedy and the Democrats for embracing civil rights. Barnett's desire to withhold the South's electoral votes from Kennedy was inspired by 1948, when Strom Thurmond's Dixiecrats had carried Mississippi and three other Deep South states in the presidential election. At that time, the Dixiecrats had tried to throw the election into the House by depriving both Truman and Dewey of a majority in the electoral college. Ultimately, the plan had failed because Thurmond won only four states where state Democrats had substituted Thurmond for Truman as the Democratic Party's nominee. Without the esteemed Democratic label, segregationists had been unable to defeat Truman in any southern state where Truman ran on the ballot as a Democrat.

Being a Democrat, for most white southerners, was a birthright as intensely felt as holding American citizenship. In 1960, most southerners approved of Democratic Party policies other than civil rights, and many Democratic officeholders resisted urging voters to desert the party's presidential candidate. If voters broke with the party in the presidential race, they might desert Democratic candidates in other contests. Besides, throwing the presidential election into the House of Representatives with a three-way split in the electoral college would not be useful. The South was weak in the House, and a northern candidate would win, even perhaps with no support from the South. In addition, a third party might encourage northern Democrats to strip southern senators and representatives of their committee chairmanships. At a rally in Shreveport, Louisiana, Senator George Smathers of Florida, who headed Kennedy's southern campaign, warned that if Kennedy won without the South senators from bolting states could expect to lose their posts.

In 1960 segregationists devised a new strategy that they believed would be superior to the Dixiecrat strategy of 1948. They rejected trying to capture the Democratic Party label for an anti–civil rights southern presidential candidate at the state level, which the national party had taken measures to discourage, and they rejected urging Democrats to shift to a third party, which would produce enormous stress inside the Democratic Party. Instead, the diehards decided to use control of state party machinery to deliver the South's electors, chosen as Democrats, to whichever national candidate would endorse southern racial views. These electors would also retain the option of voting for a third-party candidate in the electoral college. Thus, on Election Day, voters could choose between a slate of Democrats and a slate of Republicans. However, the Democratic electors, picked by each state party's machinery, would not be pledged to support the national nominee. Rather, after Election Day, but before the electoral college met, these "unpledged electors," as their advocates styled them, would bargain to deliver the South's electoral votes to the candidate who would promise to give the white South relief on the racial issue. If neither the Democrat nor the Republican would do so, then the electors might vote for a third candidate, as had happened in 1948. Thus, the plan neither precluded nor required a third-party candidate.

The beauty of the plan for unpledged electors was in the details. Voters would be asked to defend segregation, which was widely popular in the South, not to vote for a particular individual as a surrogate for a cause. Advocates believed that a vote for segregation on the customary Democratic line on the ballot would attract more votes than would a vote for any individual. If the election was close enough that independent electors held the balance of power, then political bargaining might occur. The bargainers could choose to support Kennedy, Nixon, or a third-party candidate. A reporter asked Governor Barnett, "But they could vote for Kennedy or Nixon, if they wanted to?" The Mississippian conceded, "They could, but I don't think they would." He indicated that he would like unpledged electors to vote for a conservative southern Democrat like Senators Harry Byrd of Virginia, Strom Thurmond of South Carolina, or Richard Russell of Georgia. Finally, in a close election, independent electors might throw the election into the House.[1]

The racially obsessed, archsegregationist, white Citizens' Council was the organized force that pushed for unpledged electors. By the late fifties, the Citizens' Council totally controlled politics in Mississippi. The mostly middle-class and respectable council, allied with the more rural and more violent Ku Klux Klan, held equally strong control of North Alabama, but it never gained the same lock on the southern half of that state, which was to result in a peculiar political outcome in 1960. Segregationists also held power through related organizations in Baptist northern Louisiana, in parts of Arkansas near the Mississippi River, and in much of rural southern Georgia. In the end, the independent elector movement was strong only in Alabama, Mississippi, Louisiana, Georgia, and South Carolina, five Deep South states that together had just 49 electoral votes. Five of Alabama's electors, however, became pledged to the national nominee, so a maximum of 44 votes were at stake. Each state pursued a somewhat different policy, had a different result, and has to be discussed separately.

In 1960, Alabama became the first state to take up the issue of unpledged electors, even before Kennedy's nomination. Under Alabama's plan, Democratic Party voters picked 11 electors for the November ballot in the primaries in May. North Alabama, where the Citizens' Council was strong, leaned to unpledged electors, but South Alabama wanted party loyalists. As it turned out, the winning electors were split—six were unpledged and five were pledged to the national nominee. Thus, when a voter filled out the ballot for the Democratic presidential candidate in the fall, the voter would be picking six electors pledged to no one and five pledged to Kennedy. Until late in the campaign, the six unpledged electors dodged criticism from within the Democratic Party by hinting that they might vote for Kennedy. But this was only one possibility. A woman from Birmingham showed up at the Republican National Convention with a letter allegedly from one of Alabama's unpledged electors promising to vote Republican if the party's platform was weak on civil rights. Nixon's people ignored the proposal. This strange split-elector situation allowed Alabama Democrats to avoid a party division that might have enabled Nixon to carry the state in a three-way contest.

In the summer, much of the white South was in an uproar. Southern black college students had been sitting in to protest segregated lunch counters all across the South since February, leading to 75,000 arrests within the year. Having been burned by the strong civil rights plank adopted by their formerly beloved Democratic Party in Los Angeles, southern segregationists had gotten no relief from the Republicans when Richard Nixon made his deal with Nelson Rockefeller, embracing the strongest possible civil rights plank. Polls showed an angry, seething South with Kennedy running very poorly. One Virginian wrote, "And I would rather go fishing." Many voters called themselves undecided, which was an ominous sign in a one-party region. Some politicians predicted that Kennedy would not carry a single southern state. The Deep South might boycott Kennedy through the use of independent electors, while the states with some Republican strength would all go to Nixon.[2]

Although Mississippi was in open rebellion, Governor Barnett's determination to prevent the state's electors from being delivered to Kennedy clashed with the fact that many Mississippians wanted to vote for the national nominee. Thus, the governor had to give up his original plan to substitute unpledged electors for Kennedy electors and, in effect, keep Kennedy off the ballot. On August 16, the Mississippi State Democratic Convention, reconvened by Barnett, voted to put both Kennedy electors and unpledged electors on the ballot under the Democratic label. Barnett agreed to the plan because he was convinced that Citizens' Council backing would enable unpledged electors to prevail. The Republicans were sufficiently weak in the state that they would run third. Whether enough independent electors would win throughout the South to decide the election would depend ultimately upon what happened in other southern states as well as the tally in the electoral college. "If neither party gains a majority," the governor vowed, "there won't be sit-ins, there'll be kneel-ins for Mississippi's votes." Salivating at the prospect of groveling Yankees, Barnett and his backers cultivated independent elector supporters in Louisiana, Georgia, and South Carolina.[3]

At the time, Barnett's decision to run a separate slate in Mississippi, despite support for the national ticket from Senators James Eastland and John Stennis, was seen as the first of what would likely be other gubernatorial decisions to break with the national party. However, Governors Luther Hodges of North Carolina, Buford Ellington of Tennessee, and Orval Faubus of Arkansas supported the national ticket, as did Governor-elect Terry Sanford of North Carolina. Most southern Democrats in Congress also resisted Barnett's plan. "If I would bolt the Democratic Party," explained Eastland, "I would be removed as chairman of the Judiciary Committee." A lot of frenzied and even awkward communication was taking place between bewildered southerners. Barnett sent Senator Harry Byrd of Virginia a copy of a *Jackson Daily News* editorial calling for unpledged electors. Byrd, alarmed by how events were unfolding, wrote James Byrnes of South Carolina: "Dick Russell told me today that Kennedy will implement the Democratic platform and advocate civil rights legislation beyond what is contained in the platform."[4]

The Virginia Conservative Party tried to put a Byrd-Goldwater ticket on the ballot but was forced to drop the plan after both senators objected. "The Republican Party," declared Barry Goldwater, "offers a home for conservatives. Don't waste your vote." The most popular Republican in the South due to his view that the Constitution required civil rights to be a state issue beyond federal control, Goldwater campaigned for Nixon in Richmond by denouncing the Democratic platform as the "Democratic Manifesto," a phrase that drew laughter. A lot of affection between Byrd and Goldwater had developed in their years together in the Senate. "It is a lonesome road you and I and the other Conservatives are going to travel in the coming years," the Virginian had written prophetically to the Arizonan, "but I think that if we stick together a little better than we have in the past, we can give those Liberals—or should we call them Radicals—something to think about." Byrd and Goldwater were conservative soul mates, in much the same way as were the liberal Kennedy and Rockefeller. Realignment seemed to be in the air, but southern committee chairs like Byrd, Russell, and Eastland could not afford to give up their Democratic Party seniority and the power it brought them.[5]

In contrast with Mississippi, Louisiana's independent elector movement failed. In January 1960 Jimmie Davis had been elected governor in a deal with the archsegregationists. After the Democratic National Convention, Davis tried to get the state party to adopt unpledged electors. Before the Democratic State Central Committee met, Lyndon Johnson intervened. Working through Senator Russell Long of Louisiana, Johnson insisted that Long urge the committee to keep the Kennedy-Johnson ticket on the ballot. Long, from the Protestant North, worked hard to switch northern Louisiana committee members from unpledged to Kennedy. The Catholic members from southern Louisiana were already for Kennedy. Long argued that independent electors threatened the state's taxes on offshore oil. Long's persuasion worked, and on August 11 the committee voted 51 to 49 to put Kennedy electors on the ballot. Had Louisiana voted the opposite way, several southern states might have followed. Archsegregationists did use petitions to put the States' Rights Party on the ballot.

The Louisiana result threw the movement for unpledged electors into question. If Barnett and other diehards could not persuade Louisiana, a bastion of segregation that had bolted from Truman to Thurmond in 1948, to join the crusade, what chance did these southerners have of gaining enough electors to control the outcome of the election? Furthermore, if one phone call from Johnson to Long could effectively hold one state, what would happen to the independent elector movement once Johnson began to campaign more energetically in the South? The importance of Johnson as the vice presidential nominee was less about the candidate persuading masses of angry southerners to stick with the Democratic Party than it was about the powerful majority leader quietly getting southern senators to organize the campaign for the ticket. Party organization was to be the key to Kennedy's success in the South. Putting Johnson on the ticket enabled the Kennedys to mobilize the South's existing parties.

Georgia was also in turmoil. Just after the national convention, Senator Richard Russell wrote a friend, "I frankly do not know what to do." Russell did not want to bolt, but his longtime friend and associate, Roy V. Harris, headed the Georgia Citizens' Council and had been enraged both by the platform and by Kennedy's nomination. Asked his opinion of the Kennedy-Johnson ticket in July, Harris said, "What I think about them can't be printed." Governor Ernest Vandiver, who was married to Russell's niece, controlled the state party, and he endorsed the Democratic ticket despite the "obnoxious" platform on August 22, just before Richard Nixon visited Atlanta. The governor would take Georgia in whatever direction the revered senator wanted. Vandiver's support mattered, because he was one of the state's twelve electors. Seven other Georgia electors, Vandiver loyalists, also endorsed Kennedy and Johnson at the same time.[6]

The endorsements produced fury among the state's archsegregationists. Roy V. Harris complained, "It means a collapse of the resistance movement in Georgia." The politically formidable Harris had embraced unpledged electors with a vengeance, although he also declared Nixon "less socialistic" than Kennedy. On September 14, Georgians voted in a referendum for unpledged electors, by 168,786 to 136,070. Thus, Georgia's twelve Democratic electors on the ballot in November would not formally be pledged to anyone. Most Georgia electors hedged their pledges to the national ticket, and by Election Day only two were unconditionally "in the bag" for Kennedy. Four were thought to be eager to throw the election into the House.[7]

Georgia's officially unpledged Democratic electors may have been a ruse to impress Harris and prevent the placement on the ballot of non–Democratic Party independent electors that could throw the state to the Republicans in a three-way contest. There is more than a hint of this conclusion in a "strictest confidential" letter that Russell wrote to a friend in August. "I do not think any intelligent Democrat who has thought this matter through," observed the shrewdest man in the Senate, "has any doubt as to where the twelve electors of Georgia will be found in November." On September 24, both Russell and Senator Herman Talmadge tepidly endorsed the ticket. In an action that spoke louder than words, both loaned staff members to Kennedy's campaign, and in October Talmadge campaigned with Kennedy before 10,000 people at Warm Springs. Georgia's adroit leaders kept a third party off the ballot and united both Harris's segregationists and Kennedy's supporters behind the Democrats. Kennedy's name was not on the ballot; only the electors' names and the party they represented were listed. Wary of unpledged electors, African Americans in Atlanta voted Republican.[8]

The unpledged elector movement also stalled in South Carolina. Governor Fritz Hollings, who favored Kennedy, kept the state loyal to the national party over objections from Senator Strom Thurmond, who was still a nominal Democrat but no more reconstructed than in 1948. South Carolina law gave the governor control of the party. Although Hollings,

a master politician, made public gestures of complying with the segregationists' demands for unpledged electors, he used the party apparatus
not only to have Kennedy loyalists named as electors but also to keep a
separate unpledged elector slate off the ballot. As a result, segregationists were forced to oppose Kennedy by backing Nixon, who favored civil
rights. About all that Thurmond could do was to denounce the Democratic platform as a "road-map for socialism." In a state that had no organized Republican Party and where no Republican, not even Eisenhower,
had carried the state since the end of Reconstruction, Hollings held the
upper hand.[9]

Johnson's fall strategy was to corral southern Democrats for the ticket
on grounds of self-interest. In many respects, Johnson's campaigning
was the most effective by any candidate during the fall. He proved to be
formidable. In a planning session at Hyannis Port shortly after the convention, Johnson agreed to go from "Boston to Austin." Much of Johnson's campaigning was to be in the South. Whereas Kennedy, Nixon, and
Lodge each spent 15 to 20 percent of their time in the South, Johnson
gave Dixie 44 percent of his time. Just after Labor Day, Kennedy and
Johnson traveled together for a few days in Texas. This tour allowed Kennedy to be introduced to Texas, crowd responses signaled which themes
should be emphasized, and national TV coverage linked the pair in the
public mind. Afterward, Rayburn privately described this episode as
"triumphal."[10]

The highlight of Johnson's fall campaign was a Truman-like train trip
from Washington, D.C., through most of the southern states to New
Orleans during mid-October. The train concentrated on the small towns
that were the heart and soul of the South's Democratic Party. These were
often economically poor areas, and they lacked the affluent country club
Republicans found in southern cities. By using many stops, Johnson
got excellent local publicity, and by staying on the train, he did not have
to speak in segregated buildings. Many southern towns had local ordi-
nances that required segregation in all public buildings. Johnson began
his train trip in Virginia and quickly warmed to the crowds of Democrats
who greeted his train. On the 3,800-mile trip, mostly by train but with
a side trip by plane to Florida, Johnson covered eight states in five days
and gave fifty-seven speeches at forty-nine stops. Also on board were 182
reporters.

The candidate made sure that the train loudspeaker blared his theme
song, "The Yellow Rose of Texas," as he arrived and departed at each

stop. As every white southerner knew, the song had been popular with Texas Confederate troops during the Civil War, but it did not offend Yankees and African Americans the way "Dixie" did. By blaring it from the train at his arrival, Johnson made sure that no one embarrassed him by striking up "Dixie" just as he got there—Johnson was already in trouble with some southerners for failing to stand for "Dixie" at a Washington, D.C., dinner. In contrast, when Roy V. Harris and others attended a Citizens' Council rally in Houston, the audience rose and cheered when "Dixie" was played. "Dixie" was also played when Nixon campaigned in Richmond, getting the biggest cheer at the event.

More important than the hordes of local enthusiasts who arrived to greet the train were the dozens of local, state, and federal Democratic Party elected officials that Johnson invited to ride with him. Altogether, 1,247 local party leaders were entertained on the train. These were the Democrats who organized and won elections in the South. A few stayed on board for the trip across an entire state, but most rode only for the distance between two stops, generally about twenty or thirty miles. Between stops, Johnson had private or group meetings with these leaders, who also had opportunities to have their pictures taken with Johnson. He stressed how much carrying the South meant for the Democrats in Congress. Party leaders could cut deals with Kennedy, and if Kennedy won and Johnson became vice president, he would be able to help southern politicians use the Kennedy administration to tackle rural poverty, economic development, education, and health care. These issues were not controversial among Democrats. The only real party split was about race, and the South could not win that argument within the party. Upon occasion, Johnson even explained privately that if the race problem could be solved the South would have a brighter future.

The South's power within the Democratic Party, Johnson argued, made it imperative for the South to stick with the party. There were other important local issues, including imported textiles in the Carolinas and oil in Louisiana. Johnson reassured southerners that he understood their problems much better than Nixon did and that he and Kennedy could be more effective in helping them, especially if Congress remained under Democratic control, which seemed likely. But there were also threats. At a meeting with Florida leaders in Miami, Johnson said, "This boy Kennedy is going to win. And he is going to win big. Democrats all over the nation are helping him. They've buried the differences and are pitching in to make this a united party. If, he wins without the South, I'm warning you, I'm warning you b—— are going to be dead. You'll get nothing out of the next Congress and the Kennedy administration. I can tell you. I know." It was a terrific act, and what local official would dare question the mature judgment of so potent and knowing a national leader as Lyndon Johnson?[11]

Johnson's private persuasions meant that most Democrats who went aboard the train left as enthusiasts for the ticket. As the train passed through the South, local party officials began to signal that they would work hard to make sure that their states voted for Kennedy. Considering the weakness of southern Republicans, these Democratic Party efforts promised to have a powerful impact. During October southern polls showed a gain of about 10 percent for Kennedy, which was enough to guarantee that he would carry a share of the South. Johnson's magic was bringing the South's Democrats home. Just after the national convention, Sam Rayburn had predicted as much, when he privately had written, "I believe Lyndon's nomination for vice president will certainly make Texas safe, and many of the other southern states. Some of them always have to kick up a little but they usually come home before election time."[12]

The public part of the train trip was also extraordinary. Johnson established the major theme at the first stop in Culpeper, Virginia, not far from Washington, when he shouted, as the train pulled out, "What has Dick Nixon ever done for Culpeper?" As everyone in the town knew, the answer was literally nothing. Johnson signaled that he and Kennedy would do more. The Texan played upon the traditional southern resentment, which he shared, that a northeastern establishment identified with the Republican Party and big business had long dominated the country. Could anyone doubt that Nixon would dance to Wall Street's tune? How could Nixon possibly be good for Culpeper? To build rapport with his small-town southern audiences, Johnson "talked southern." The sophisticated reporters covering the train trip derisively referred to it as the "Cornpone Special." Some of them missed the effectiveness of Johnson's folksy approach.[13]

Johnson spoke in the words southerners understood. (Johnson had a rule for his speechwriters: No word with more than seven letters. No sentence with more than six words. No paragraph with more than three sentences.) He also put on a thick southern accent not heard by those who knew Johnson on Capitol Hill. When he arrived at Culpeper, he began by drawling, "We're mighty glad you came out to howdy and shake with us." At some stops he mentioned his Confederate granddaddy, and how his great-granddaddy, a prominent Baptist preacher, had baptized Sam Houston. In Alabama, Lady Bird, who accompanied Lyndon on the trip, called out to cousins in the audience. "We could feel minds being changed as he spoke," recalled Johnson's aide George Reedy. "They had received a glorious revelation."[14]

Johnson talked about Kennedy as a war hero, and he liked to tell the story of young Joe Kennedy's death, and how no one had asked Joe what his religion was when he had volunteered for a dangerous and ultimately fatal mission. "If a man is barred from public office because of the way he worships his God," Johnson said in Mississippi, "the time will come when a Methodist, Baptist, or Church of Christ member can't hold office because of religious intolerance." Much of politics is talking about issues in ways that please constituents, but on this issue Johnson had the passion of righteousness. There was, of course, another reason to attack religious bigotry. It was akin to racism, a subject that could be talked about only with a certain delicacy. In attacking religious prejudice, Johnson suggested that all forms of bigotry were loathsome. His remarks decrying prejudice were noticed by African Americans, who had plenty of reason to be skeptical about Johnson, and therefore, in the process of seeking to win white southern votes, Johnson also acted to draw black southern votes.[15]

Johnson also tackled the race issue. He had no choice, since his decision to join the ticket had required him to accept the total platform, including the strong civil rights plank. From the rear of the train, addressing audiences that were often racially mixed (train stations were often close to black neighborhoods), Johnson reaffirmed the party's endorsement of civil rights with vague, noble language. At many stops he gingerly said, "We think all men are equal under the law." He only said this after the audience had been warmed up. Occasionally, as at a party rally in Richmond, he spoke more candidly: "We must protect the rights of everyone, regardless of the color of his skin." To white southerners, he sometimes offered empathy. In Mississippi he said, "I love Mississippi. I understand your problems, and I want to work with people from all sections of this nation." Although he did not say so, Johnson knew that the world, the nation, and the South would all be better places when people were judged by merit rather than by skin color.[16]

Although the trip was brilliantly conceived and executed, it was an ordeal for Johnson. A megalomaniac who loved to surround himself with sycophants in his "Taj Mahal" office in the Senate or at his beloved Texas ranch, Johnson found the cramped quarters, the constant speeches, and the cozy interviews with men he had to pretend to like to be almost more than he could stand. Whenever Johnson felt heavy pressure, he gritted his teeth, bore it with resolution, and drank heavily. Aides found him angry and drunk at the end of almost every evening, offended by something that this person or that had said, or by some foul-up in the train schedule, or by an inadequate crowd at some stop, or worse, an apathetic crowd that did not adore his entreaties. Some evenings he threatened to quit the trip, or even to resign from the ticket, and on many mornings he had such a hangover that the staff had trouble coaxing the great man to gulp enough coffee to get him sober enough for the day's ordeal.

As Johnson's train made its way through Virginia, North Carolina, and South Carolina, he did much to bring those states back to the Democratic Party. One big disappointment was that Senator Harry Byrd and his intimates had declined to greet the train in Virginia. Without Byrd's support, it was hard to see how Kennedy could carry Virginia, which had an active Republican Party. After a short trip in Georgia, where the Democrats were far ahead, the train was sent without the Johnsons to Alabama, while Lyndon and Lady Byrd made a detour by airplane into Florida. The Johnsons rejoined the train for the final trip through Alabama, Mississippi, and a bit of Louisiana to a major rally at the train station in New Orleans. In Mississippi, Senators Eastland and Stennis rode on the train and publicly endorsed the ticket. Local party leaders seemed energized, and one reporter concluded, "The big push is on." This was even better than in Georgia, where Senators Russell and Talmadge had issued terse statements saying that they would vote the straight party ticket as they had always done. In New Orleans practically every important Democrat greeted the train, and 100,000 people attended a parade.[17]

Most of the remainder of Johnson's campaign was spent in Texas, where polls in the fall showed Democrats, angry over Kennedy's nomination and the liberal platform, gradually returning home to their party. But many voters remained undecided. Texas had voted for Eisenhower in both 1952 and 1956, and former governor Allan Shivers headed the organization Democrats for Nixon. Shivers's energetic campaigning across the state gave Nixon a real boost. The state's Democrats were divided, and Governor Price Daniel declared, "We're going to have harmony if we have to fight for it." From Johnson's viewpoint, whether Kennedy won the national election was less important than Johnson's ability to carry the Lone Star State for Kennedy. Johnson wrote John Connally, "We just must not win the nation and lose Texas." There would be "tremendous shock," Sam Rayburn warned, if the Republicans carried Texas. If Johnson failed in his home state, his own future presidential nomination would be unlikely and his post as majority leader in the Senate would be in jeopardy. As Election Day approached, the Texas contest tightened. Both sides went all out to excite their supporters and get them to the polls. In the last two weeks, the Democratic National Committee brought in nineteen senators, including Estes Kefauver, Tom Dodd, and John Stennis, to campaign for the ticket in all of Texas's congressional districts.[18]

Politics sometimes turns on odd moments. On the Friday before the election, the Johnsons attended a political event at the Adolphus Hotel in downtown Dallas. A group of right-wing Republicans protested the event by gathering in the hotel lobby. Among the protesters was John Tower, who was challenging Johnson for the Senate; Johnson was both seeking reelection and running for vice president. Also present were Representative Bruce Alger, Texas's only elected Republican Party official, and many women, who were not political pros. Sensing the dramatic possibilities, Alger had notified the media about the protest, and live television covered the unfolding event. Suddenly, Lyndon and Lady Bird appeared at the hotel entrance and had to make their way through the crowd in the lobby to reach a staircase. The angry and hostile crowd pushed and jostled. The physically large and agile Johnson rose to the challenge, fully prepared to jostle back, with Lady Bird following along.

It took half an hour for the Johnsons to cross the lobby, and Lyndon was in no hurry to deprive the TV cameras of the story. Hecklers chanted, "We want Nixon," and Alger swung a sign close to Lady Bird that read, "LBJ Sold Out to Yankee Socialists." Lady Bird was hit over the head by another sign, "Lyndon is a Judas." Amid increasing shouts and shoves, some protesters began to spit. One angry woman drenched Lady Bird's face in spit, but she projected serenity as she glided, blinded by spit, behind Lyndon. Television coverage suggested that Nixon's supporters were ill-mannered kooks. The next day Johnson told a Democratic rally that it was "outrageous that in a large civilized city, a man's wife can be subjected to such treatment." He added, "The Republicans are attacking the women, and the children will probably be next." Alger denied that there had been "discourtesy, profanity or jostling," but television viewers could draw their own conclusions. To viewers, Lady Bird's calm courage

On November 3, John Kennedy and Lyndon Johnson campaigned together in Wichita Falls, Texas. Senator Ralph Yarborough joined the two candidates. (LBJ Library photo by Frank Muto)

had been dignified and magnificent. After the election, Robert Kennedy said, "Lady Bird carried Texas."[19]

The televised Adolphus Hotel incident enabled Texas Democrats to get their voters to the polls in order to vote for Kennedy and Johnson to protest the treatment of Lady Bird. More important, Johnson used the incident to make three phone calls to Senator Richard Russell, who had sat out the campaign. Later, after the election, Russell explained his behavior. He needed 20 Republican votes in the Senate to block liberal Democrats from passing bills that he opposed. By staying out of the campaign, it had been easier to keep a friendly relationship with the Republicans. However, after the Republican National Convention, Russell had also concluded that Kennedy was likely to win. Both Kennedy and Johnson knew that they would lose without the South, and Russell was now in the position, late in the campaign, of offering his valuable services in order to save the ticket. Such help would have to be acknowledged if the Democrats won.

As for the decision to go with Kennedy, Russell years later said, "I accepted Kennedy as the lesser of two evils." During Johnson's third call to Russell, who adored Lady Bird, the Georgian agreed to campaign for the ticket "on the basis of our personal relations." Georgia was safe for Kennedy, and Russell had no desire to rile his old friend Roy V. Harris. So Russell spent two days campaigning in conservative East Texas, an area where Nixon had expected to do well. Russell not only helped there, but because he had many relatives in South Carolina, news of his activity, widely carried in Georgia and South Carolina, stimulated Democratic turnout in South Carolina as well. A little spit had done quite a bit to tip the election.[20]

Thus, Johnson was able to use Long to keep Louisiana Democratic, and bringing Russell on board had helped in Texas, South Carolina, and Georgia, but Johnson was not successful everywhere. Johnson's campaigning could not save Florida, and despite the support of Eastland and Stennis, Mississippi narrowly went for Barnett's unpledged electors on Election Day. Johnson's biggest disappointment was probably Virginia. He had counted on being able to lure Senator Harry Byrd, whose personal political machine ran the state, in the same way that he had appealed to Long or Russell, but Johnson was not personally close to Byrd in the same way that Johnson was close to Russell, and the congruence of Louisiana and Texas state interests had created bonds between Johnson and Long that could not be repeated where Virginia and Texas were concerned. Byrd later admitted that he had not voted for a Democrat for president since 1936. "I just wonder," observed Sam Rayburn, "how long some of these people will have to vote Republican in order to acknowledge that they are Republicans." Byrd, however, was not a Republican but a states' rights Democrat.[21]

Byrd's rural-based political machine seethed with hostility toward Kennedy. In early August, Senator Byrd's son, who edited the *Winchester Evening Star*, denounced Kennedy and the liberal Democratic Party platform. At the annual political picnic at his apple orchard, Senator Byrd announced his position on the presidential contest by declaring that "silence is golden." Closer to Election Day, Byrd took important steps to give Virginia to Nixon. He widely circulated a Senate speech defending state right-to-work laws that made it hard for unions to organize in the South. Kennedy opposed the Taft-Hartley provision that allowed Virginia and other southern states to keep an open shop. Byrd privately accused Kennedy of wanting "a labor controlled government." The senator also appeared on statewide television with Eisenhower when the president spoke at Mary Baldwin College on October 27. Byrd then played the race card. He had a henchman, Blackie Moore, a close friend and the Speaker of the Virginia House of Delegates, issue a public letter, conveniently published in the *Winchester Evening Star*, condemning Kennedy for a promise to appoint black federal judges. Before the Kennedy forces in Virginia could recover from this barrage, former governor Allan Shivers of Texas arrived in Richmond to denounce Kennedy as a "stargazer" who favored a "managed economy." Hit from all sides, the state's loyal Democrats reeled into incoherence. Nixon carried Virginia. Byrd remained king of his realm.[22]

Virginia proved to be an exception. On Election Day most of the South voted Democratic. Although Nixon carried Tennessee (11 electoral votes), Virginia (12), and Florida (10), all states twice won by Eisenhower, he made no further inroads into the former Confederacy. Johnson enabled Kennedy to carry Texas (24), a state that otherwise would have been lost, and Johnson's intervention with Russell Long saved Louisiana (10). Johnson's appeal to Richard Russell guaranteed Georgia (12), where Johnson's presence on the ticket overcame the pressure for independent electors. Hollings's support, the black vote, Johnson's train trip, and Russell's campaigning delivered South Carolina (8). Without Johnson on the ticket, North Carolina (14) also would have most likely gone to Nixon, and Barnett's independent electors would have easily swept Mississippi

(8). Kennedy's only safe southern state was heavily Democratic Arkansas (8).

With Johnson, Kennedy took six whole states and gained five of Alabama's electors (a total of 81). Nixon won three states (a total of 33), and the independent electors were marginalized in the electoral college by carrying only Mississippi plus six from Alabama (a total of 14). Had Johnson not been on the ticket, Nixon would have won Tennessee, Virginia, Florida, Texas, South Carolina, and probably North Carolina (a total of 79). Independent electors would have carried Mississippi, Louisiana, and a share of Alabama (a total of 24). Kennedy would have been reduced to winning Arkansas and part of Alabama (a total of 13). The outcome in Georgia, if Johnson had not been on the ticket, cannot be predicted. To carry enough of the South, including Texas, to win the election, Kennedy needed Johnson as a running mate, but Johnson's adroit campaigning also mattered. So did effective Democratic Party organizations throughout the South. All year, the Kennedys' emphasis upon organization played a role. Sam Rayburn believed that Johnson was the first vice president on a ticket to have made much of a difference since Teddy Roosevelt ran with William McKinley in 1900.

6
THE FALL CAMPAIGN

The postconvention campaign can be divided into four segments. First, in August, both candidates tested themes and ideas in minor campaign swings. Richard Nixon got a big bounce from his convention acceptance speech and led John Kennedy in the early August Gallup poll, 50 percent to 44 percent. Then, during early September, the religious issue exploded, to the dismay of both Kennedy and Nixon. Toward the end of the month and well into October, the first-ever televised presidential debates enabled Kennedy to establish a definite lead, and Kennedy's superior organization enabled him to retain the lead. In early October, Gallup reported Kennedy ahead, 49 percent to 46 percent. Finally, during the last two weeks, Nixon surged, with a massive barrage of television advertising and effective campaigning with President Eisenhower. For both candidates, money, organization, and television drove the result. By Election Day, the race was a dead heat.[1]

Despite Lyndon Johnson's presence on the Democratic ticket, some Republicans urged Nixon to run a southern-oriented campaign, and in mid-August Nixon made trips to Greensboro, North Carolina; Birmingham, Alabama; and Atlanta, Georgia, three New South cities with lively and prosperous business communities and growing numbers of so-called country club Republicans, many of whom were recent transplants from the North. In all three cities, Nixon drew unprecedented crowds, reaching 15,000 in Greensboro, 25,000 in Birmingham, and 150,000 in Atlanta, one-quarter of whom were black. "We now believe that the Kennedy-Johnson ticket is in great trouble in the South," he said in Atlanta. "The size of the crowds and their enthusiasm exceeded the highest estimates we had received in advance." In Greensboro, Nixon declared race a national issue, endorsed civil rights, and approved sit-ins. He would not run separate campaigns in different sections, but he also did not intend to write the South off just because Johnson was Kennedy's running mate. Nixon's reception committees at the airports in Birmingham and Atlanta were integrated.[2]

The most important event during Nixon's southern trips occurred in Greensboro, where the Republican nominee on August 17 scraped his knee on a car door as he got out of a vehicle. Within a few days, a massive staphylococcus infection had set in that could only be treated in a hospital. While the vice president was hospitalized from August 29 to September 9, Kennedy launched his formal campaign in Detroit with an AFL-CIO–sponsored rally on Labor Day, September 5. For the Nixon campaign, the candidate's hospitalization was a disaster. Every day, Kennedy was on the campaign trail exciting local crowds, cultivating fellow politicians, making national headlines, and dominating television, while the incapacitated Republican was stuck in bed hooked up to drip medications. After seeing a poll that showed Kennedy leading 51 percent to 49 percent, Nixon left the hospital, on Friday, September 9.

Furthermore, Nixon's pledge to visit all fifty states now hung over the campaign like a curse. There were only nine weeks between Labor Day and Election Day, and almost two weeks had been ripped out of the schedule. It was hard to reschedule Nixon without throwing off the campaign's pacing, upsetting local Republican Party plans, and causing further scheduling problems. If the fifty-state pledge was to be kept, it would become difficult to make the repeat visits that were needed in the large, close states that were key to winning. To keep as many commitments as possible, Nixon scheduled visits to thirty-seven states in just three weeks. Beginning on Monday, September 12, Nixon flew 9,000 miles to cover fourteen states in five days. After a rally at the Baltimore airport, Nixon made short stops in Indiana, Texas, and California. Pausing a bit in his home state, in a single day he covered Washington, Oregon, and Idaho. Then it was on to North Dakota, Illinois, and Missouri, before heading east to New Jersey, turning south to Virginia, then retracing halfway across the continent to Nebraska, and ending with a day visiting rural Iowa.

Friday, September 16, in Iowa proved too much. Trapped in a car on bad roads connecting numerous tiny towns in safely Republican Iowa where he met few voters and got virtually no national news coverage, Nixon finally exploded. On a lonely stretch of highway, the candidate, who was sitting in the back seat on the right side, began to kick the front seat violently, jabbing his aide and friend Don Hughes in the kidneys. Finally, the driver pulled over, and Hughes leapt out and began to walk down the road ready to desert the campaign and his berserk boss. Another aide had to fetch Hughes back to the car, but Hughes refused to sit in the now-useless front seat, which Nixon had kicked so hard that it had broken from its moorings. The seething, angry candidate did not say another word. To the relief of Nixon's aides, the press was nowhere to be seen.[3]

Still ill when the trip started, Nixon caught a cold en route, had little time to rest, and ended the week ten pounds lighter, with a 103-degree temperature, night fever, and chills. A friend, Earl Blaik, had warned Nixon that a national campaign was a physical endurance contest that needed the same care demanded of a great athlete preparing for an Olympic competition. "It is just as important to plan your campaign with the understanding of possible physical attrition as it is to plan the presentation of issues," advised Blaik. "Since the campaign is a continuous series of television performances you must always project as the relaxed, confident, fresh and unwearied candidate. Issues are important, but far more important is the impression created by the candidate." It was wise advice, but Nixon's hospitalization had caused Nixon to ignore Blaik's warning.[4]

After Iowa, Nixon spent September 19 to 25 in punishing travels to another nine states: Minnesota, Pennsylvania, Michigan, Kentucky, Wisconsin, South Dakota, Kansas, Louisiana, and Mississippi, as well as returning to Indiana, Missouri, and Illinois. Nixon's frantic travels were matched by Kennedy's jetting across the country from September 2 to 25 to twenty-six states: New Hampshire, Maine, California, Alaska, Michigan (for Labor Day), Idaho, Washington, Oregon, Texas (with Johnson), Missouri (a fund-raiser in St. Louis), New York, New Jersey, Pennsylvania, Maryland, North Carolina, West Virginia, Virginia, Tennessee, Iowa, the Dakotas, Montana, Wyoming, Colorado, Utah, and Ohio. Comparison of the two lists shows that Kennedy's travels were more efficient. Unlike Nixon, he tended to concentrate on two or three states in the same region before a long hop. Nixon's more exhausting schedule was the result of mixing in locations that had been rescheduled from early September with other commitments.

Nixon was eager to regain the initiative because during his time in the hospital the religious issue had surfaced in an alarming way. In August and early September, mounds of scurrilous anti-Catholic literature began to appear across heavily Protestant parts of the South and Midwest, especially in the key state of Texas. More than 300 separate anti-Catholic tracts were identified, and five million copies of eleven pamphlets were circulated. Most of this literature seems to have originated with rural Protestant clergy in the Bible Belt. It was estimated that 95 percent of 3,700 Southern Baptist preachers in Texas would support Nixon and advise their congregations to do so. These rural Protestants argued that a Catholic president would represent un-American, alien values. To Americans who lived in large cities or in polyglot regions of the East, Midwest, and West, where Protestants, Catholics, and Jews had long resided together, the country was not the kind of monocultural Protestant society that these rural preachers imagined it to be.[5]

The Nixon campaign had nothing to do with this material, and Nixon seems to have been shocked by its virulence. He described himself as "distressed" in a letter to the Catholic Republican journalist Clare Boothe Luce. Raised in the often-persecuted Quaker faith, Nixon understood religious prejudice. Just after the Republican nominee was released from the hospital, he told *Meet the Press* that it would be "tragic" if religion affected the election. He then declared that he would not mention the topic again. Nixon had personal reasons to be offended by religious bigotry, but his high-mindedness also coincided with political calculation. Like Hubert Humphrey in the spring, Nixon knew that Protestant bigots would vote for him in any case, but he also recognized that anti-Catholic propaganda threatened to alienate Catholic voters who might otherwise support him. After all, Nixon's anti-Communism appealed to many Catholics. Nixon could do nothing about the religious issue except to hope that it would die out.[6]

The religious issue had gained attention on September 8, when major newspapers publicized a statement by 150 Protestant clergy attacking Kennedy's candidacy and opposing any Catholic as president. Although many of the signatories were obscure, one person stood out: Dr. Norman Vincent Peale. The chief pastor of New York's prestigious Marble Collegiate Church, Peale was the most prominent Protestant in New York City. The author of a best seller, *The Power of Positive Thinking* (1952), he wrote a weekly religious column carried in hundreds of newspapers, and he frequently represented the mainstream Protestant view on national television. Peale's name gave the anti-Catholic group seriousness, respectability, and legitimacy, and the statement produced a firestorm of opposition. The witty Adlai Stevenson said, "Paul is appealing but Peale is appalling." Robert Kennedy declared that religion was "the number one question." However, one top Democrat was pleased. "This may have been our first big break," he said, adding that Kennedy could now tackle the religious issue head-on. Within two days, Peale had withdrawn his support for the group and declared that he had been "stupid" for being witlessly maneuvered into supporting something with which he did not agree. Once Peale saw the hostility against his having signed the statement, he had little choice but to capitulate.[7]

Nixon and his staff were alarmed by Peale's antics. In key northern states, Nixon expected Kennedy to gain Catholic votes, and Nixon also knew that he would gain anti-Catholic votes in the South and in conservative parts of the Midwest. In other words, there was a trade-off. Democrats agreed with this assessment. During September, the Gallup poll found Nixon overall drawing 50 percent, 8 percent below Eisenhower's victory in 1956. The drop, however, was uneven. Nixon was down 2 percent among Protestants but down 22 percent among Catholics. From Nixon's viewpoint, the problem was that Kennedy could now reintroduce the religious issue to his own advantage and do so by claiming that he was merely responding to anti-Catholic prejudice. The more that Kennedy was able to campaign on the issue in this way the more likely it was that he would attract Catholics who had voted for Eisenhower in 1952 and 1956. Unless Nixon could hold a good proportion of those Catholics, his presidential bid was doomed.[8]

Almost immediately after the Peale fiasco, Kennedy accepted an invitation to address the Greater Houston Ministerial Association on September 12—not a friendly audience. Before the event, Speaker Sam Rayburn warned Kennedy, "These are not ministers. These are politicians. . . . They hate your guts and they're going to tear you to pieces." Composed of about 300 white preachers, many of them Baptists, the association had a wary, negative view of the candidate. Johnson and Rayburn accompanied Kennedy to the event, which took place as part of a short swing through Texas by Kennedy and Johnson.[9]

In a high-risk gamble, the Kennedy campaign had the event broadcast live on a statewide television hookup. Kennedy never lacked self-confidence when he used television. Nor did he ever use it more brilliantly. It was the highlight of the entire fall campaign, the best single event by either candidate. Kennedy opened by noting that the U.S. Constitution supported a separation of church and state and that he agreed heartily with the concept. He said pointedly, "I am not the Catholic candidate for president, I am the Democratic Party's candidate for president who happens also to be a Catholic." That line alone was designed to coax many Democrats to stick with their party. The senator explained that he was not under Catholic Church discipline in his political capacity. "I do not speak for my church on public matters," he said, "and the church does not speak for me." More than anyone else, Rayburn had been afraid of the religious issue, but after the event, the Speaker said simply, "He ate 'em blood raw." Many voters who cared little about religion saw Kennedy as courageous for doing the event. One California businessman said, "Kennedy shows a young fighting spirit, he seems so assured. He has what America has lost."[10]

The Kennedy campaign videotaped the Houston event, and some 300 to 400 copies were made for circulation. Cut and edited into one-minute clips, a five-minute version, and a thirty-minute version, the tape was shown on local television stations in most parts of the country, often repeatedly in close states. It was never shown on network television; local stations were used to prevent the national media from giving the event too much prominence after the original broadcast. Kennedy did not want a general discussion about the religious issue, because too much focus might drive Protestants to the Republicans. In other words, he wanted to avoid media "noise." Kennedy's main goal was to rally Democrats, an effective position to take considering the majority party's popularity. Local television also enabled Kennedy to target areas where the tape might be played beneficially. The video was used in key cities just before Kennedy arrived for a campaign event, a strategy that enabled Kennedy to keep the focus on his own version of the "religious issue," which emphasized tolerance for different religions.

There is abundant evidence that Catholics were the targeted audience. For one thing, the short spots tended to be played on television in Protestant areas, while the thirty-minute version was used most often in Catholic areas. Kennedy knew that he could not convert anti-Catholic bigots into supporters. But it was necessary for the senator to structure the appeal in this fashion. In other words, while Kennedy's overt appeal was for Protestants to be tolerant, the greatest impact of the message was on fellow Catholics, especially Republican-leaning Catholics torn between a desire to back their usual party and religious pride that led them to want a Catholic president. The video was played most often not in the South but in Catholic areas outside the South, which provides evidence that the Kennedy campaign saw the real audience for the film as Catholic. Since anti-Catholic bigotry was uncommon in much of the rural North, it is especially significant that the show was replayed frequently in upstate New York (eight times), Illinois (seven), Pennsylvania (eight), and Ohio (seven). All were pivotal and populous states with many Catholics.[11]

The tape made one other subtle appeal. By calling for religious tolerance, Kennedy seemed to suggest that religion ought not to play much of a role in political life. This theme appealed to Jews, who had their own reasons for distrusting Kennedy, primarily Joe Kennedy's desire to appease Hitler in the late 1930s. Kennedy had received little support from Jews for the nomination. Although most Jews were Democrats, a significant minority had voted for Eisenhower in 1956, and during the summer of 1960 polls showed that many Jewish voters were undecided. Kennedy's Houston tape reassured Jews that Kennedy understood the problem of being a member of a minority group. On Election Day, Jews returned to the Democratic fold in record numbers. The Houston tape could also be read as a racial appeal to African Americans. Kennedy's appearance registered with black Americans in a way that produced sympathy for Kennedy. Like the white Baptist preachers at the event, many black Baptists had reservations about a Catholic president. On the telecast, Kennedy conveyed that he wanted to preside over a country where tolerance would be the norm.

The Houston speech and its effective use in local rebroadcasts showed the increasing power of television in the presidential campaign. Nixon prided himself on being an expert on the new medium, largely on the basis of his success with the Checkers Speech in 1952 and with his Kitchen Debate with Khrushchev in 1959. But television was evolving rapidly, and Nixon was less expert than he believed. "You know," Nixon told the journalist Stewart Alsop in 1959, "I've never heard a speech I've made [on television] played back, never seen myself on television." Television, Nixon's friend Earl Blaik warned, was about projecting personality, not about content. Near the end of the campaign, Nixon told Nelson Rockefeller, Senator Jacob Javits, and Leonard Hall, "Look, I am and am going to be Nixon. I will not change to please TV or Madison Avenue. I'm going to be what I am, for good or bad." This stubborn sentiment no doubt seemed much less compelling to Nixon after he lost, and in 1968 he ran a much more media-savvy campaign.[12]

Television drove politics in 1960, much more so than in the past. Half-hour paid political broadcasts were the norm, even though consultants recommended five-minute infomercials at the end of slightly shortened popular shows. Few realized that potent messages could be conveyed at lower cost using thirty-second spots. After the election, 87 percent of Americans said that they had followed the presidential contest on TV. Only 80 percent had read about the campaign in newspapers, just 42 percent had followed it on the radio, and 41 percent had gotten information on the campaign from magazines. The heavy use of TV increased turnout, which reached an all-time high as a percentage of potential voters. The Republicans spent $5.4 million on paid national television advertising; the Democrats spent $4.4 million. These amounts exclude Kennedy's frequent local rebroadcasts of the Houston speech. For radio, the numbers were $2.1 million for the Republicans and $1.8 million for the Democrats. Exclusive of debates and free interview shows, Nixon was on the air nationally, in paid time that lasted at least five minutes, for fifteen hours and fifty-three minutes, Kennedy for fourteen hours and fifty-seven minutes. Lodge got five hours and forty-seven minutes, but the not very telegenic Johnson received only two hours and twenty-four minutes of exposure. In addition to these appearances, the Republicans ran 198 one-minute national spots; the Democrats ran 202.[13]

All of this paid advertising escalated campaign costs. Only rarely do we get a glimpse into the shadowy underworld of campaign finance as it truly existed in 1960. In the fall Kennedy held a fund-raiser in St. Louis. After the event, Tip O'Neill, who had helped organize it, met Kennedy in the men's room. The candidate asked, "How did we do?" Tip replied, "I got $29,000: twelve in cash and seventeen in checks. What will I do with it?" Kennedy said, "Give me the cash. And give Kenny O'Donnell the checks." Tip thought, "Jeez. This business is the same whether you're running for ward alderman or whether you're running for president of the United States." A friendly *Boston Globe* reporter, Bob Healy, was covering the trip. On the flight out of St. Louis, Kennedy called him to the airplane stateroom where there was $100,000 in cash on the bed. Kennedy said to Healy, "Did you ever see anything like that?"[14]

Kennedy understood the power of television. A gifted performer, he used as much television as possible. It is doubtful that Kennedy would have run in 1960 had TV not been available—with his thin record in the Senate he was otherwise an unlikely candidate. One of Kennedy's talents was a capacity for cold, accurate analysis of his own performances. Early in the campaign, Kennedy's staff arranged for all events to be taped on a portable video recorder. These new machines were quite rare at the time. Costing about $100,000, they were so expensive that many small television stations did not own one, and very few machines were in private hands. The networks first used videotape, which had only recently been invented, during the Democratic National Convention in July. Beginning in Wisconsin, Kennedy videotaped all rallies and speeches. He then carefully reviewed the tapes, noticing flubbed lines, thinking of better ways to make a point, and especially watching crowd reactions. The Nixon campaign declined to use a video recorder.

In 1960, 88 percent of American homes had television, and the CBS, NBC, and ABC networks drove popular culture. By 1960 the price of buying time had soared, and both parties were eager to find ways to reduce campaign costs. Under the law as it then existed, paid time had to be equally available at the same price to all candidates. As a practical matter, only prominent candidates could afford to buy airtime, and no candidate could get much free airtime because a station or network had to make equal free time available to all candidates. Thus, a station that interviewed Kennedy would have to talk at equal length with Nixon and with each minor party candidate. A panel discussion had to include all candidates, no matter how minor. The only exceptions to the rule of equal access were news broadcasts and regularly scheduled press panel shows, which could interview a single newsworthy candidate, so long as all newsworthy candidates appeared in the course of the campaign. For example, *Meet the Press* could skip minor candidates, but the program had to air in turn Kennedy, Nixon, Johnson, and Lodge. The law barred debates between the two major presidential candidates without including minor candidates.

By 1960 commercial advertisers were saturating the air in major media markets such as New York and Los Angeles, and escalating prices were rationing scarce airtime. Even so, huge sums of money were much less important then than would be true later in the century. Full-time fund-raising and the commitments to special interests that resulted were in the future, and the parties and candidates were still trying to operate within the lower budgets that had existed in the pretelevision era. Yet the power of television could not be denied. Not only did the new medium allow a candidate to become well known in a hurry, but the shrewd use of television could go a long way to shaping an image. Negative campaign advertising barely existed. Television could easily reach the politically apathetic, and it was possible to use the new medium to stimulate interest and encourage the registration of new voters and their subsequent turnout. The parties, politicians, and some network executives were drawn to the idea of televised debates by excitement about the new medium of television, by the potential cost savings to each party, and by the realization that putting both major presidential candidates on the air simultaneously would greatly increase audience size. As it turned out, a two-way debate tripled the audience compared to a show with a single candidate.

In August 1960 Congress suspended the equal time rules for the remainder of the 1960 presidential contest. Indeed, the "Great Debates" of 1960 would be the only presidential debates until 1976, when a desperate incumbent, Gerald Ford, badly trailing in the polls, agreed to debate Jimmy Carter in the hope of catching up. Kennedy, who understood his own excellent projection on television, was eager to confront Nixon in 1960. "Every time we get those two fellows on the screen side by side," observed Kennedy's media adviser, "we're going to gain and he's going to lose." The little-known senator knew that a debate was a superb way to gain public attention, and appearing on the same stage with Nixon would create an aura of equality and erode Nixon's claim to greater "experience." Without successful debates, Kennedy was unlikely to win. In September, Gallup found that 55 percent of Americans were keenly interested in the projected debates. Interest was especially strong in the East (63 percent), among Americans in their twenties (60 percent), and among Catholics (66 percent).[15]

For Nixon, the debates were problematic. Eisenhower advised Nixon, "Don't build him up by appearing with him on television." The vice president, however, was under pressure to debate. The Republican Party did not find it easy to raise money for Nixon's campaign. Many corporate leaders were hedging their bets by backing both parties. Because the Republicans had done poorly in 1958, they lacked the governors and senators who were big draws at fund-raisers. The party needed to spend money on congressional candidates, and party leaders wanted Nixon to cut campaign costs by agreeing to debate. Nixon also feared constant criticism from Kennedy and the media if he refused to debate. Finally, the vice president believed that he could demolish his opponent. After watching Kennedy's mediocre acceptance speech, Nixon told friends, "I can take this man." Nixon had been a champion debater in high school and college; in 1946 he had overwhelmed Jerry Voorhis in a series of debates. No one parsed arguments better with cold logic or scored more points with debating judges. But Nixon failed to understand that the proposed "debates" would be mere theatrical shows in which a projected image on television would be more important than debating talent.[16]

The candidates' staffs and the networks agreed to four debates. The presidential contenders would meet on CBS in Chicago on September 26, on NBC in Washington on October 7, on ABC using a split screen— with Nixon in Los Angeles and Kennedy in New York—on October 13, and on ABC in New York on October 21. Thus, debates would dominate the news neither during the early campaign, when themes were being set, nor during the important wrap-up of the last two weeks. This schedule suited Nixon's campaign theory. Each debate would last sixty minutes and would be shown on all three networks. Altogether, the debates cost the networks $4 million to $5 million in production costs and lost advertising revenue. The debates in effect substituted for several expensive half-hour paid broadcasts.

Neither side wanted vice presidential debates. Lodge and Johnson performed poorly on television, and both turned down an offer from CBS to stage a vice presidential debate. Had Nixon not wanted to debate Kennedy, the best strategy would have been to insist on one vice presidential debate. To avoid showcasing Johnson, the Kennedy campaign almost certainly would have rejected a vice presidential debate. In one joint Kennedy-Johnson paid program, the Kennedy campaign cut Johnson off after only a few minutes of airtime. To gain an edge with his stronger foreign policy credentials, Nixon demanded that one debate be devoted to foreign policy. The Kennedy staff reluctantly agreed but insisted that the first debate be about domestic issues, which favored the Democrats. Nixon acceded to this idea because his staff believed, quite wrongly and naively, that audiences for the debates would grow over time, with the first debate having the smallest audience.

Nixon insisted that there be no audience in the studio; the reporters who were covering the campaigns were annoyed at being forced to watch the debates at the stations on monitors in adjacent rooms. The absence of a live audience flattened the debaters' emotional responses, which, ironically, hurt Nixon. The naturally cool and laconic Kennedy could make his appeal directly into the camera with impressive effect, but Nixon needed a live audience to come across as warm and empathetic. In the 1968 campaign, Nixon used question-and-answer sessions before handpicked studio audiences with great success. In a decision that turned out to work to Nixon's disadvantage, the networks insisted on the right to show reaction shots of each candidate while the other was speaking, out of fear that not to do so would bore the audience.

The first debate, on domestic issues, was set for Chicago for Monday night, September 26. Far from that of a formal debate, the format called for several reporters in rotation to ask each candidate a question. In addition, each candidate was allowed to respond to the other candidate's answers. In the first and last debates, each nominee also gave opening and closing statements. For several days prior to the first debate, Kennedy spent any spare time as he campaigned going over a staff briefing book. On the day of the debate, the candidate engaged in mock debates with his staff. In contrast, an exhausted Nixon arrived in Chicago very late on Sunday night, underweight and with a temperature of 101 degrees from the infection that had put him in the hospital. The next morning, Nixon retreated to his hotel room and barred entry to anyone. Although he reviewed notes for the debate, he made no effective advance preparation. The staff had compiled a briefing book, but no time had been found to discuss its contents with Nixon.

The middle-aged Nixon's pronounced jowls, receding hairline, and deep-set eye sockets made him less than appealing to television viewers. The remedy was facial lighting projected strongly upward against the powerful downward studio lighting. Nixon also sweated profusely under television's hot overhead lights. Then, too, Nixon had pale skin with a dark beard, and the television camera literally probed beneath the surface like an X-ray machine and presented Nixon's subsurface dark facial hairs on camera even when he had closely shaved just prior to a broadcast. The solution was to wear heavy makeup, but the candidate refused to do so and arrived at the studio too close to airtime to be made up in any case. Instead, Nixon used light facial powder that turned his face gray, which matched both his suit and the studio's background. When the studio lights were turned on, Kennedy's white face, dark suit, and gray background presented a sharp, handsome visual that contrasted with Nixon's grayed face, ill-fitting gray suit, and gray background. One candidate stood out, and the other faded away, even before a word had been spoken. Nixon probably lost the debate before it started.

Kennedy's sparkling opening statement began: "In the election of 1860, Abraham Lincoln said the question was whether this nation could exist half-slave or half-free. In the election of 1960, and with the world around us, the question is whether the world will exist half-slave or half-free. . . . If we do well here, if we meet our obligations, if we're moving ahead, then I think freedom will be secure around the world. If we fail, then freedom fails. Therefore, I think the question before the American people is: Are we doing as much as we can do? . . . I should make it very clear that I do not think we're doing enough. . . . I think it's time America started moving again."[17]

Jarred by Kennedy's statement, Nixon responded defensively: "The things that Senator Kennedy has said many of us can agree with." Affirming his rival's campaign theme, Nixon declared: "The only way to stay ahead is to move ahead. And I subscribe completely to the spirit that Senator Kennedy has expressed tonight, the spirit that the United States should move ahead. . . . A record is never something to stand on. It's something to build on." He concluded: "I know Senator Kennedy feels as deeply about these problems as I do, but our disagreement is not about the goals for America but only about the means to reach those goals." The senator talked to the television audience, but the vice president seemed to be addressing only the senator. Nixon disappointed his own supporters by suggesting that he was a weak copy of Kennedy.[18]

For Nixon, the debate only got worse. Throughout, Kennedy rallied reluctant Democrats and independents, while the senator's presence rattled the vice president. Nixon never went on the offensive. To Republicans, Nixon seemed too wan and too much engaged in "me-tooism," that is, adopting or acceding to Democratic proposals. Nixon's former adviser Murray Chotiner told the press that Nixon had shown "no animation, no life, enthusiasm, spirit." He warned, "Be the real Nixon or you'll lose." Conservative columnist Holmes Alexander declared, "His tryout for the role of Little Gentleman is an atrocious bit of miscasting. . . . Down with the New Nixon! Let's have the Old Nixon!" One Nixon aide, Meade Alcorn, privately urged his candidate to be more aggressive in the next debate. "You are at your best," he noted, "when you pack some emotion into the conviction which you so well convey."[19]

The TV reaction shots favored Kennedy. During the debate, Nixon frequently looked off stage, which suggested shiftiness, licked sweat from his upper lip, which suggested that he could not handle pressure, or nodded in agreement with his rival. In contrast, Kennedy either looked intently at Nixon or took notes. Then the studio lights heated up the candidates, and Nixon began to sweat profusely. CBS broadcast one reaction shot of Nixon mopping his brow while Kennedy made telling points. The visual impact was devastating, because it suggested that an

Kennedy and Nixon shook hands before the first-ever televised candidates' debate. (Ollie Atkins Photo Collection, Special Collections and Archives, George Mason University Libraries, Fairfax, Virginia)

outmatched vice president had been made to sweat by Kennedy's shrewd words. Worse, Nixon's facial powder began to streak down his face, causing parallel lines of gray and white with black hairs appearing to poke through the white. Before the show was over, Nixon resembled a Halloween ghoul.

At the studio, Mayor Richard Daley blurted out, "My God, they've embalmed him before he even died." Ralph Barstow, an old friend of Nixon, wrote, "Your make-up man betrayed you." Alice Roosevelt Longworth, Teddy Roosevelt's daughter and a staunch Republican, told her cousin Joe Alsop, "Dick has finished himself off." Lodge, watching the debate on television in Texas, shouted, "That son-of-a-bitch just lost us the election!" After the event, Hannah Nixon called from California and asked, "Is Richard ill?" Nixon's press secretary, Herb Klein, was forced to issue a statement: "Mr. Nixon is in excellent health and looks good in person."[20]

Kennedy and his staff were pleased. At breakfast the next morning, the senator said, "Boy, did I nail him." Johnson publicly noted that Nixon blamed his makeup but "all you hear is that poor Richard has cracked up." Adlai Stevenson crowed, "There is no surer way to lose confidence in Nixon than to see him." About the vice president, Senator Russell Long told the press, "He looked like a man who knew he was taking a bad beating." Ten southern Democratic governors had watched the debate together at their annual gathering at Hot Springs, Arkansas. Deeply worried about the effect of Kennedy's candidacy on the party in the South, they watched with apprehension. The senator's strong performance elated them, and they sent Kennedy a warm congratulatory wire. "Unless Kennedy won the debate," said Governor Lindsay Almond of Virginia, "there would have been no telegram." The governors' subsequent vigorous support for the campaign mattered a lot in the South.[21]

Despite Nixon's poor appearance and his defensive posture, the debate was not so one-sided as it has sometimes been made out to be. Most viewers remained committed to the candidate that they had favored before the debate. Among radio listeners, Nixon was judged the winner. But a majority of television viewers, and there were an estimated 70 million or more of them, one of the largest audiences ever recorded, felt that Kennedy had won, regardless of whom they personally favored. Republicans were demoralized, and Nixon's campaign, already off track, was thrown further into chaos. Kennedy's crowds doubled or even tripled in size. From this one television appearance, Kennedy gained the quality of a movie star, a phenomenon new to politics that bemused the candidate and puzzled old-line politicians. When his motorcade traveled along a street, excitement and frenzy rippled through the crowd, especially among young women and girls. "Screamers" let loose deliriously as his vehicle passed, "jumpers" bounced hysterically up and down, and "touchers" reached into the car to grab Kennedy's clothes or body. Unfortunately for the nominee, many of these fans were not old enough to vote. Kennedy was beginning to reach nonvoters or persons who voted only rarely.

The main effect of the debate was to raise the level of excitement and thereby increase turnout for the election. Democrats believed that a high turnout favored their party because occasional voters tended to vote Democratic more than did regular voters. According to Elmo Roper's survey, the debates netted Kennedy about 2 million votes, mostly due to the first debate. These voters were often independents or conservative Democrats who had had misgivings about Kennedy. Nixon's "experience" argument, which had worked well for him, had been severely weakened. It was hard to see how a confident, articulate Kennedy was less experienced than a hesitant, visually unappealing Nixon.[22]

The three later debates had little impact on the contest. The candidates tangled over how the United States should keep Quemoy and Matsu, two tiny islands off the coast of Communist China that Taiwan controlled, from falling into Communist hands. Nixon got the better of that particular exchange, but Kennedy effectively countered with the charge that American strength and prestige had deteriorated. Each candidate consistently presented himself as a militant cold warrior. Contrary to Nixon's prediction, the number of viewers, although still impressive, dropped off. At least 80 percent of Americans saw or heard at least one debate. Pollsters found that the later debates caused few voters to change their views. After the second debate, Nixon received a thousand telegrams urging him to "keep slugging." The vice president was no longer sick, had regained lost weight, wore a dark suit, used proper makeup, and, to the thrill of his supporters, parried Kennedy's thrusts with counterthrusts that sometimes drew blood. Nixon's antics annoyed Kennedy, who privately said, "The man is a shit—a total shit." To many viewers who watched all four performances, the candidates appeared to be evenly matched.[23]

On the day of the final debate, Nixon's friend Earl Blaik analyzed the overall political situation: The debates had been a gift to Kennedy,

After the first television debate, Kennedy's crowds grew.
(Ollie Atkins Photo Collection, Special Collections and Archives,
George Mason University Libraries, Fairfax, Virginia)

because on television he had shown a facile ability to turn a phrase, to distort statistics, and to evade issues with "irrelevant chatter." Nixon had declined in the polls because in the debates he had failed to show how "shallow and callow" the young senator was, out of fear of making him into a martyr. The Nixon campaign seemed to be marking time, merely "awaiting a Kennedy fumble." Such a mistake was unlikely. Blaik urged, "It is time to take this young senator to the cleaners."[24]

Kennedy had a theory about how to win an election. The key was organization, which had several dimensions. Serious planning took a superb staff, and one of Nixon's friends, Dillon Anderson, observed that Kennedy always had the best staff that money could buy. Ted Sorensen was a brilliant speechwriter, Louis Harris was an excellent pollster, and, in a bit of luck, Robert Kennedy was a superior campaign manager. A top staff could then organize the country, identifying potential supporters, registering them to vote, and making sure that they voted. In early 1960, there were 67 million registered voters; another 40 million eligible Americans were not registered. It was estimated that 70 percent of the unregistered voters were Democrats, and voter registration was a major part of the Kennedy campaign's efforts in 1960. A considerable amount of money was spent on this effort, thus demonstrating how money and organization worked together. Labor unions, especially the United Auto Workers, also played a pivotal role in this effort.[25]

Democrats netted a gain in new registrations over Republicans of 212,000 in California, 200,000 in Chicago, and 500,000 in New York City. For the first time, Democrats outnumbered Republicans in Pennsylvania and Connecticut. By early October, Democrats had signed up 8.5 million new voters. New registrations often produced strains between Kennedy's forces and old-fashioned urban Democratic political machines, which did not necessarily want to register more voters. The Kennedys calculated that New York State could be won by registering new black and Puerto Rican voters. When Tammany Hall boss Carmine De Sapio refused to do so, because he could not control these voters, the Kennedys used their own Citizens for Kennedy organization to undertake the registrations. Without these new voters, Kennedy would have lost New York State. In Cleveland, 57 percent of new voters favored Kennedy. Most were under age twenty-five.[26]

Kennedy also identified both a general theme and specific issues to rally supporters, calculating that a single theme along with a small number of appealing issues could give the campaign a clear overall message that would fairly easily prevail against a rival's campaign. "The policies I advocate," Kennedy said, "are the result of the rule of reason." The public could see Kennedy on his own terms as a serious candidate with concrete proposals, and criticism would tend to be deflected by the campaign's simplicity and clarity. Although this approach was easier to propose than to execute, the well-organized Kennedy campaign carried if off elegantly and flawlessly. Throughout 1960, Kennedy declared, "It is time to get this country moving again." This simple theme turned Kennedy's youth, which had been perceived to be a negative, into a virtue.[27]

Youth represented action, and this progressive theme appealed to liberals. In part, Kennedy had to campaign on the left because Nixon already occupied the middle ground. The *New Republic*'s Richard Strout observed that Nixon was already for "moderate change," which meant that Kennedy had to offer even more change. The issue for voters, Strout concluded, was: "How much change do you want?" A *Wall Street Journal* reporter wrote that the threat of a revolt by Democrats in the South meant that Kennedy had to move left in order to win the large, liberal, and heavily unionized industrial states. Columnist Walter Lippmann noted that Kennedy, like Franklin Roosevelt, offered "a time of renewal," but Kennedy was less "radical" than Roosevelt and did not wish to upset the socioeconomic structure as the New Dealers had.[28]

A campaign promoting change, however, could only work if it contained specific details. Otherwise, change might be perceived as threatening, and on Election Day voters might opt for the status quo by voting for Nixon. Kennedy wisely promoted only a few key programs. And he was shrewd in another way. Even as he announced support for several expensive liberal proposals, he declared that his campaign was about getting the country to face challenges and not about offering promises. This call for sacrifice undermined Nixon's ability to charge that Kennedy's liberal programs were just a form of pandering. Humphrey's failure in the spring had demonstrated that the public mood was less liberal than some liberals thought. Thus, Kennedy did not call for national health insurance, a complex and expensive idea vehemently opposed by the medical establishment. Truman had proposed a plan in the 1940s, and the result was that he had obtained no health care insurance legislation at all.

Kennedy instead called for what would eventually be called Medicare, that is, national health insurance for the elderly. In 1960 medical costs were rising, and older Americans were often losing their homes, their only real assets, in order to pay high hospital bills. Polling data showed that Medicare was popular, and Republicans, tied closely to the American Medical Association lobby, which opposed the idea, were on the defensive. Because Nixon had no credible counterproposal, it was a good idea for Kennedy to stress Medicare. Research data showed that Kennedy effectively used the debates to sell Medicare. One elderly woman in California told the pollster Samuel Lubell, "We were Republicans but are switching to get this socialized medicine." A policeman on Long Island said, "My father-in-law lives with us. We have to pay his Blue Shield and Blue Cross. Under Kennedy's plan social security would pay for it."[29]

Kennedy also urged federal aid to school districts and the creation of a program to assist college students. Education aid appealed both to middle-class voters, especially in the suburbs, and to working-class voters who had aspirations for higher education for their children. Republicans, worried about high costs and possible tax increases, generally dodged new federal programs, but Nixon crafted his own education proposal to curry favor in the normally Republican suburbs. Both candidates advocated federal construction grants to school districts and aid for college students. Construction grants were especially appealing to suburban districts with growing enrollments. However, Nixon opposed Kennedy's proposal for federal grants to school district operating budgets. To do so, Nixon felt, was to invite federal control of education. A Republican candidate had to worry that conservatives inside his own party would oppose federal aid for operating costs.

In contrast with Medicare, research data showed that Kennedy failed in the debates to make his position on education issues clearly distinct from Nixon's position. In fact, both candidates confused voters. Kennedy's strong support for civil rights was designed to gain both black votes and the support of white Americans who believed that racial justice was the country's most pressing current problem. The Democrats had the stronger platform on civil rights and Kennedy talked more about the issue in the campaign, but Johnson proved to be a burden for Kennedy on this issue. What Medicare, aid to education, and civil rights had in common was that all three represented a liberal commitment to activist government consistent with the larger theme of "moving again." Thus, Kennedy's issues projected an image of liberalism, even though the senator's record was moderate.

By mid-October, the Kennedy campaign was quietly optimistic. Kennedy had made gains while Nixon was in the hospital. Then, during the debates, Kennedy had opened a small but definite lead. In mid-October, Gallup reported Kennedy ahead, 49 percent to 45 percent. However, the Kennedy team put less emphasis on the debates than did the media. The campaign's optimism was rooted in the registration of new voters, largely done through the efforts of the AFL-CIO. For example, New York State had 7.7 million registered voters in 1956 and 9.5 million in 1960. The Democrat was also drawing larger, friendlier crowds, a sign of growing campaign momentum. At the same time, polls showed that Kennedy was beginning to beat Nixon decisively in the nation's large cities and in the suburbs that surrounded those cities. Unlike many Democrats, Kennedy targeted the suburbs, especially seeking to reach new voters who had only recently moved from the cities. In contrast with earlier times, there were now many Catholics in suburbia—for example, of persons moving to suburban Long Island after World War II, 60 percent were Catholic.[30]

Reporters who accompanied the Kennedy campaign, caught up in the excitement and manipulated by Kennedy's superb organization, wrote about a possible Kennedy tidal wave on Election Day. Because the Nixon campaign was disorganized, discouraged, and foundering, many doubted that the operation could be revamped in time to catch up with the smoothly running Kennedy organization. Kennedy operatives felt that the remaining undecided voters would gradually slide their way. By Election Day, some were heard to say, Kennedy might win by 5 million votes, which would be enough to be considered a landslide. On November 5, political analyst Ted Lewis of the *New York Daily News* forecast that Kennedy would carry thirty-one states, with 415 electoral votes.

Neither John Kennedy nor Robert Kennedy ever bought the scenario of a landslide. "Do you figure," the nominee asked a reporter, "this was how it was for Dewey in . . . 1948?" On balance, the Kennedys preferred having the small but widening lead that Kennedy held in mid-October to being in Nixon's position, but they also recognized that much could go wrong during the last three weeks of the campaign, and Kennedy continued to run all out. Robert Kennedy later observed, "We simply had to run and fight and scramble for ten weeks all the way, and then we would win. We got on top with the debates, we fought to stay on top, and we did win." Many doubts remained concerning the religious issue, the black vote, and the South. Also, any last-minute foreign policy crisis was bound to help Nixon, who remained competitive in the polls almost entirely because of the perception on the part of many Americans that the Democrats were not to be trusted with foreign affairs.[31]

Indeed, state-by-state analysis in late October suggested that Kennedy's narrow national lead could easily evaporate. But Kennedy was ahead in New York, and there were many who believed that New York would decide the election. New York remained Kennedy's best big state throughout the rest of the campaign, and its probable loss remained Nixon's greatest frustration. Since 1876 no Republican had won the presidency without the Empire State. Atlanta editor Ralph McGill declared Nixon's campaign in "near panic" over New York. Johnson's southern train trip had helped Kennedy, but whether enough of the South could be won to carry the election was far from clear. Kennedy needed to win at least half the electoral votes in the South, and to do so, he had to take Texas, which was uncertain. Other key states were also in play. Kennedy was considered narrowly ahead in Pennsylvania, Ohio, and California, but Michigan, Minnesota, and Missouri were too close to call, and Nixon was ahead in Illinois. A Nixon surge might easily tip all or many of these states his way, and it was difficult to see how Kennedy could then win.[32]

Nevertheless, Kennedy's position was stronger in mid-October than was Nixon's. Plagued by tangled lines of authority within the staff, by the candidate's moodiness and unwillingness to be disrupted while traveling, and by the continuing fallout from the candidate's hospitalization and subsequent rescheduling, the Nixon campaign also suffered from other, more fundamental problems. The Nixon campaign had to be organized around the inconvenient fact that there were 50 million Democrats and only 33 million Republicans. To win, Nixon had to put together an unnatural coalition. Like Kennedy, Nixon understood the importance of registering new voters, and Robert Finch had undertaken this important task in Los Angeles, as had Ray Bliss in Ohio. However, Republicans could not match Democrats in new registrants because most of the unregistered were Democrats. In the end, the Democrats probably registered close to twice as many new voters, a fact that goes a long way toward explaining Kennedy's victory. Then, too, the Republican Party was notoriously weak, as shown by its inability to elect governors in 1958. With a Republican governor, a state had a party organization capable of registering voters, running a campaign, and getting out the vote. Unfortunately for Nixon, most key states had Democratic governors.

Nixon's problem was rooted in numbers. "To win," he observed, "we have to get most of the Republicans, more than half of the independents, and 20 percent or more of the Democrats." Putting together a winning bipartisan coalition was Nixon's greatest challenge. Nixon was confident that he could appeal to enough Democrats and independents to win, but he could not run a campaign on specific domestic issues because his potential voters disagreed on those issues. If he moved to the left on domestic issues by adopting the same positions that Kennedy took, in order to appeal to Democrats and independents strictly on foreign policy grounds, he risked losing conservative Republicans, who would sit out the election.[33]

The conservative *National Review* condemned Nixon's "vapid generalities" and suspected him of "liberal tendencies." Although some on the Right grated their teeth, Nixon did benefit from fear of Kennedy's liberalism. One apprehensive conservative business executive wrote Nixon, "The trail that Mr. Kennedy threatens to blaze really frightens me. It means the road to socialism." On this letter a Nixon staff member wrote the annotation: "Articulate MOSSBACK [that is, a reactionary]." The conservative editor of *Newsweek* privately confessed, "Frankly, I shudder to think of what would happen to the country with four or eight years of Democratic control." Nixon could do or say nothing that would antagonize these sorts of voters. In any case, strong support from conservative Republicans was necessary to do party work on Election Day. The only viable strategy for Nixon was to blur domestic issues by saying little about them and by offering vague compromises a bit to the right of Kennedy. This strategy also posed problems. Nixon's pollster Claude Robinson warned the nominee to avoid the phrase "middle-of-the-road" because it suggested straddling. In October, Eisenhower privately advised Nixon that the campaign needed more "zip," that it should be "more hardhitting," but not in a personal way, and that more concrete plans for future programs needed to be presented.[34]

Observers had different takes on Nixon's approach to the campaign. Journalist Stewart Alsop felt that Nixon was an "instinctive conservative" without any ideological commitment. Max Lerner correctly understood that Nixon's "moderation" was an attempt to get independent voters, but the columnist shrewdly warned that voters would prefer Kennedy's "energy and clarity" to Nixon's "trimming and tailoring." Seeking to have it both ways, Nixon's campaign emphasized conservative means to liberal ends. Unfortunately for the vice president, the zigzagging that resulted only reinforced the "Tricky Dick" label. Nixon's attempt to promote a new image also provoked ridicule. To Kennedy's aide Arthur Schlesinger, Nixon's behavior was proof that he was a "chameleon" with no underlying political philosophy and preoccupied only with his public image.[35]

Columnist Joseph Alsop found Nixon's stump speech bland, devoid of details, which might offend, and revealing no viewpoint on the issues. John Kennedy privately observed, "You know, Nixon is really smart—how can he talk such shit?" Having agreed with Nelson Rockefeller on pushing the Republican Party to adopt a liberal platform, Nixon on the campaign trail avoided saying anything that Barry Goldwater might dispute. Nixon, Goldwater thought, was "anxious to please everyone." Rockefeller's adviser Emmet John Hughes offered a deeper analysis of Nixon's lack of a moral center. The more important the issue, the greater was Nixon's ambiguity and hesitation. The result, according to Hughes, was that Nixon came across in the campaign as an angry man hiding his own private doubts. In public, he was banal; in private, he was laconic, reflective, withdrawn, and lacking in confidence. "This unseen personality," thought Hughes, "ruled much of the spirit and the conduct of the 1960 campaign."[36]

The Republican nominee believed that 19 million unsophisticated voters remained undecided in the fall. Nixon's campaign was designed to win their support not by ideology or policy positions but by creating an atmosphere of confidence around the candidate. Nixon was trying to convince voters that he was the next Eisenhower, the mellow moderate, and the safer choice in the risky nuclear age. Largely ignoring domestic issues, the vice president ran strenuously on foreign policy in order to rally a coalition of Republicans, independents, and Democrats who believed that the Democratic Party could not be trusted with management of the Cold War. The contrast between Eisenhower's eight years of peace and Truman's bogged-down war in Korea did not have to be mentioned in order for it to be understood.

The code word to imply Democratic incompetence that Nixon had adopted was Nixon's greater foreign policy "experience." Just as almost every Kennedy speech all year had included some reference to "moving again," so too did Nixon's speeches stress the vice president's "experience." Privately, the vice president acknowledged that "experience" was not quite the correct word for what he wanted to convey: He wanted

Americans to see that "he is at his best when the going is toughest." Even Kennedy's declaration that the sixties would be a hard decade for the United States internationally could be made into an argument for Democrats and independents to vote for Nixon. Although the candidate met Republicans at rallies, he wooed swing voters mostly with television. Like Kennedy, Nixon understood the power of television, but he lacked insight into its subtleties. As the *Washington Post* observed, Nixon needed "perfect balance" in his campaign to excite party workers and to get nonparty votes.[37]

Whereas Kennedy used a domestic agenda to fill in the details of what "moving again" meant, Nixon could not develop the "experience" argument with reference to specific foreign policy proposals. Because his supporters did not agree upon policies, Nixon was left using anti-Communist rhetoric, but this rhetoric no longer seemed fresh in 1960. Having been a fresh face who had discovered Communism in 1947, Nixon was now a dated old fogy, who did not seem to be willing to get the country "moving again." Still, the "experience" argument was powerful, because it highlighted the true difference between Kennedy and Nixon: The vice president had participated in the highest councils of government, had traveled the world, and had been Eisenhower's apprentice. As a St. Louis taxi driver told pollster Samuel Lubell, "Nixon has already stood up to the Russians. I don't know what Kennedy will do." Many voters, however, felt that both Nixon and Kennedy were too young and too small for the task. Eisenhower remained unusually popular, and Nixon promised to extend the current administration and its numerous overseas successes by maintaining peace through strength. Whenever Nixon mentioned Ike's name, the crowd applauded.[38]

Although Kennedy had elevated himself with the first debate, he had not completely overcome Nixon's "experience" argument. The vice president was the vice president, and the junior senator was still the junior senator. About Nixon, Senator Styles Bridges of New Hampshire declared, "He is as tough and ruthless with Khrushchev as he was with Alger Hiss. His experience and his opponent's experience is like comparing an airplane carrier with a sailboat." As the campaign continued into early November, Nixon pushed his "experience" claim as the only possible footing for his election. He intended to make the public understand that, although voters might prefer the Democrats' domestic agenda, the life or death decision in the nuclear age was about foreign policy. Nixon wanted voters to see that a vote for the inexperienced Kennedy was risky.

Thus, in a single day near the end of the campaign, Nixon denounced Kennedy as "shockingly reckless," "woolly and fuzzy," "irresponsible," and "totally lacking in judgment." A week later, Johnson said, "Name calling is in vogue. Day by day we see more of the old Nixon." Nevertheless, Nixon's approach was having an effect.[39]

Nixon also had a theory on how to win an election, and it was quite different from Kennedy's. According to the vice president, the key was pacing. Because no candidate could have enough ideas, energy, or money to dominate all the time, it was important to expend these scarce resources in a careful way. For a candidate to look competent, every thrust had to be parried, but a candidate might choose to fight for a time on the opponent's turf so as to exhaust media interest in a particular topic. Nixon could gain nothing from the religious issue, and thus it was better to have it discussed in mid-September rather than later in the campaign. By November, neither the public nor the media would show much interest. A candidate might be wise to hold back the best issues for a last-minute television barrage. The other side might then be so befuddled that it could not effectively counterattack.

Like a long-distance runner, it was necessary to stay close throughout the race, but the key to victory was a burst of energy during the last three weeks that allowed for the surprise lunge across the finish line. Harold Macmillan had told Nixon that he had won in Britain in 1959 by allowing Labour to overreach with "pie in the sky promises." The Tories had then launched an effective counterattack during the last three weeks and won. Indeed, the Democrats worried deeply about a powerful Nixon surge. "I cannot, of course, ever feel safe till the last week is over," warned Eleanor Roosevelt, "because with Mr. Nixon I always have the feeling that he will pull some trick at the last minute." Nixon believed that Kennedy had peaked in late October, and on Halloween he declared, "The tide has turned."[40]

Nixon's theory assumed that the candidate could control events, and, although Nixon generally was able to pace his campaign in 1960 in the way that he wanted, he faced two costly, unplanned incidents. On October 12, vice presidential nominee Henry Cabot Lodge made a "pledge" to an audience in Spanish Harlem that Nixon would name an African American to his cabinet. "Whoever recommended that Harlem speech," said one Republican, "ought to have been thrown out of an airplane from 25,000 feet." Nixon and Lodge had never discussed cabinet appointments, and Nixon had not authorized Lodge to make this promise.

In one sense, the statement was mundane. A longtime practitioner of the urban ethnic politics of the Northeast, Lodge was operating in the old Boston tradition, according to which each racial or ethnic group was entitled to an office—the Irish police chief, the Jewish health inspector, the Italian public works superintendent, the African American sanitation director, and so on.[41]

No one at the Spanish Harlem street rally greeted the remark with much enthusiasm or took it seriously. Of course, many of the Puerto Ricans who had been lured to the street festival at which Lodge spoke did not know English. White politicians often visited Harlem and made all sorts of promises, most of which were never kept. Furthermore, whether Nixon appointed a black cabinet officer mattered little to the average Harlem resident, who had serious problems with housing, unemployment, and bad schools. Lodge failed to understand that his remark was extremely offensive in those parts of the United States where racial and ethnic spoils of office were seen as proof of the special pandering typical of corrupt urban political machines. Kennedy and Johnson quickly deplored cheap racial promises and vowed that only the best persons, regardless of race, would be appointed to high office.

Lodge's remark exploded in the headlines. Clearly peeved by Lodge's blunder, Nixon declared, "I will attempt to appoint the best man possible without regard to race, creed, or color." The media, of course, jumped on the differences between the two Republicans, which gave more play to the story. The following day, Lodge, campaigning in North Carolina, retreated by saying, "I cannot pledge anything." Democrats then used Nixon's denial of Lodge's original promise to warn African Americans to stay away from the Republicans' dodgy promises. Although there is no evidence that Lodge's original promise would have gained any black votes, Nixon's repudiation almost certainly cost the Republicans black votes. In addition, Nixon's southern polls dropped sharply. As the controversy swirled on for several days, Johnson suggested that Nixon and Lodge debate the issue. Lodge managed to cost Nixon votes both in the North and in the South, quite an achievement.[42]

The larger issue was Nixon's ambivalence about going after white votes in the South while simultaneously seeking black votes in the North. When Nixon had yielded to Rockefeller's demand for a strong civil rights platform and had picked Lodge as his running mate, he had signaled that he would pursue a northern strategy. But Kennedy's unpopularity in the South, Nixon's large crowds in the South in August, and favorable polls had led the vice president to shift toward a southern strategy. Still, he could not win the election without a decent share of the northern black vote. If, as many believed, New York was the key, and if Catholic voters in New York went overwhelmingly to Kennedy, then Nixon needed black votes to carry New York.

Polls suggested that African Americans, who admired Eisenhower for sending troops to Little Rock and who were suspicious of Johnson, could be enticed to vote Republican. Nelson Rockefeller had eagerly sought and won the African American vote in 1958, and Nixon made a serious effort to get black votes. He tried to register black Republicans, spent a lot of money on paid advertising in the black press, and made effective use of his most important black supporter, baseball hero Jackie Robinson. In addition, Nixon had a positive relationship with Martin Luther King Jr., whom Nixon had first met in Ghana during that country's independence celebration. In contrast, King and Kennedy had never met. King's father was a staunch Republican leader in Atlanta.

Another unanticipated event further complicated the issue of the black vote when, on Wednesday, October 19, just three weeks before the election, Rev. Martin Luther King Jr. joined a small group of Atlanta University students in protesting segregation with a sit-in at a department store restaurant. Everyone at King's particular sit-in was arrested, but Democratic mayor Bill Hartsfield pressured the city jail to release the students quickly without bail. The jail, however, had been full, and some arrestees had been taken to the Fulton County jail. The mayor had more difficulty getting the demonstrators held there released, but by Sunday, October 23, all except King were free. King remained in the county jail due to a hold placed on him by adjacent suburban Dekalb County, where Hartsfield had no influence.

King had recently moved from Montgomery to Atlanta, and Georgia police previously had stopped and cited him for not having a Georgia state driving license. He had been put on parole for this violation, and on Tuesday, October 25, DeKalb County judge Oscar Mitchell, a rabid reactionary, revoked King's parole and sentenced him to four months of hard labor at the state penitentiary at Reidsville. Before Hartsfield, the NAACP, or anyone else in Atlanta could intervene, King had been thrown into a state patrol car and driven at high speed in the middle of the night to Reidsville. Mrs. King, who was six months pregnant, went into near-hysterics when she learned that her husband had been shipped out of Atlanta. She called Kennedy aide Harris Wofford and said, "They are going to kill him, I know they are going to kill him."[43]

Hartsfield, a Kennedy loyalist, was alarmed at how King's arrest might affect the election. Most Americans did not believe that someone driving with a license issued by the wrong state should be sent to state prison, and the Republicans could point out that all the officials in Georgia who were harassing King were Democrats. In the North, Republicans might pick up the votes of undecided voters, and African Americans might well swing behind Nixon to protest King's arrest. On Wednesday, October 26, Wofford talked with Louis Martin in Washington. An African American, a former editor of the *Chicago Defender*, and a key organizer of Kennedy's campaign among African Americans, Martin had already done much to win black votes for Kennedy. He had placed advertising in the black-owned media, but, unlike Nixon's generic ads, which were identical to those in the mainstream press, Kennedy's ads featured celebrity endorsements by Lena Horne, Cab Calloway, and Nat King Cole, along with Martin's own copy stressing civil rights. Horne was portrayed saying, "Republicans talk pretty but Kennedy will do something about all the problems."[44]

After Wofford recounted Mrs. King's frantic telephone call, both Wofford and Martin agreed that Kennedy should call her to express concern. However, Wofford also knew that Kennedy's top political aides, Larry O'Brien and Kenny O'Donnell, would be unsympathetic to Kennedy taking any action out of fear of riling southern white voters. To circumvent the "Irish mafia," Wofford called Sargent Shriver, Kennedy family member and the aide most sympathetic to civil rights. Shriver strategically maneuvered to gain a minute alone with Kennedy while O'Donnell stepped out of the room in order to explain what had happened in Atlanta.

At Wofford's request, Shriver asked Kennedy to call Coretta Scott King. About African Americans, Shriver told Kennedy, "You will reach their hearts." On Wednesday, October 26, the Democratic nominee placed the brief call and told Mrs. King, "This must be pretty hard on you, and I want to let you know that I'm thinking about you and will do all I can to help." Wofford and Martin immediately informed the media about the call. Contacted by the press, Mrs. King said, "It certainly made me feel good." Asked about Richard Nixon, she said, "He's been very quiet." When the media later asked Kennedy why he had called her, the nominee said simply that she was a friend of the family. This was an almost comical lie, but it had political utility. The two had never met and, in fact, never did. O'Donnell and O'Brien were unhappy with the telephone call; O'Donnell fumed, "You just lost us the election."[45]

When Robert Kennedy learned what had happened, he was furious, because he felt that his brother's call had lost the southern white vote. Bobby warned Shriver and Wofford, "You bomb throwers better not do anything more in the campaign." After reflecting, however, Bobby changed his mind. He then called the local judge in Georgia and demanded that King be released immediately, which the judge did, after conferring with Governor Ernest Vandiver. The governor, who was supporting Kennedy, had already made a similar request to the judge, who agreed to release King, provided that the judge could say publicly that he was acting at the request of the Kennedys. Mayor Hartsfield claimed that King had been freed due to pressure from the Kennedy campaign. This was not entirely true, but the mayor knew it was a good way to get black votes for Kennedy. On Thursday evening, King was released from Reidsville state prison and returned to Atlanta.[46]

Kennedy's compassionate call made little impression in the mainstream media or on white voters. In 1960, King was not the towering national figure that he later became. White southerners saw the call as an expression of Kennedy's concern for King's safety and for the pregnant Mrs. King's health, and Kennedy lost few white votes as a result of his call. Robert Kennedy's call to the judge, which could have been construed as an illegal attempt to influence a judge, received only minor coverage. Richard Nixon later said it was "unethical." President Eisenhower and Nixon remained quiet throughout the episode, although both had staff members who urged that one or the other also make a call or at least issue some statement protesting King's unfair treatment.[47]

Nixon's inaction was rooted in his desire throughout the campaign to seek both northern black votes and southern white votes. Having been outmaneuvered by Kennedy with Kennedy's initial call, any action that Nixon took after the press had reported on that call would look like racial pandering. The vice president's behavior was typical of his paralysis all year, his insistence on playing it safe, and his general unwillingness to take risks. For a man who claimed to be as strong for civil rights as Kennedy, Nixon's inaction spoke volumes, and the persons most concerned about the issue, African Americans, noticed. Thus, Kennedy's action and Nixon's inaction had little effect on the white vote, but the same could not be said of the black vote. The brilliance of the Kennedy campaign was its capacity for seizing sudden opportunities, which was just one advantage of having a gifted staff. Kennedy had engineered a powerful appeal to African Americans without sacrificing southern white votes, and, to win, he needed both groups.

The black press treated Kennedy's call to Mrs. King as a major story. Even the *Atlanta Daily World*, a black-owned Republican paper that strongly supported Nixon editorially, gave the issue major play. Martin Luther King Jr.'s father, also an Atlanta Baptist preacher and a major political figure, had, like the rest of the Atlanta black establishment, long supported Republicans (although he supported Hartsfield, a Democrat and a racial moderate, in local elections). The senior King had serious doubts about the election of a Catholic as president, and he had already endorsed Nixon. The phone call to his daughter-in-law, however, changed everything. At a meeting of 800 people at Ebenezer Baptist Church, the elder King said, "It took courage to call my daughter at a time like this. He has the moral courage to stand up for what he knows is right." Then he added, "I've got a suitcase of votes, and I'm going to take them to Mr. Kennedy and dump them in his lap." The junior King stayed decidedly neutral in the contest.[48]

Black voters shifted to Kennedy as a result of Kennedy's phone call. The Kennedy forces saw to that as an effective, well-financed organization moved into high gear. Shriver and Wofford prepared a leaflet entitled "'No Comment' Nixon Versus a Candidate with a Heart, Senator Kennedy." Joe Kennedy wrote a large personal check to pay the printer in Chicago for the midwestern copies. Two million leaflets were shipped across the country and passed around just outside black churches on the Sunday before the election. In Tallahassee, Florida, 16 percent of blacks switched from Nixon to Kennedy in the last two weeks; 5 percent of whites changed to Nixon; and undecided voters of both races went to Kennedy. African Americans ranked race as the number one issue, but whites rated it only fifth.[49]

During the last week, the Republicans launched a television blitz. Nixon was on the air every night with a rally, a speech, or an event with Lodge or Eisenhower. The Republicans presented nine hours of paid shows plus fifteen five-minute spots; the Democrats presented only three hours plus eighteen spots. One-quarter of the Nixon campaign's total TV budget was spent in the last week. As part of Nixon's theory of pacing, the blitz was designed to drown out last-minute Democratic messages, to stress Nixon's foreign policy experience, and to lead voters to the polls to affirm Eisenhower's presidency, peace, and prosperity. No candidate had ever before spent so much money to saturate the airwaves. As Nixon anticipated, the blitz did have an effect, although it was probably not a good omen that the highest-rated show starred Eisenhower—neither Nixon nor Lodge could reach the public in the way that the incumbent did. There was little Kennedy could do to counter the blitz.[50]

As part of the blitz, Nixon also brought the popular Eisenhower into the campaign in a major way. Robert Kennedy declared that the last-minute use of Eisenhower showed "panic," but the president had a tremendous impact. On Wednesday, November 2, Eisenhower joined Nixon, Lodge, and Rockefeller for a full day of campaigning in the New York City area. Beginning with short visits to a number of Republican suburbs, the presidential party then motored into the city to enjoy a ticker tape parade seen by more than 500,000 people. The president reveled in crowds, and they reveled in his presence. Whenever Eisenhower passed along a block riding in the motorcade, a wave of happiness passed across the masses. The secret to his political success was that his mere presence made people happy. Many Democrats cheered Ike. Ominously, they carried signs that read "We like Ike—We back Jack." The Republicans released balloons that said, "Experience Counts—Vote Nixon-Lodge." At a short rally in front of Macy's, Nixon asked, "Are we going to build on the progress we have made?" But he also whined, "I'm getting sick and tired of this whimpering and yammering and wringing the towel and saying America is second best." As Nixon passed beneath a high-rise building under construction, workers shouted down, "We want Jack." The day's campaigning concluded that evening with a massive Republican rally at the New York Coliseum that was broadcast on national television.[51]

Exasperated by and fearful about Eisenhower's campaigning, Kennedy tried to blunt the effect with humor. In California, Kennedy commented on Eisenhower, Nixon, Lodge, and Rockefeller appearing together in New York. "We have all seen these circus elephants," he said, "complete with tusks, ivory on their head and thick skins, who move around the circus ring and grab the tail of the elephant ahead of them." The audience laughed. He continued, "Dick Nixon grabbed that tail in 1952 and 1956, but this year he faces the American people alone. . . . And the American people have to choose between Mr. Nixon and the Republican Party and the Democratic Party and progress." Kennedy's best hope was to portray the election as a party contest.[52]

On November 2, Henry Cabot Lodge, Richard Nixon,
and President Eisenhower campaigned before large crowds
in New York City. (©Bettmann Corbis)

In a nationally televised dinner speech, Eisenhower took the gloves off. He denounced Kennedy's "phony schemes" and said that the "young genius" was not ready to be president. On the night before the election, Eisenhower, Nixon, and Lodge made major television addresses arguing for Nixon's election. On the same night, Kennedy laid down his challenge at a Boston Garden rally: "I run for the presidency of the United States," he said, "because it is the center of action." Kennedy's change versus Nixon's continuity was still the choice. Eisenhower's campaigning appeared to be a great success, but he did not have a decisive impact on the states where he visited. Kennedy carried Pennsylvania and New York, and Ohio easily went to Nixon. Suppose Eisenhower had instead been used in Illinois, Missouri, Michigan, or Texas? After the election, the question haunted the Republicans.[53]

In fact, the Republican blitz may have failed due to a declining economy during the last half of 1960—the country would be in a recession by early 1961. Kennedy made faster economic growth a major campaign theme, calling for 5 percent growth to create jobs. He argued for a full employment policy in Youngstown, Ohio, where 15,000 people were out of work, suggesting that low interest rates would stimulate the economy. Not everyone was convinced. A Minnesota housewife observed, "Kennedy has a lot of high ideas but they're also high-priced." In August, unemployment was at a worrisome 5 percent, auto sales had slipped, and steel production was at a low 55 percent of capacity. By October, it was revealed that industrial production, sales, and jobs had declined from the year's second quarter to the third quarter. Amid rising unemployment, widespread fear of layoffs spurred unprecedented union election efforts. Just after Election Day, October joblessness was reported at 6.4 percent; Michigan reached 9.3 percent. Indeed, unemployment during October rose by 452,000, a number considerably larger than Kennedy's margin of victory. Kennedy did well in economically struggling northern cities such as Chicago, Detroit, Pittsburgh, and Cleveland.[54]

Throughout the campaign, Kennedy also enjoyed the advantage of being able to charm and manipulate the media. Phil Graham, *Washington Post* publisher, privately wrote, "Joe [Alsop] and I float along on an idolatrous cloud." Walter Lippmann praised Kennedy so much that Arthur Krock said, "At least I don't fall in love with boys like Walter Lippmann." About Graham, Alsop, Lippmann, and James Reston, Arthur Schlesinger observed, "They cannot stand the thought of a Nixon victory." During the last week, Robert Novak of the *Wall Street Journal* and

Bill Lawrence of the *New York Times* both covered the Nixon campaign. In a hotel bar, another reporter remarked that it was tough having to cover Nixon. "No," said Lawrence, "I think I can do Jack more good when I'm with Nixon." The Kennedys, according to Russell Baker, had seduced Lawrence. "People did things for Jack Kennedy," observed Ohio governor Michael DiSalle, "because they wanted to be his friends." Senator Barry Goldwater deplored the "sycophantic attitude of the national press." Kennedy knew that a reporter appreciated a few choice words for a good quote. His publicity staff provided accurate handouts describing Kennedy's major speeches so that reporters could meet deadlines easily.[55]

Nixon had long had a strained relationship with the press. He estimated that 80 percent of the working reporters in Washington, D.C., disliked him, and he saw no reason to cultivate them. Instead of trying to charm or manipulate reporters, the vice president quietly held them in contempt or harassed them. Nixon told his pollster, "They never miss an opportunity to give us the needle." Nor did he seek to make reporters' lives easier. For much of the campaign, the staff provided no handouts of Nixon's speeches. But press disgruntlement produced hostile stories, so it is hard to see how Nixon benefited from his war against the press. After the election, Nixon privately wrote, "It was pretty difficult for me to get my positions across to the voters in view of the attitude of some of the reporters covering the campaign." Although most reporters favored Kennedy, 78 percent of newspapers endorsed Nixon. Most magazines that did endorsements, including *Life*, supported Nixon. One of the few major newspapers to endorse Kennedy was the *New York Times*, which had backed Dewey in 1948 and Eisenhower in 1952 and 1956. After the election, Kennedy repeated a *Times* advertising slogan by joking, "I got my job through the *New York Times*." There was a grain of truth in the joke.[56]

By the end of the campaign, both candidates were exhausted. Nixon had traveled 65,000 miles and visited all fifty states; Kennedy had traveled 44,000 miles and visited forty-five states. Each believed that all that could be done had been done. The Republicans had spent $11.3 million on the national presidential campaign; the Democrats had spent $10.6 million. In addition, organized labor had spent an additional $2.3 million, mostly helping the Democratic campaign; this amount excludes the money labor spent to register voters. This was one of the few presidential elections where, after union money is taken into account, more money was spent on behalf of the Democrat than on behalf of the Republican.

Democrats ended with a $3.8 million debt; the Republicans ended with a debt of $700,000. The tabulation for the national presidential campaign excludes local party and candidate spending. Total political spending on all elections throughout the country in 1960 was probably about $175 million. Kennedy privately told Ben Bradlee that his own campaign cost $13 million. Louis Harris estimated that parties and candidates altogether spent $1 million to $1.5 million on private polls; Kennedy paid Harris about $300,000 in 1960.[57]

Polls released just before the election predicted a close outcome. Three prominent pollsters gave a narrow edge to Kennedy and one put Nixon ahead, but all the estimates were within the margin of error. George Gallup refused to make a formal prediction, stating that his final poll, which favored Kennedy by 1 percentage point, was within the margin of sampling error. Forecasts were difficult because the election was close in so many states. A difference in turnout between Democrats and Republicans could affect the result, and Kennedy's perceived gains among African Americans as a result of the phone call to Mrs. King might be offset by Nixon's television blitz plus Eisenhower's late campaigning. Both Kennedy and Nixon recognized that the greatest uncertainty was the religious issue, which was difficult to capture in polls. Americans tended to hide prejudices when participating in polls, but deeply held feelings often had a way of expressing themselves in the voting booth, even if they were unacknowledged and rationalized. A Protestant might vote for Nixon because he was "experienced," and a Catholic might vote for Kennedy to get the country "moving again." What went into a vote for president was often complicated, subtle, and personal. On November 8 the voters finally had their say.[58]

7 KENNEDY'S VICTORY

The 1960 election turned out to be one of the closest in history. As this chapter shows, John Fitzgerald Kennedy surged into the lead on election night, lost ground in later returns, and finally won a narrow victory based on strong eastern and urban support. After the election, controversy swirled around the vote count, and Kennedy shrewdly used his cabinet appointments and Inaugural Address to rally the country behind the new administration. Early in the morning on Election Day, Jack and Jackie Kennedy voted at the precinct that served Kennedy's official legal residence in Boston. Jackie later said that she had voted only for her husband because to vote in any of the other races would be to diminish her devotion to him. It was the first time Jackie had ever voted. She intensely disliked politics. While the Kennedys voted in Boston, Dick and Pat Nixon voted in the early morning in Whittier, California, their legal residence before Nixon entered Congress. They, too, posed for the press. The photographs of the candidates voting would remind other Americans to exercise the right to vote. For both campaigns, it was the final photo opportunity.

In a close election like 1960, the perceived trend could easily shift on election night. Early on, around 6 P.M. in the East, Nixon led in the raw vote count, which was composed of a few lightly populated precincts in rural areas where polls closed exceptionally early. Nixon's lead mirrored Eisenhower's in 1956 in these precincts. At 7 P.M., the polls closed in Connecticut, a two-party state whose voters flip-flopped from election to election. The Nutmeg State used mechanical voting machines, and within an hour it was reported that Kennedy would carry the state by 90,000, a significant majority in a state that Eisenhower had won by 306,000 votes. Kennedy had run exceptionally well in grimy industrial cities like Bridgeport, Waterbury, and Danbury and had cut into the usual Republican margin in the suburbs, except for the most affluent suburbs. The small towns had stayed Republican. Kennedy won a big black vote in New Haven and Hartford and a strong vote in Jewish precincts and in Catholic areas, including many suburbs. Furthermore, the areas that Kennedy carried had a high turnout. The Connecticut results suggested that Kennedy would do well in New York, New Jersey, and Pennsylvania.

By 10:30 P.M., Kennedy's lead in the national popular vote had reached 1.5 million. Fans began to celebrate, but Bobby Kennedy's private phone calls showed a race that was tightening as the South and Midwest began to report. Although Nixon was giving Kennedy a run for his money, Republican leaders were not happy. For most of the year, they had been quietly confident about winning this election, due to peace and prosperity. A loss, they believed, would be the fault of an inept candidate and a poorly executed campaign. In 1961, a still-irate Senator Styles Bridges of New Hampshire blamed Nixon, saying, "He virtually threw away the election." From midnight to 3 A.M., Bobby and Jack Kennedy sat in Bobby's command center in Hyannis Port with growing unease. At midnight, Kennedy's lead in the popular vote peaked at 2 million but then began to drop alarmingly as rural votes and western votes were counted. Sometime after midnight, Bobby called Lyndon Johnson on the private line to Texas. Johnson chortled, "I hear you're losing Ohio, but we're doing fine in Pennsylvania." He could afford to gloat, since Texas was safe. By 12:45 A.M., Kennedy led nationally by only 1.6 million votes, and 45 minutes later by just 1.1 million.[1]

At 2 A.M. eastern time, Richard Nixon met with his staff in Los Angeles. He had taken Ohio and believed that he would carry California based upon absentee ballots. Kennedy had won New York, Pennsylvania, Texas, and Michigan. It all came down to Illinois and Minnesota. Kennedy could win with either state, but Nixon needed both, and even both might not be enough because of the fourteen unpledged electors from Mississippi and Alabama. The election might go to the House of Representatives, a possibility that neither candidate wanted. Always a realist capable of cold-blooded calculation, Nixon concluded an hour later that he had almost certainly lost. At 3:20 A.M. eastern time, Nixon told the television cameras, "If the present trend continues, Senator Kennedy will be the next president of the United States." The crowd yelled, "Don't give up!" Nixon also thanked his supporters. Although some in the Kennedy compound were angry at Nixon's failure to concede, Jack Kennedy was more guarded. "Why should he concede?" said Kennedy. "I wouldn't." Then both Jack Kennedy and Dick Nixon went to bed. In the morning Kennedy awoke to the news that he had won.[2]

By 9 A.M. Kennedy's lead had shrunk to half a million votes, but most of the media had declared him the winner in the crucial electoral college. Vote counting would continue for several days and even into December. Absentee ballots had to be processed, write-in votes had to be tallied, and errors had to be corrected, and, more than in most elections, these changes to the count favored one candidate. Nixon ran strong in rural areas where paper ballots took longer to handle and among older voters who were more likely to use absentee ballots. Final certification by the states found that 68,833,243 Americans had voted for president. Another 224,931 voters had gone to the polls but declined to vote for president. Turnout had been high. Of registered voters, 82 percent cast ballots, and of those eligible to be registered, 64.3 percent voted, the highest percentage in modern times.

Kennedy got 34,221,349 votes, and Nixon got 34,108,546, a difference in the popular vote of only 112,803. Kennedy's margin was less than one-half vote per precinct. Other candidates received 503,348 votes, the most significant of which were 116,248 for segregationist unpledged electors in Mississippi and 169,572 for the States' Rights Party in Louisiana. In percentage terms, Kennedy had 49.7 percent of the total vote, Nixon had 49.6 percent, and the remainder amounted to .7 percent. Kennedy, like Lincoln, Wilson, and Truman, would be a minority president elected by less than half of the electorate. (In 1968 Nixon would win the presidency in a three-way contest with 43 percent of the vote.) Many states were close. A switch of just 4,430 votes in Illinois and 4,991 in Missouri would have thrown the election into the House, and another shift of 1,247 in Nevada, 1,148 in New Mexico, and 58 in Hawaii would have made Nixon president (for details, see Appendix D).

In the electoral college, Kennedy fared better than in the popular vote, carrying twenty-three states, if Alabama is credited with its five Kennedy electors, for a total of 303 electoral votes. Although Kennedy won fewer states, the Democrat won in the more populous states, where his campaign had been focused. Senator Barry Goldwater bitterly noted that Nixon might have won the election had he skipped a last-minute long flight to Alaska and campaigned instead in Illinois, Michigan, and Texas. A week after the election, Kennedy lost California when absentee ballots went heavily to Nixon. The vice president won his home state by 35,623 votes. In December, a recount gave Hawaii to Kennedy by 115 votes. Nixon took twenty-six states and received 219 electoral votes.

On December 10, Alabama's six unpledged Democratic electors said that they would not vote for Kennedy unless he repudiated the party's national platform and especially its civil rights plank. Three days later, the six Alabama electors, along with Mississippi's eight unpledged electors, announced that they would cast their votes for president for a conservative southern Democrat, Senator Harry Byrd of Virginia. They urged the thirty-eight Democratic electors from Georgia, Louisiana, Arkansas, and South Carolina, all of whom were technically unpledged, to desert Kennedy and join them. If enough had done so, the election would have been thrown into the House. But there were no Democratic Party desertions. On December 19, Mississippi's eight electors joined Alabama's six to vote for Byrd for president and Senator Strom Thurmond of South Carolina for vice president. In Oklahoma, one Republican elector defected to Byrd and voted for Senator Barry Goldwater of Arizona for vice president.

A study of the election returns reveals how the 1960 election marked several significant changes from 1956. The cities were beginning to turn much more strongly Democratic, which was mostly a result of white middle-class flight to the suburbs. Of the ten most populous Rust Belt cities, Eisenhower had carried Chicago, Baltimore, and Milwaukee. Kennedy swept all ten with a combined 65.3 percent and a victory margin of 2.5 million votes. The cities were the bulwark of Kennedy's support, and the greater the population, the greater the numerical edge. Kennedy's largest victory margins were in the four largest cities: New York City, 791,120; Chicago, 456,312; Philadelphia, 331,544; and Detroit, 311,721. In each of these cities, as well as in Cleveland and Boston, Kennedy's *local* margin exceeded his *national* popular vote margin. Furthermore, the margins by which he won New York City, Chicago, Philadelphia, Detroit, Baltimore, and St. Louis exceeded the margins by which he won in the states of New York, Illinois, Pennsylvania, Michigan, Maryland, and Missouri. Kennedy's urban support did not translate into victory in every state; for example, despite sizable victories in Cleveland and Milwaukee, he lost Ohio and Wisconsin. He also ran poorly in Cincinnati and Minneapolis, although he carried Minnesota narrowly.

Six populous Sun Belt cities produced quite different results. Although Kennedy carried four of the six, losing only Houston and Dallas, his margins in Los Angeles and Denver were miniscule. Kennedy did outpace Nixon in San Francisco and New Orleans, both of which Eisenhower had taken. Because Kennedy ran poorly in urban areas in California and Colorado, he lost both states, and he won Texas only with rural votes. The suburbs also produced a new pattern in 1960. In the fourteen largest metropolitan areas that cast about one-third of the national vote, the suburbs showed a dramatic swing. In 1956 Eisenhower had won 62 percent of this suburban vote, but Nixon got only 51 percent four years later, an 11 percent drop. In the nation as a whole, Nixon ran 8 percent behind Eisenhower. Unlike many Democrats, Kennedy targeted suburban voters. His education, polish, and wit appealed to suburban sophisticates, who were also attracted to parts of his program. Certainly many of those who moved to the suburbs were Republicans, but others were Democrats, and the growing suburban vote was much less Republican than it had been in the fifties. In New York, Philadelphia, and Chicago, many suburbanites were Catholics who voted heavily for Kennedy.[3]

Of Catholics who had voted for Eisenhower in 1956, 62 percent voted for Kennedy, which was a far greater party shift than for any other group in the electorate. Many of these voters, however, had been Eisenhower Democrats. Many Catholics chose Kennedy because they were Democrats, not because they were Catholics. In 1960, Catholics were 72 percent Democrats, 18 percent Republicans, and 10 percent independents. Many Catholic Democrats lived in declining industrial cities, and their votes for Kennedy may have been mostly about poor local economies. Of Catholic Democrats, 95 percent voted for Kennedy. Although Kennedy also appealed strongly to Catholic independents (72 percent), he drew only limited support from Catholic Republicans (18 percent). Overall, 78 percent of Catholics voted for Kennedy. This was the highest percentage of Catholics backing a Democratic presidential candidate from 1952, when analysis of group voting began, through 2004.[4]

Of the fifteen most heavily Catholic states, where Catholics roughly equaled or outnumbered Protestants, Kennedy won eleven, losing only traditionally Republican rural upper New England and Nixon's home state of California. Of sixteen predominantly Protestant southern or border states, including Texas, Kennedy took ten, six of which were overwhelmingly Democratic ex-Confederate states largely held for the ticket by Johnson. Of nineteen predominantly Protestant states outside the South, Kennedy carried only Minnesota and Nevada. Campaigning for reelection, Senator Hubert Humphrey sold Kennedy to skeptical Scandinavian Lutherans by noting that the Vikings had conquered Ireland. Referring to Kennedy's fair skin and reddish hair, Humphrey exclaimed: "Why, he is one of us!" After the election, Humphrey concluded that the argument had worked in the areas where the Minnesota senator had personally campaigned.[5]

Although Kennedy's religion helped in some places, especially among suburban Catholics in the Northeast, in many parts of the country it hurt. Losses among Protestant Democrats and independents may have been as high as 4.4 million votes, offset by perhaps 2.9 million Catholic votes for Kennedy. However, these numbers have been hotly disputed, and any exact calculation is impossible because of the difficulty of establishing a baseline. The *percentage* of Protestants who switched to Nixon was smaller than was the Catholic percentage shift to Kennedy, but because Protestants outnumbered Catholics 66 percent to 26 percent, according to a 1957 census, the *number* of Protestant voters who voted against Kennedy for religious reasons probably did exceed the number of Catholics who voted for Kennedy for religious reasons. However, concentration of Catholic voters in key states may have helped Kennedy in the electoral college. "The bigots were maldistributed," complained Bryce Harlow, an Eisenhower aide. Without the Catholic swing to Kennedy, Nixon would probably have carried Illinois, New Jersey, Michigan, and Pennsylvania (95 total electors). Had Kennedy been Protestant, he would probably have won Tennessee, Florida, and Kentucky and possibly Virginia and Oklahoma (51 total).[6]

The shift of Catholics to Kennedy and of Bible Belt Protestants to Nixon has one other dimension. In later elections, where there was no Catholic presidential candidate, Catholics returned to more normal voting patterns, but 1960 marked the year when conservative, traditionally Democratic Bible Belt Protestants began to shift permanently to the Republicans at the presidential level. A comparison of the Democratic percentage of the two-party vote in 1960 with 1968 shows this trend. Nixon was on the ballot both years, and Hubert Humphrey's vote in 1968 largely mirrored Kennedy's in 1960. In these two elections the Democratic share varied by less than 2 percent in nineteen states and by less than 5 percent in another sixteen states. Furthermore, Kennedy ran ahead of Humphrey in only seven of fifteen highly Catholic states, but Kennedy did better than Humphrey in fourteen of sixteen southern or border Protestant states. Conservative southerners deserted the liberal Humphrey in droves, but that process began in 1960. *Liberalism*, as expressed in the 1960 Democratic Party platform, rather than *Catholicism* may explain why so many Bible Belt Protestants objected to Kennedy. In fact, a case can be made that, despite all the talk about religion during the campaign, the number of both Catholics and Protestants who voted on the basis of religion in 1960 was very tiny and proved to be so offsetting that the overall effect was *no* net religious vote in 1960.

At the same time, African Americans began to move to the Democrats, a trend that would lead to huge Democratic margins later in the century. Kennedy received 68 percent of the black vote, compared to Stevenson's 61 percent in 1956. The swing to Kennedy was especially strong in the South, where many African Americans had protested against local segregationist Democrats by voting for Eisenhower in 1956. Black votes enabled Kennedy to carry South Carolina, North Carolina, and Texas, as well as Illinois, Michigan, Missouri, New Jersey, and Pennsylvania. In Illinois, Kennedy may have won 250,000 black votes, and his phone call to Coretta Scott King influenced this result. In large urban areas, Kennedy's black support reached 75 percent. In Harlem, Kennedy got 80 percent, whereas Stevenson had won only about two-thirds. In other areas, the black vote was around 60 percent Democratic. Despite Kennedy's call to Mrs. King, much of Kennedy's black vote may have been about jobs rather than about civil rights. One black Ohioan said, "I'll vote for the Democrats because they'll give me a job." Then, too, employment could be seen as part of the rights issue. Black union members were especially strong Democrats, giving Kennedy 77 percent. Younger African Americans were also more likely to favor Kennedy (73 percent).[7]

Jewish voters gave Kennedy 81 percent, which was higher than the percentage among Catholics. In 1956, 75 percent of Jews had voted for Stevenson. Union members were 65 percent for Kennedy, and this percentage rose to 85 percent among Catholic union members. This intense labor support was strongest in the East (68 percent) and weakest in the South (59 percent); it was also pronounced in metropolitan areas (70 percent). Voters age twenty-one to twenty-nine favored Kennedy with 54 percent, and among young women the percentage was 55 percent. In contrast, only 44 percent of women over age fifty voted for Kennedy.

Although Kennedy received the votes of only 38 percent of the nation's Protestants, he received more votes from Protestants than from Catholics and Jews combined. Overall, 49 percent of whites voted for Kennedy; in the South he got 48 percent, which showed that the South was beginning to vote like the rest of the country.[8]

Certain regional trends also began in this election. The East was deserting the Republican Party, which had dominated there since the 1850s. Even in eastern rural areas, the party was in decline. Kennedy took nine of twelve states, including vote-rich New York, New Jersey, and Pennsylvania. Kennedy's 141 electoral votes overshadowed Nixon's pathetic 12 from rural upper New England. Kennedy was popular in his home region, and eastern liberal Republicans were increasingly at odds with the rest of their party. Liberal governor Nelson Rockefeller had campaigned for Nixon but had not been able to deliver New York. Rocky's conservative rival, Senator Barry Goldwater of Arizona, taunted, "If Mr. Rockefeller can't carry New York, he can't be reckoned a figure to be contended with in the Republican Party." If the party could not win in the increasingly liberal East, then conservative Republicans argued that the party should become a more conservative party based in the Midwest, West, and South.[9]

Despite Lyndon Johnson's presence on the ticket, Nixon did well enough in the South to run even with Eisenhower in that region. Although Kennedy carried Texas and five other southern states, plus getting five of Alabama's electors, Nixon took Virginia, Florida, and Tennessee, as well as the border states of Kentucky and Oklahoma. Within the thirteen-state region, Kennedy won 81 electoral votes to Nixon's 50 and Byrd's 15. Nixon's performance was strong, considering that the South had long been a one-party region, that the Republicans were not organized in many southern states, and that Nixon lacked personal popularity in Dixie. In an ominous sign of racial battles to come, Mississippi voted for unpledged electors. In the long run, the rise of the Republican Party in the South promised to reshape the national political landscape. A Georgia Democrat warned, "This Republican habit is going to spread like the pox."[10]

The West voted Republican. Of the thirteen western states, Kennedy narrowly carried only New Mexico, Nevada, and Hawaii, and Senator Clinton Anderson credited the New Mexico win to Lyndon Johnson. Kennedy's 10 electoral votes contrasted with Nixon's 75. The endorsement by the president of the Mormon Church of Nixon enabled Nixon to win Utah and Idaho and began a long cozy relationship between that organization and the Republican Party. In liberal Washington State, Governor Albert Rosellini, who faced a tough reelection, did not want to remind voters that two Catholic Democrats were on the ballot. The state party headquarters, under the governor's control, displayed no Kennedy posters. Some pundits blamed Kennedy's Washington loss on anti-Catholicism, but Rosellini won reelection. Tens of thousands of voters split tickets for Nixon and Rosellini, which would be a strange way to express anti-Catholicism. Kennedy's eastern brand of politics played poorly throughout the West. California was Kennedy's biggest regional disappointment. In Los Angeles County, Kennedy ran 200,000 votes behind his party's legislative candidates because he lacked enthusiastic support from the California Democratic Clubs. Kennedy operatives' high-pressure tactics had deeply offended local Democrats.

Finally, the Midwest emerged as a closely contested battleground, which it would remain for the next forty years. As Kennedy expected, Nixon swept the Farm Belt from Kansas to North Dakota, and the two candidates split the remaining eight midwestern states. Kennedy took Illinois, Michigan, Missouri, and Minnesota; Nixon got Ohio, Indiana, Wisconsin, and Iowa. Kennedy won 71 regional electoral votes to Nixon's 82. The vice president won the Midwest's popular vote. In popular percentage terms, Middle America was Nixon's best region.

Kennedy carried only 206 congressional districts; Nixon won 228. Unpledged electors prevailed in three Mississippi districts. Kennedy ran poorly in such a large number of districts because they were gerrymandered to favor rural voters. The Supreme Court had not yet required districts to have the same number of residents. Then, too, Kennedy's support, heavily concentrated in urban areas, simply was not spread across as many districts. In other words, Kennedy prevailed in the districts that he won by a greater margin on average than Nixon did in his districts. The Democrats retained control of the Senate and easily won the House, 262 to 175. However, ninety-nine Democrats were from the South, and seventy or more were conservatives. Conservatives, not liberals, held a majority in the House. The new Senate was more liberal than the House, but liberals could pass nothing in the Senate because it took a two-thirds vote to end a filibuster.[11]

In all parts of the country, Democratic candidates for Senate or House ran ahead of Kennedy. Kennedy outpaced Democratic congressional candidates in only 134 districts. Kennedy got 49.7 percent of the total vote; Democratic candidates for the House got 55 percent. Democratic members, mostly moderates or conservatives who had run ahead of him, showed little interest in liberal legislation. Kennedy's winning coalition was composed of contradictory elements: conservative Catholics, organized labor, liberals from the East, and conservatives from the South. Kennedy's overall lack of popularity at the ballot box, combined with his running behind other Democratic Party candidates, undermined his capacity for governance. However, Kennedy did not run poorly everywhere. His strong showing in major cities and in many suburbs provided coattails in a few places.

In 1958 the Democrats had gained forty-nine seats in the House (and they had also lost one). Of these seats, twenty were in the East, twenty-three were in the Midwest, five were in the West, and only one was in the South. The industrial recession with its heavy loss of unionized factory jobs played a major role in these gains. In 1960, a more prosperous year, the Democrats lost twenty-two of these seats, giving up seven seats in the East, thirteen in the Midwest, and two in the West. The fact that the Republicans were able to make a better comeback in the Midwest (thirteen of twenty-three) than in the East (seven of twenty) was important, because it shifted the party's center of gravity away from the East. In 1960 the Republicans also picked up another seven seats (one in the East, four in the Midwest, and two in the West) that had been Democratic both in 1956 and in 1958. These new seats, like the twenty-two seats recaptured in 1960, were mostly in rural areas dominated by a small city—for example, Portland, Maine; York, Pennsylvania; Racine, Wisconsin; and Dubuque, Iowa. Kennedy ran poorly in most of these districts.

In contrast, the Democrats in 1960 held twenty-seven of the seats that they had first won in 1958, and they picked up another eight seats. Many of these thirty-five seats were urban or suburban districts. In 1960 the Democrats retained seats first won in 1958 in Baltimore, Philadelphia, Chicago (two), and Oakland-Berkeley in California; in medium-size cities Louisville, Des Moines, and Salt Lake City; in an industrial area outside Buffalo, New York; in the more urban parts of Connecticut (four); and in suburbs of Boston, Detroit, and northern New Jersey. In 1960 the Democrats gained eight new seats—four in the East and four in the West. Two were in New York City, and two were in New York's suburbs (one in New York, one in New Jersey). Another gain was in Los Angeles. Kennedy coattails accounted for some of these holds and gains in 1960. Considering both gains and losses in 1960, the Democrats overall lost four seats in the East and seventeen in the Midwest, with a draw in the South and West.

In 1960, Senate Democrats lost two seats, which was another sign that Kennedy generally lacked coattails. The Senate elections, unlike 1958, favored incumbents. Of nineteen Democratic senators who sought reelection, eighteen were returned. Conservative Democratic senator J. Allen Frear of Delaware lost to a Republican moderate, J. Caleb Boggs, who had the AFL-CIO endorsement. All ten Republican incumbents won reelection. A Republican won the only Republican open seat, while Democrats retained control of three of four open seats that Democrats had previously held, losing only in Wyoming. The 64-to-36 Senate did not last long, however, because Wyoming's Republican senator-elect Keith Thomson died of a heart attack in December and was succeeded by an appointed Democrat. In January 1961 the new Senate opened with sixty-five Democrats and thirty-five Republicans.

The 1960 gubernatorial elections showed no clear pattern. In the late 1950s, state governments were thrown into fiscal turmoil by the rising costs of paying for the huge increase in the number of baby boomers attending school. States raised taxes, but tax increases proved to be unpopular. In 1960 many governors chose not to run for reelection, while others hoped to defy the odds. Of eight Democratic governors seeking reelection, four won. Of six similarly situated Republicans, four also won. Overall, only eight of fourteen incumbents were reelected. One prominent casualty was Orville Freeman, who had been promoted as a possible Kennedy vice president. A very large tax increase killed him. Of seven open governorships previously held by Democrats, the party retained five. For Republicans, the rate was two of six. For open seats, the party in power retained control in only seven of thirteen cases.

In any close election, as can be seen in the year 2000, the most important question is whether the losing side can reverse the result. Because TV reports during election night showed Kennedy substantially ahead, neither Nixon nor the Republicans at first contemplated any election challenge. However, as Kennedy's lead dwindled from a half million votes on Wednesday morning to a little over 100,000 weeks later, some Republicans believed that a careful review of the returns might elect Nixon. Such an idea especially appealed to persons who believed that Kennedy had received numerous fraudulent votes: Perhaps Kennedy's entire margin of victory was composed of the votes of dead people, illegal voters, and repeaters. Senator Barry Goldwater concluded that Kennedy's final margin was less than the number of votes that had been stolen in Illinois and Texas. Republicans questioned the results because of reports of fraud that poured into the headquarters of the Republican National Committee from all over the country. Senator Thruston Morton of Kentucky, the party chair, said that more than 135,000 letters and wires concerning fraud had been received. Because the Republican Party was the weaker party, Republicans were less likely to control election machinery at the precinct, county, or state level, which left them vulnerable to being taken advantage of by Democrats.

After the election, the greatest complaints concerned Illinois and Texas. If both states had voted for Nixon, he would have won. Virtually all locally elected officials in Texas were Democrats. So were the precinct judges. Furthermore, Texas law made no provision for challenging a presidential election. In fact, in many places there were more votes cast than registered voters in the jurisdiction. In Fannin County, 4,895 voters cast 6,138 ballots. In Navarro County, Dawson Precinct, 479 registered voters cast 315 votes for Kennedy and 219 for Nixon. In some heavily Democratic jurisdictions, votes for president and vice president were added, giving each side double the number of votes. In Angelina County, Precinct 27, 86 people voted. Kennedy got 147 votes and Nixon got 24. The judge had added 74 votes for Kennedy to 73 votes for Johnson. In Lee County, Precinct 15, 39 people voted but 64 votes were counted for president. By comparing poll books to the vote count, it was clear that 100,000 votes had been counted that simply did not exist, but Republicans were prevented from seeing any actual ballots.[12]

Texas voting law also contained one oddity, which resulted in an ingenious way to manipulate the result. Although thirteen counties containing about half of Texas voters used mechanical voting machines, the rest of the state voted with "negative" paper ballots. In 1957 the law had been changed to require that voters strike out the names of all the candidates they opposed. In 1960 there were four candidates on the Texas presidential ballot. Thus, a voter had to cross out three names to cast a valid vote. In some counties, it was charged, Democratic election officials disallowed votes that had only Kennedy struck out, but they counted votes for Kennedy that had only Nixon struck out. In Wichita Falls, middle-class Eagle Lake gave Nixon 475, Kennedy 357, and had 234 voided, while lower-class Precinct 54, which went to Kennedy by six to one, presented only two voided ballots. A certain amount of variation simply reflected the whim of the officials in each precinct. In rural Wichita County, Precinct 34, 3 percent of ballots were invalidated. In adjacent Precinct 35, an essentially identical rural precinct, 22 percent of ballots were invalidated.

The evidence suggests that Democratic officials purposely used different standards in different kinds of precincts or counties in order to manipulate the overall result. For example, in some precincts that voted heavily for Nixon, 40 percent of the votes were voided, while in Starr County, a poor county on the Mexican border that voted more than 93 percent for Kennedy, only 1.5 percent were thrown out. In Fort Bend County, Precinct 1, Nixon drew 458, Kennedy drew 350, and 182 were disallowed. In Precinct 2, Kennedy received 68 votes, Nixon 1, and none were voided. In one strong Kennedy precinct where a recount in a local election allowed outside observers to see the ballots, about 200 Kennedy votes were seen that should have been voided for striking out only Nixon. Republicans charged that more than 100,000 Republican ballots had been disallowed in Texas, and thousands of Democratic ballots with the same type of error had been added in. Kennedy's margin was 46,000. However, without an official investigation, there was no way to know whether this kind of vote counting fraud provided Kennedy's margin of victory in the Lone Star State. The national media showed little interest in this story.

Illinois was more complicated. The state had long had vote fraud, often but not exclusively associated with Chicago. In a later election, a Chicago precinct captain explained the Illinois mind-set: "We don't know how many we got until we find out how many we need." Some Republican suburban areas were eager to offset thefts that they believed took place in the city, a corrupt Democratic machine in East St. Louis also practiced fraud, and a few rural Republican counties also had crooked machines. Cook County, dominated by Chicago, cast almost half the state's total vote, so fraud there mattered a lot in the statewide totals. To Chicago Democrats, "downstate" meant any other county, including suburban Republican Lake County, which was north of Cook County.[13]

Mayor Richard Daley had been elected in 1955, and he had not yet consolidated his power when he won a second term in 1959. Daley wanted badly to carry Illinois for Kennedy. In addition to Irish pride, the mayor had made a promise to Joe Kennedy. Daley also recognized that Kennedy could bring Chicago the federal financial assistance that it needed. But the inexperienced Daley did not realize until the 1960 election the heavy burden that charges of vote fraud would place on his own leadership. As a result of the events in 1960, he tried to run a cleaner operation in later elections. In 1960 Daley put pressure on the precinct captains and ward bosses to produce fixed vote margins for each precinct and ward for Kennedy. Any member of the organization that failed to produce was likely to lose both his political party post and his city job. Efficient precinct captains identified voters, made sure they were registered, and got them to the polls on Election Day. In 1960, Chicago had an impressive 89.3 percent turnout, far above the national average. The problem was that some precinct captains who needed to produce fixed victory margins for Kennedy had not cultivated enough actual voters. So they turned to other measures.

Many tricks were used in Chicago. Republicans were removed from the rolls, a fact that they only discovered when they tried to vote. One turned out to be an irate columnist for the *Chicago Tribune*. Persons who had been dead for years often were found to have voted. In Ward 4, Precinct 31, both a dead man and a son who had taken care of the man and then moved away performed their civic duty. Rolls could be padded in other ways. In Ward 5, Precinct 46, registration closed with 636 voters listed. But on Election Day the poll book contained 751 names, the extra 115 names having been added at city hall. Of these fraudulent registrants, 49 voted. The total vote in the precinct was 640, four more than on the registration list. Democrats paid cheap boardinghouses one dollar per head for each resident who voted. Managers also got an additional twenty-five dollars to fifty dollars to keep Republicans from entering to talk with the tenants. Vans carried "floaters" from precinct to precinct to cast multiple votes, electioneering sometimes took place inside polling places, and votes were bought just outside the door.

In Ward 4, Precinct 77, the Democratic precinct captain voted twice and then went outside to pay voters on their way in. In Ward 5, Precinct 22, one voter put six ballots in the box. Many precincts had fake Republican election judges. In Ward 4, Precinct 6, the "Republican" judge tried to assist a Republican voter in voting a straight Democratic ticket. The judge had to be physically restrained from casting the ballot for the voter on the machine. Final results were Kennedy 451, Nixon 67. In Ward 6, Precinct 38, the voting machine at 10:15 A.M. showed 121 votes, but only 43 voters had signed in. The final total was Kennedy 408, Nixon 79. In half a dozen precincts, the number of votes counted exceeded the number of registered voters by more than 75. In Ward 2, Precinct 50, with 22 or 54 registered voters (the parties disputed the number), 82 persons signed in, and 84 ballots were cast. Kennedy had 78 votes, and Nixon had 4. The area was undergoing urban renewal, and former residents had been allowed to vote. Contrary to law, no Republican judges were present. When a grand jury subpoenaed the sign-in list, it disappeared from the election office vault.

Chicago Republicans paid for a partial recount. In many of the city's 3,317 voting machine precincts, the numbers that remained visible on the machines disagreed with the official tally sheets. The bigger problem, however, was in the 634 precincts that used paper ballots, where numbers on the tally sheets often bore no relationship to the ballots in the ballot box, when they were recounted at the courthouse in the presence of Republicans. In 1960 vote counting on election night in most jurisdictions in the United States was done in the precincts with counted ballots and completed tallies then taken to the courthouse. Nor was it reassuring that about 60 percent of the ballot boxes either had seals that were missing or broken when they were brought from storage into the counting room. Ward 23, Precinct 70, was reported as Kennedy, 372, and Nixon, 144. The recount found Kennedy, 341, and Nixon, 170. It looked like the numbers had more or less been transposed to improve Kennedy's margin. Sometimes the changes were arbitrary. Ward 29, Precinct 18, officially was Kennedy, 338, and Nixon, 30. The recount was Kennedy, 327, and Nixon, 45. Kennedy won Ward 29, Precinct 23, 328 to 50, and in the recount, the result was 289 to 72. Ward 42, Precinct 41, went from 433 to 113 to 335 to 115.

In many precincts, an inspection of the ballots showed that Republican votes had been erased. In Ward 27, Precinct 20, there were fifteen straight Republican ballots in a row that had been spoiled by an extra X being placed into the Socialist Labor Party column. Although impossible to prove, it was easy to conclude that the marks had been added during the counting. The tally sheets almost always favored Democrats more than did the recount of the actual ballots. Apparently, local precinct officials had simply made up results to provide the margins that Daley had demanded. The press identified 677 election judges in 133 precincts who had stolen votes. The investigation, however, accomplished little. One Chicago politician told the journalist Alistair Cooke, "When a vote is stolen in Chicago, it stays stolen." In justifying existing practices, Sidney Holzman, Chicago's chief election official, said, "The Republicans are stealing so much downstate, that all we do is balance it out."[14]

Despite the evidence in Illinois, Nixon did not challenge the election. The main purpose of the Republican investigation appears to have been to persuade Democrats to treat Republican candidates better in the future. There was no mechanism to make a challenge in Texas. Also, even if Illinois had gone to Nixon, Kennedy would still have won in the electoral college. Entangling Illinois in court might have dropped Kennedy down to 273 electors, and if as few as five southern state electors had then defected from the ticket, the election would have been thrown into the House. Denouncing the unpledged electors as "brigands," the Republican *Chicago Tribune* noted that more than 99 percent of Americans had voted for either Kennedy or Nixon. The vice president did not want to take any action that might throw the election into the House. It was possible that five electors in Georgia or Arkansas could have been persuaded to defect from Kennedy to unpledged, but this result would not have helped Nixon. There was no way Nixon could have won in the House: Democrats controlled 29 state delegations; Republicans controlled only 17.[15]

Nixon recognized that being a gracious loser in 1960 would enable him to run for president again. In both of his memoirs, Nixon suggests that President Eisenhower wanted to challenge the election but that Nixon refused to do so because he believed that the Cold War required the United States to have continuous, strong leadership. An election challenge might leave a vacancy in the presidency and a power vacuum for months. However, conservative journalist Ralph de Toledano claimed that the actual roles were reversed. According to his account, Nixon, egged on by some party leaders, was prepared to challenge the result, but Eisenhower cited national security to demand that Nixon drop the issue. In any case, the issue was dropped. When Earl Mazo, a reporter sympathetic to Nixon, started to write a twelve-part series in the *New York Herald Tribune* detailing examples of election fraud around the United States, especially in Texas and Illinois, Nixon asked Mazo to cancel the series, and Mazo agreed to do so. The fourth installment was the last.

Kennedy understood that the narrow win meant that he lacked a mandate to govern as a liberal. His thin edge in the popular vote, the conservative majority in the House, and the ability of conservatives to wield the filibuster in the Senate caused a conservative president-elect to replace the preelection liberal nominee. On the Thursday after the election, Kennedy announced that two members of the Eisenhower administration would be staying on: J. Edgar Hoover, age sixty-five, of the FBI, and Allen Dulles, age sixty-seven, of the CIA. Kennedy had good reasons to retain both officials. Hoover had been a close friend of Joe Kennedy for years.

In addition, the director had a thick file on Jack Kennedy, beginning with his wartime romance with the suspected Nazi spy, Inga Arvad. The public knew nothing about Kennedy's very active sex life; if that information had been revealed, there would have been demands for Kennedy to resign. Kennedy kept Allen Dulles at the CIA because the plan to use Cuban exiles to invade Cuba at the Bay of Pigs and overthrow Castro was nearing its launch date. Kennedy wanted Dulles to stay until the invasion had taken place.

Kennedy's appointees were virtually all white men. A very high proportion had served as junior officers in World War II, especially in the U.S. Navy. These veterans spoke the common language of their generation and expressed its values. Patriotic, proud to be tough, and having a "can-do" attitude, they were eager to get the country "moving again." They made the seasoned committee chairs on Capitol Hill nervous. When Lyndon Johnson, age fifty-two, told Speaker Sam Rayburn, seventy-eight, how impressed he was with the appointees, the Speaker said, "Well Lyndon, you might be right and they may be every bit as intelligent as you say, but I'd feel a whole lot better about them if just one of them had run for sheriff once." In the South, the sheriff was the most important elected official in any county. He knew the score and where all the bodies were buried. He knew when to pursue a crime, and when not to press too hard. He was a local political impresario. Rayburn worried that Kennedy's appointees lacked caution, political sense, a grasp of reality, and popular appeal.[16]

Kennedy decided, in effect, to be his own secretary of state. Foreign policy was Kennedy's passion, and given the conservative control of Congress, it was the only area where the president could be decisive. To run the State Department, which had more than 24,000 employees and produced masses of paper work, Kennedy tapped Dean Rusk, fifty-one years old. A soft-spoken Rhodes scholar whose words expressed great nuance and subtlety, Rusk had little in common with the impatient, action-oriented Kennedy. Adlai Stevenson, age sixty, became the UN ambassador, a cabinet-rank ceremonial post with no policy-making function. Defense, with more than 3.5 million employees and a $43.7 billion budget, more than half the federal budget, went to Robert McNamara, age forty-four, the president of Ford Motor Company. Although a registered Republican, he had campaigned for Kennedy. For Treasury, Kennedy picked C. Douglas Dillon, a fifty-one-year-old Wall Street investment banker who had served in the Eisenhower administration. Also a Republican,

Dillon had donated $26,000 to the Nixon campaign. Dillon's appointment reassured Wall Street about the Kennedy administration's commitment to sound economic policies. For attorney general, Joe Kennedy insisted that Jack appoint Robert Kennedy.

The minor cabinet posts proved easier to staff. Interior went to conservationist congressman Stewart Udall, age forty, who had stolen the Arizona delegation for Kennedy before the convention; the post of agriculture secretary was filled by Minnesota's governor Orville Freeman, age forty-two, who had lost his reelection bid; Arthur Goldberg, fifty-two, an early Kennedy supporter who was legal counsel to the Steelworkers Union, became the secretary of labor; the secretary of commerce post went to North Carolina's governor Luther Hodges, sixty-two, a leading southern supporter; Connecticut's governor Abraham Ribicoff, fifty, one of Kennedy's earliest backers, became health, education, and welfare secretary; and the Post Office post went to J. Edward Day, age forty-six, a Los Angeles businessman.

The White House staff included the "Irish Mafia," Larry O'Brien, forty-three, and Kenny O'Donnell, thirty-six, as well as Ted Sorensen, thirty-two, and Arthur Schlesinger Jr., forty-three. The new president made himself the focal point for the staff. He refused to have a chief of staff, because he feared that the person would wield vast power by blocking access to the president. All White House aides were given the same job title and paid the same salary. On the first day on the job, aides put their belongings into whichever office they wanted. No offices were assigned, at least at the beginning. This lack of hierarchy manifested itself in other ways. As president, Kennedy frequently called staff, cabinet, or bureaucratic subordinates to seek advice, to ask questions, to give praise, to prod into action, or to heap disapproval. Kennedy referred to this method of operation as "a wheel and a series of spokes," but this process caused mischief. Circumvention of the chain of command unsettled the people who had been cut out, and the lack of coordination caused confusion. Unable to orchestrate itself to pursue a common agenda, the staff generated few workable policies or programs. It was ironic that a campaign noted for its superb organization produced an administration without organization.[17]

Substantively, Kennedy's presidency lacked achievement. He had the lowest percentage of bills sent to Congress approved by Congress of any president in the twentieth century. "All those Bostons and Harvards," said Lyndon Johnson, "don't know anymore about Capitol Hill than an

On a cold day in January, President John F. Kennedy delivered his Inaugural Address. (Ollie Atkins Photo Collection, Special Collections and Archives, George Mason University Libraries, Fairfax, Virginia)

old maid does about fuckin'." Kennedy's ineffective foreign policy came from the brilliant, arrogant McGeorge Bundy, forty-one, assisted by the anti-Communist ideologue, Walt Rostow, forty-four. Together, they planned the Vietnam War. The Cuban invasion at the Bay of Pigs was the most disastrous single incident of the entire Cold War, and the Cuban Missile Crisis nearly produced a nuclear holocaust. The administration did establish the Peace Corps, begin the program to put an American on the moon, and sign the Nuclear Test Ban Treaty. Despite a weak record, Kennedy was a master of public relations. In a brilliant stroke, press secretary Pierre Salinger, thirty-five, proposed holding live press conferences on television. Kennedy scored heavily with the public on television, expressing an unusual amount of candor for a president and frequently showing his sardonic wit.[18]

In early January, as inauguration day approached, Washington hummed with excitement. Thousands of Democrats had made their way to the capital to celebrate. In 1960, anticipation was strong among Democrats, who were thrilled by the young, telegenic president-elect. Cabinet and staff appointments had been well received. Kennedy's administration, composed of younger World War II veterans, signaled a shift in power from the generation that had commanded during the war, signified by Eisenhower, to those who had served as junior officers. Resourceful, confident, even cocky, these veterans had learned certain lessons: Power mattered, and force could be useful. Restless, dynamic, and progressive, they looked upon the older generation's caution with contempt. Bill Haddad, who helped Sargent Shriver found the Peace Corps, later said, "We were guys of the Fifties who thought there was nothing we, or America, couldn't do."[19]

On the morning of the inauguration, which broke cold and clear with a fresh carpet of glistening snow, the Kennedys called on the Eisenhowers at the White House, and both couples then rode to the ceremony at the Capitol's inaugural stand. Lyndon and Lady Bird Johnson were also on the platform, along with Richard and Pat Nixon. Kennedy's family and cabinet were present, too. Jackie Kennedy drew attention with her fur-trimmed beige coat, mink muff, and striking pillbox hat. Designed by Oleg Cassini, the incoming first lady's outfit marked the beginning of her domination of style in the United States. Within weeks, the "Jackie look" swept the country. At about 12:30, a bit behind schedule, Chief Justice Earl Warren swore in John Fitzgerald Kennedy as the thirty-fifth president. Even though it was only twenty-two degrees, the president had cast aside his top hat and removed his coat. Because of the cortisone-derivative pills that he took for his Addison's disease, he was often over-heated. Television viewers who looked carefully at the facial close-ups could see sweat on the new president's face.

In a moving Inaugural Address, Kennedy spoke only about foreign policy, except for two words. He pledged support for human rights around the world, and, in words appended shortly before the speech was given, he added the words "at home." James Meredith, a black U.S. Air Force veteran who watched Kennedy's speech on television, immediately decided to apply to all-white Ole Miss on the grounds that the new administration would help him win admission. But most Americans missed the significance of those brief words. Kennedy talked about the transfer of power not in personal terms from Eisenhower to Kennedy but in generational terms: "Let the word go forth . . . that the torch has been passed to a new generation of Americans. . . ." Concentrating on the Cold War, he vowed, "We shall pay any price, bear any burden, meet any hardship, support any friend, oppose any foe to assure the survival and the success of liberty." The speech had a fierce quality that fitted the mood of the moment. He intoned, "Ask not what your country can do for you. Ask what you can do for your country."[20]

Kennedy's militant Inaugural Address was an immediate hit, receiving praise from persons as diverse as Adlai Stevenson and Barry Goldwater. Senator Wayne Morse, who was hard to impress, said, "This guy is going to be a wonderful president." Richard Nixon found the speech "very effective." The former vice president noted, "It had a great impact on almost everyone, although not on Eisenhower. As I stood beside him, I could hear his teeth grating." Columnist Richard Strout found the address "a tingling, exhilarating start." Former president Truman called it "marvelous." In the first Gallup poll taken after the inauguration, Kennedy won 72 percent approval. This was tremendous support for a man who had received only 49.7 percent of the vote just three months earlier. Kennedy's presidency was off to a flying start.[21]

CONCLUSION

When John Fitzgerald Kennedy won the presidency in 1960, he also won the right to put his own interpretation (or "spin") upon his victory. Aided by enthusiastic journalists who had rooted for Kennedy throughout the campaign, the Kennedy camp told the tale either as that of an underdog's heroic personal triumph or as that of a liberal crusader slashing his way through the thicket of special interests until Kennedy met and vanquished the sinister Richard Nixon. In this telling, the brilliant Kennedy bested Nixon with powerful rhetoric and went on to win an inevitable victory that would advance truth, justice, and the American way. Kennedy's narrow margin of victory was usually passed over, unless it was cited to prove that such a close contest showed that Kennedy was a heroic fighter.

No person did more to promote this storyline than Teddy White in *The Making of the President, 1960*. So began the myth about Kennedy's election, which would form a substantial part of the larger Kennedy myth. White recounted the election mostly as a morality tale in which the virtuous, liberal Kennedy conquered the morally ambiguous Nixon. As would have to be true for any portrait that gained widespread currency, there had to be a grain of truth in it. Indeed, Nixon's lack of commitment could be seen throughout 1960, and his moral failings became painfully clear during his unfortunate presidency. But White was less evenhanded about Kennedy. Portraying Kennedy as a flawless hero, White ignored many of the political realities about Kennedy's campaign for the White House. This book has tried to go beyond White's mythmaking to discuss more honestly the nuts-and-bolts politics that enabled Kennedy to win in 1960.

Thus, a number of conclusions can be drawn about the 1960 election. On the surface, much of the election contest appeared to be about religion, and Kennedy's victory, no matter how narrow, established that a Catholic could be elected president. Catholics took pride in breaking an important barrier, and women, African Americans, Jews, and other minorities could imagine that other barriers eventually would fall in what was rapidly becoming the civil rights era. Kennedy's victory, therefore, offered a hopeful sign.

Kennedy also won because he exuded an unusual amount of charm on the campaign trail, especially on television. The charm was a striking personal trait that evoked glamour and excited people just as a film star did. Kennedy was the first celebrity politician. Without television, this phenomenon would have been impossible. Kennedy's intelligence, style, and wit were captivating, and a great many people, particularly new, young voters, were attracted by Kennedy's public personality. After 1960, both parties would search for telegenic candidates who exhibited the undefined quality that could only be called charm. Kennedy had it, and so did Ronald Reagan and Bill Clinton. On the other hand, neither Richard Nixon nor Lyndon Johnson had charm, and at least some of the grief of their television age presidencies can be traced to public distrust rooted in the lack of charm. Charm cannot make a successful presidency, since it has little to do with substance, but its absence can go a long way to inhibiting success.

Under the surface, other conclusions concerning Kennedy's 1960 campaign can be identified. Perhaps the most important new ingredient that Kennedy introduced into politics was vast hordes of money. Money, of course, was not new to politics, but the Kennedys had the ability to spend freely, they did spend freely, and they recognized shrewdly how money could be used effectively and efficiently. As Hubert Humphrey lamented afterward, the 1960 campaign had proven that no financially poor candidate, unless there were rich backers, would ever again be able to run for president. In the old presidential election system, candidates, usually governors or senators, offered themselves to politically savvy state leaders and bosses, who gathered at the national conventions to put together tickets that they believed would help the party. In that system, Harry Truman or Adlai Stevenson, neither of whom had much money, might gain a presidential nomination.

Kennedy rewrote the rules of American politics. He knew that the older party leaders would pass him over for the nomination in 1960 as too young and too inexperienced, as well as being a Catholic who could not be elected. Even Catholic leaders harbored these views. So he decided to win the primaries to prove that a Catholic could be elected. After 1960, it was rare to be nominated without winning many state primary elections. But such elections were inevitably expensive, and personal wealth or rich supporters were a necessity. The result was candidates like the George Bushes, Al Gore, or John Kerry, all of whom came from exceptionally affluent backgrounds. Whether such a money-driven system has produced better candidates or better presidents is doubtful, as a thoughtful Senator George Smathers concluded in an interview done after he retired from politics.

One should be careful about how one expresses the idea that Kennedy changed politics by spending money. After all, campaigns have always been expensive. But the Kennedy method of using money was different. Not only did he spend more money than previous candidates in winning the nomination, but he also used money in new, interesting, and powerful ways. It is incorrect to suggest that Kennedy bought the nomination, since a certain amount of popularity was necessary to gain a party nomination, but the Kennedys did transform vast sums of money into votes. As we have seen, much of this expenditure was ingenious. For example, flying to campaign stops in a private, chartered airplane saved travel time and allowed for smoother scheduling. Then, too, when Kennedy traveled around the country as early as late 1956 seeking support for the 1960 nomination, he had to spend a considerable amount of his own money at this early date before money could be raised from the usual political sources. This political networking was expensive, although its success ultimately depended upon Kennedy's charm when he delivered the message in person. To Kennedy, money was a means, not an end.

At the same time, money had a lot to do with Kennedy's ability to build a successful campaign organization. Private wealth enabled Kennedy to hire a highly competent staff at an early date and to hone them for a campaign long before other candidates were prepared. Being geared up with an expanded, seasoned staff before 1960 was a considerable advantage, as could be seen in the Kennedy-Humphrey primaries. When the contest heated up in early 1960, money could be used to buy television advertising. One of the most important consequences of Kennedy's vast family resources was that he did not waste precious campaign time dialing for dollars. The Kennedys did the usual fund-raisers, but they never had to sacrifice vote-getting opportunities for money-raising efforts. Nor did the staff worry that a paycheck would bounce, and vendors could be confident that they would be paid. In contrast, some of Humphrey's West Virginia vendors were never paid.

Decisions about the Kennedy campaign were made with reference to political effectiveness, not with reference to cost. For example, at the end of the campaign Joe Kennedy wrote a six-figure personal check to print huge numbers of pamphlets about Kennedy's phone call to Coretta Scott King for distribution at black churches. Few candidates can write personal checks of that size. Whether the expenditure was cost-effective was not considered, nor did it suffer from bureaucratic delay while awaiting approval by the finance chair, as would have been true in the Nixon campaign.

Kennedy might have spent a lot of money and received little political benefit from it. In 1976 John Connally spent more than $10 million to seek the Republican nomination and got just one delegate. One reason that Kennedy was able to turn his cash into political support was his superb staff. Speechwriter Ted Sorensen, pollster Louis Harris, and campaign manager Robert Kennedy were exceptionally able. Acquiring and retaining top talent was partly about Kennedy's charm, since the candidate attracted talent, but it was also partly about having the financial means to pay staff. A key hire was the still photographer Jacques Lowe. Money was important in hiring Lowe, but Joe Kennedy was also a shrewd talent scout. In contrast, Adlai Stevenson, Stuart Symington, and Hubert Humphrey depended upon friends, fans, and amateurs for their ineffective campaign organizations. Had Nelson Rockefeller run, his staff would have been large, high quality, and well organized.

After the election, Richard Nixon mused that Kennedy's organization was one of Kennedy's main advantages. Kennedy's early start enabled him to put together a smooth operation long before the fall campaign, but having a paid staff for such a long period also cost a lot of money. Nixon lacked the money to pay top talent in the first place, and he certainly could not afford to hire a large staff before early 1960. Of course, Nixon also lacked charm, and many talented people would have declined to work for Nixon at any price. Nixon also sabotaged the effectiveness of his own organization with a strange managerial troika. However, Nixon was correct that his staff was not of the highest quality. Robert Finch's letters reveal a manager too often caught up in trivia, and after the campaign was over some unspent funds were found that could have been used to buy last-minute television advertising. When Nixon ran in 1968, he had a much more effective organization. Kennedy-style professional organization became the norm for future successful presidential campaigns.

Kennedy's organization was used in part to present the candidate to potential delegates at party meetings across the country At the same time, the staff organized the country for Kennedy. Thus, the staff identified Kennedy supporters and coaxed them to set up local volunteer groups in areas where party leaders were not enthusiastic about Kennedy's candidacy. It may sound paradoxical, but money and organization are necessary to mount an effective political campaign using volunteers. The volunteers, many drawn to Kennedy by the candidate's charm, were powerful both in winning the nomination and in organizing the fall campaign. Kennedy's religion helped stimulate volunteers. Volunteers were most important in nonprimary states, where they pushed state conventions toward Kennedy. In contrast, primary states were won with television. Volunteers usually operated under the direction of a paid staff member. Finally, Kennedy spent a lot of money and staff effort registering new voters, another form of organizing that required considerable amounts of money. With varying degrees of success, most presidential campaigns after 1960 have emphasized voter registration drives.

Without television, Kennedy would have been neither nominated nor elected. Kennedy recognized his own natural talent in the new medium, but he also worked hard to maximize his own impact. Having the talent to be an Olympic athlete does not guarantee a gold medal. Talent must be combined with strenuous effort. Kennedy was careful about his appearance, learned how to talk to a television audience, and studied videotapes of his own campaign events. In contrast, Nixon seemed both cocky and naive about television, a lethal combination in the devastating first debate. In 1960, as in later elections, the use of television was mostly about paid advertising. Hiring top ad agencies to make the ads cost a lot of money and buying airtime was expensive, but Kennedy understood the importance. Again, money mattered. Although Nixon edged out Kennedy in hours of national television ads, if one adds in Kennedy's frequent local rebroadcasts of the powerful Houston speech on religion, Kennedy in 1960 was seen on TV more than was Nixon. In 1968, Nixon paid much closer attention to television. In 1976, the little-known Jimmy Carter used television to achieve victory, only to lose four years later to a television master, Ronald Reagan. No presidential winner since 1960, except for Lyndon Johnson, has been awkward on television. Kennedy's election established the power of the new medium.

Politics always has a darker side. Like other politicians, Kennedy was manipulative. After polls showed that he would defeat Governor Michael DiSalle in the Ohio primary, Kennedy persuaded DiSalle to hand over control of the delegation. Kennedy used the same ploy with Governor Pat Brown of California, but the result was less successful. In both cases, Kennedy's arm-twisting produced hard feelings that help explain why he lost Ohio and California in November. Kennedy's attempts to coerce support from Hubert Humphrey and Adlai Stevenson failed—even more than in the DiSalle and Brown cases, the bullying backfired. As a manipulator of politicians, Kennedy was only partially successful. The charm that he used on the public did not always work on professionals, who resented Kennedy's money, youth, and inexperience.

At the same time, Kennedy brilliantly manipulated the media. Joe Kennedy's pressure on newspaper and magazine publishers played a role in this success, but so did Kennedy's charm with reporters. His ability to mesmerize journalists was amazing. As a former reporter, Kennedy understood that reporters wanted stories, and he provided good copy, always spun to his own benefit. One Kennedy success was the cultivation of Teddy White. A wonderful writer, White knew little about the inner workings of politics. The Kennedy organization fed White anecdotes that promoted Kennedy, while they carefully avoided stories that made Kennedy look bad. The result was a book, *The Making of the President, 1960*, in which Kennedy appeared as a flawless shining hero, a white knight clashing with the sinister Richard Nixon.

Politics often has an unsavory side that practitioners like to keep hidden from public view. Deceit and deception are the norm, to some extent, in a democratic political system in which candidates are required to appeal for votes from many groups of voters who disagree with each other. Thus, Kennedy presented himself to African Americans as sympathetic on civil rights; at the same time, he reassured southern whites that he was a racial moderate. Kennedy wanted Adlai Stevenson's followers to vote for him in the belief that Kennedy would name Stevenson as a peace-oriented secretary of state, but Kennedy told hardliners that he would be tough on the Soviet Union in the Cold War. One of Ted Sorensen's main duties was to craft speeches that could appeal to all Democratic Party factions.

Although the fall campaign between Kennedy and Nixon was remarkably clean, Kennedy was not above using dirty tricks during the primaries when he faced a possibly fatal loss to Hubert Humphrey. In Wisconsin, a Kennedy staff member apparently mailed anti-Catholic literature to Catholics. When this fact was discovered, the person quietly disappeared from the campaign. The pro-Kennedy media showed no interest in the story. Later, in West Virginia, the Kennedys coerced Franklin Roosevelt Jr. into falsely charging that Humphrey was a draft dodger in World War II. Although Roosevelt later apologized to Humphrey, the Minnesotan carried his resentment to the end of his life. Again, reporters gave Kennedy a pass, just as they did on the massive vote buying in West Virginia. To be fair, Humphrey bought votes, too. He just had less money with which to do so. Kennedy's use of dirty tricks in 1960 can be compared with the Nixon administration's dirty campaign in 1972, although Nixon operated in a league of his own. In any case, the high standards for clean campaigns that Adlai Stevenson and Dwight Eisenhower had set in the 1950s failed to become the norm.

As can be seen throughout this book, neither Kennedy nor Nixon had much use for political ideologies. In truth, both were moderates, as evidenced by their behavior in the White House. Nixon, lacking charm, never succeeded in bridging the conservative-liberal gap inside the Republican Party. All through 1960, he clumsily tacked from right to left and back again to try to be all things to all voters. In contrast with Nixon's artless maneuvering, Kennedy's powerful organization, polished presentations, and charm enabled him to package himself in the election as a moderate liberal, even though he was no more ideologically committed than was Nixon. Kennedy's decision to run as a liberal was dictated by the powerful influence of liberals inside the Democratic Party, by the sense that the party's victory in 1958 might be heralding a new liberal age (which proved untrue), and by the fact that Lyndon Johnson had strong support from the more conservative southern branch of the party at the convention. As a true liberal, Kennedy was unconvincing, as evidenced by his lifelong refusal to condemn Senator Joseph McCarthy's excesses. To win in the fall, Kennedy had to hold his own diverse party together. One reason both Kennedy and Nixon talked so much about the Cold War was that foreign policy united supporters in a way that domestic issues did not.

Since 1960, voters generally have preferred moderate candidates who have disdained ideology. Few hard-edged conservatives or liberals have been nominated. The two most stridently ideological nominees, Barry Goldwater in 1964 and George McGovern in 1972, lost in landslides because their shrill rhetoric, while appealing to many in the base of their respective parties, scared middle-of-the-road voters. Jimmy Carter won as a moderate in 1976, a fact that produced such restlessness inside the Democratic Party that he was nearly blocked from renomination in 1980. Ronald Reagan might be seen as the one winner who broke this moderate mold, but Reagan, as Californians knew from his governorship, was always less conservative in deeds than in words, and his reelection in 1984 was an affirmation of his successful foreign policy and moderately conservative domestic agenda. For the most part, Bill Clinton and both George Bushes governed as moderates, although each at times tilted toward his party base, especially on issues that the base considered of greatest importance.

Kennedy's victory taught lessons for future presidential candidates. First, start with plenty of money, either your own or someone else's. You will need it. Second, build an organization at an early date. Hire as much talent as you can, even more than you need, since it prevents opponents from hiring that same talent. Use the staff to build volunteer organizations loyal to you, and register lots of new voters. Get those voters to the polls both in the primaries and in November. Winning primaries is a necessity. Third, master the art of television. This, too, will require a lot of money to hire top staff and put ads on the air. Fourth, use pressure, flattery, deals, and charm to push opponents aside or lure important people into endorsements. Also, cultivate the media. Their opposition, as evidenced by Richard Nixon and George W. Bush, is poisonous to any presidency. Fifth, avoid dirty tricks if you can, but recognize that politics ultimately is about winning. The public does not mind dirt, if it means telling lies about your opponent, unless matters get out of hand, as happened with Watergate. Stay out of jail. Finally, forget ideology. You need to use key phrases and ideas to reassure the ideologically oriented base inside your own party, but go lightly for fear of frightening middle-of-the-road voters who decide most elections. Remember Eisenhower's popularity, but also remember Kennedy's. Be charming. In the television age, it is crucial. If you are not charming, don't run.

1960 DEMOCRATIC PRESIDENTIAL PRIMARIES, NUMBERS OF VOTES FOR EACH CANDIDATE, BY STATE

		Kennedy	Humphrey	Stevenson	Johnson	Symington	Other	
NH	Mar. 8	**43,372**	—	168*		183^	Fisher:	6,853
							Nixon:	164*
							Other:	159*
WI	Apr. 5	**476,024**	366,753	—	—	—		
IL	Apr. 12	**34,332***	4,283*	8,029*	442*	5,744*	Other:	337*
NJ	Apr. 19	—	—	—	—	—	Other:	**217,608****
MA	Apr. 26	**91,507***	794*	4,684*	268*	443*	Nixon:	646*
							Other:	721*
PA	Apr. 26	**183,073***	13,860*	29,660*	2,918*	6,791*	Nixon:	15,136*
							Rocky:	1,078*
							Other:	4,297*
DC	May 3	—	**8,239**	—	—	—	Morse:	6,127
IN	May 3	**353,832**	—	—	—	—	Latham:	42,084
							Daly:	40,853
OH	May 3	—	—	—	—	—	DiSalle:	**315,312**
NE	May 10	**80,408**	3,202*	1,368*	962*	4,083*	Nixon:	241*
							Other:	428*
WV	May 10	**236,510**	152,187	—	—	—		
MD	May 17	**201,769**	—	—	—	—	Morse:	49,420
							Daly:	7,536
							Easter:	3,881
							Uninstructed:	24,350
OR	May 20	**146,332**	16,319	7,924*	11,101	12,496	Morse:	91,715
							Nixon:	712*
							Other:	498*
FL	May 24	—	—	—	—	—	Smathers:	**322,235**
CA	June 7	—	—	—	—	—	Brown:	**1,354,031**
							McLain:	646,387
SD	June 7	—	**24,773**	—	—	—		

Source: Congressional Quarterly, *Presidential Elections since 1789,* 4th ed. (Washington, D.C.: Congressional Quarterly, 1975), 144–145. Additional information is in "Convention Guide," *Congressional Quarterly,* June 24, 1960, suppl., 12–13; and John H. Runyon, Jennefer Verdini, and Sally S. Runyon, eds., *Source Book of American Presidential Campaign and Election Statistics, 1948–1968* (New York: Frederick Ungar, 1971), 14–15.

Note: Winners are in bold.

*Write-in votes.

**Votes for unpledged delegates at large.

1960 REPUBLICAN PRESIDENTIAL PRIMARIES, NUMBERS OF VOTES FOR EACH CANDIDATE, BY STATE

		Nixon	Rockefeller	Goldwater	Other	
NH	Mar. 8	**65,204**	2,745*	—	Fisher:	2,388*
					Kennedy:	2,196*
					Lodge:	141*
					Other:	357*
WI	Apr. 5	**339,383**	—	—		
IL	Apr. 12	**782,849**	—	—	Other:	442*
NJ	Apr. 19	—	—	—	Other:	**304,766****
MA	Apr. 26	**53,164***	4,068*	221*	Lodge:	373*
					Kennedy:	2,989*
					Stevenson:	266*
					Others:	764*
PA	Apr. 26	**968,538**	12,491*	286*	Kennedy:	3,886*
					Stevenson:	428*
					Other:	1,202*
DC	May 3	—	—	—	Uninstructed:	**9,468**
IN	May 3	**408,408**	—	—	Beckwith:	19,677
OH	May 3	—	—	—	Other:	**504,072****
NE	May 10	**74,356***	2,028*	1,068*	Kennedy:	882*
					Other:	923*
WV	May 10	—	—	—	Other:	**123,756****
OR	May 20	**211,276**	9,307*	1,571*	Kennedy:	2,864*
					Other:	2,015*
FL	May 24	**51,036**	—	—		
CA	June 7	**1,517,652**	—	—		
SD	June 7	—	—	—	Unpledged:	**48,461**

Source: Congressional Quarterly, *Presidential Elections since 1789*, 4th ed. (Washington, D.C.: Congressional Quarterly, 1975), 144–145. Additional information is in "Convention Guide," *Congressional Quarterly*, June 24, 1960, suppl., 12–13; and John H. Runyon, Jennefer Verdini, and Sally S. Runyon, eds., *Source Book of American Presidential Campaign and Election Statistics, 1948–1968* (New York: Frederick Ungar, 1971), 16.

Note: Winners are in bold.

*Write-in votes.

**Votes for unpledged delegates at large.

1960 DEMOCRATIC NATIONAL CONVENTION VOTE

State	Votes	Kennedy	Johnson	Symington	Stevenson	Other	
AL	29	3.5	20	3.5	.5	1.5	split
AK	9	9	—	—	—	—	
AZ	17	17	—	—	—		
AR	27	—	27	—	—	—	
CA	81	33.5	7.5	8	31.5	.5	Brown
CO	21	13.5	—	2	5.5	—	
CT	21	21	—	—	—	—	
DE	11	—	11	—	—	—	
FL	29	—	—	—	—	29	Smathers
GA	33	—	33	—	—	—	
HI	9	1.5	3	1	3.5	—	
ID	13	6	4.5	2	.5	—	
IL	69	61.5	—	5.5	2	—	
IN	34	34	—	—	—	—	
IA	26	21.5	.5	.5	2	1.5	Loveless
KS	21	21	—	—	—	—	
KY	31	3.5	25.5	.5	1.5	—	
LA	26	—	26	—	—	—	
ME	15	15	—	—	—	—	
MD	24	24	—	—	—	—	
MA	41	41	—	—	—	—	
MI	51	42.5	—	6	2.5	—	
MN	31	—	—	—	—	31	Pass
MS	23	—	—	—	—	23	Barnett
MO	39	—	—	39	—	—	
MT	17	10	2	2.5	2.5	—	
NE	16	11	.5	4	—	.5	Humphrey
NV	15	5.5	6.5	.5	2.5	—	
NH	11	11	—	—	—	—	
NJ	41	—	—	—	—	41	Meyner
NM	17	4	13	—	—	—	
NY	114	104.5	3.5	2.5	3.5	—	
NC	37	6	27.5	—	3	.5	Smathers
ND	11	11	—	—	—	—	
OH	64	64	—	—	—	—	
OK	29	—	29	—	—	—	
OR	17	16.5	—	—	—	.5	
PA	81	68	4	—	7.5	1.5	Meyner
RI	17	17	—	—	—	—	
SC	21	—	21	—	—	—	

State	Votes	Kennedy	Johnson	Symington	Stevenson	Other	
SD	11	4	2	2.5	1	1.5	Humphrey
TN	33	—	33	—	—	—	
TX	61	—	61	—	—	—	
UT	13	8	3	1.5	—	.5	Humphrey
VT	9	9	—	—	—	—	
VA	33	—	33	—	—	—	
WA	27	14.5	2.5	3	6.5	.5	Rosellini
WV	25	15	5.5	1.5	3	—	
WI	31	23	—	—	—	8	Humphrey
WY	15	15	—	—	—	—	
DC	9	9	—	—	—	—	
CZ	4	—	4	—	—	—	
PR	7	7	—	—	—	—	
VI	4	4	—	—	—	—	
Totals	1,521	806	409	86	79	141	

Source: *San Francisco Chronicle*, July 14, 1960, 6.

1960 PRESIDENTIAL ELECTION RETURNS: NUMBERS OF VOTES, PERCENTAGE OF VOTE, ELECTORAL VOTES (TOTAL VOTE = 68,833,243)

	Kennedy (Dem.)		Nixon (Rep.)		Others		Electoral Vote		
	Votes	Percent	Votes	Percent	Votes	Percent	Dem.	Rep.	Others
AL	318,303*	56.4	237,981	42.2	8,194	1.5	5	—	6
	—	—	—	—	(324,050*)	—	—	—	—
AK	29,809	49.1	30,953	50.9	—	—	—	3	—
AZ	176,781	44.4	221,241	55.5	469	.1	—	4	—
AR	215,049	50.2	184,508	43.1	28,952	6.8	8	—	—
CA	3,224,099	49.6	3,259,722	50.1	22,757	.3	—	32	—
CO	330,629	44.9	402,242	54.6	3,375	.5	—	6	—
CT	657,055	53.7	565,813	46.3	15	—	8	—	—
DE	99,590	50.6	96,373	49.0	720	.4	3	—	—
FL	748,700	48.5	795,476	51.5	—	—	—	10	—
GA	458,638	62.5	274,472	37.4	239	—	12	—	—
HI	92,410	50.0	92,295	50.0	—	—	3	—	—
ID	138,853	46.2	161,597	53.8	—	—	—	4	—
IL	2,377,846	50.0	2,368,988	49.8	10,575	.2	27	—	—
IN	952,358	44.6	1,175,120	55.0	7,882	.4	—	13	—
IA	550,565	43.2	722,381	56.7	864	.1	—	10	—
KS	363,213	39.1	561,474	60.4	4,138	.4	—	8	—
KY	521,855	46.4	602,607	53.6	—	—	—	10	—
LA	407,339	50.4	230,980	28.6	169,572*	21.0	10	—	—
ME	181,159	43.0	240,608	57.0	—	—	—	5	—
MD	565,808	53.6	489,538	46.4	3	—	9	—	—
MA	1,487,174	60.2	976,750	39.6	5,556	.2	16	—	—
MI	1,687,269	50.9	1,620,428	48.8	10,400	.3	20	—	—
MN	779,933	50.6	757,915	49.2	4,039	.3	11	—	—
MS	108,362	36.3	73,561	24.7	116,248	39.0	—	—	8
MO	972,201	50.3	962,221	49.7	—	—	13	—	—
MT	134,891	48.6	141,841	51.1	847	.3	—	4	—
NE	232,542	37.9	380,553	62.1	—	—	—	6	—
NV	54,880	51.2	52,387	48.8	—	—	3	—	—
NH	137,772	46.6	157,989	53.4	—	—	—	4	—
NJ	1,385,415	50.0	1,363,324	49.2	24,372	.9	16	—	—
NM	156,027	50.2	153,733	49.4	1,347	.4	4	—	—
NY	3,830,085*	52.5	3,446,419	47.3	14,575	.2	45	—	—
NC	713,136	52.1	655,420	47.9	—	—	14	—	—
ND	123,963	44.5	154,310	55.4	158	.1	—	4	—
OH	1,944,248	46.7	2,217,611	53.3	—	—	—	25	—
OK	370,111	41.0	533,039	59.0	—	—	—	7	1

	Kennedy (Dem.)		Nixon (Rep.)		Others		Electoral Vote		
	Votes	Percent	Votes	Percent	Votes	Percent	Dem.	Rep.	Others
OR	367,402	47.3	**408,060**	52.6	959	.1	—	6	—
PA	**2,556,282**	51.1	2,439,956	48.7	10,303	.2	32	—	—
RI	**258,032**	63.6	147,502	36.4	1	—	4	—	—
SC	**198,129**	51.2	188,558	48.8	1	—	8	—	—
SD	128,070	41.8	**178,417**	58.2	—	—	—	4	—
TN	481,453	45.8	**556,577**	52.9	13,762	1.3	—	11	—
TX	**1,167,932**	50.5	1,121,699	48.5	22,214	1.0	24	—	—
UT	169,248	45.2	**205,361**	54.8	100	—	—	4	—
VT	69,186	41.3	**98,131**	58.6	7	—	—	3	—
VA	362,327	47.0	**404,521**	52.4	4,601	.6	—	12	—
WA	599,298	48.3	**629,273**	50.7	13,001	1.0	—	9	—
WV	**441,786**	52.7	395,995	47.3	—	—	8	—	—
WI	830,805	48.0	**895,175**	51.8	3,102	.2	—	12	—
WY	63,331	45.0	**77,451**	55.0	—	—	—	3	—
Totals									
	34,221,349	49.7	34,108,546	49.6	503,348	.7	**303**	219	15

Sources: Official returns are from "Dave Leip's Atlas of U.S. Presidential Elections," uselectionatlas.org/, except Texas returns, which are online at the web site of the Texas Secretary of State, www.sos.state.tx.us/elections/historical/index.shtml.

Note: Winners are in bold. There is no single official source for presidential election returns for 1960. The earliest compilation from official state sources is *CQ Weekly Report*, December 16, 1960, p. 1972, but this report contains some errors. In 1960 Alabama was one of several states where voters could choose to vote for individual electors. In the spring, before the Democratic Convention had nominated Kennedy, Alabama Democrats picked electors. Five electors were elected who were pledged to back the national ticket, and all supported Kennedy. Six electors were elected as unpledged, and after the Democratic Convention they announced that they would not back Kennedy unless he repudiated the national party platform's civil rights plank. Thus, in November, Alabama voters could choose to back some or all of these eleven electors. *Congressional Quarterly* followed the principle laid down by the journalist Horace Greeley in the nineteenth century that, in those states where voters voted for individual electors, the candidate should be credited with the vote that was cast for the elector who favored that candidate who received the highest number of votes. It is on this basis that *Congressional Quarterly* credited Kennedy with 318,303 votes in Alabama. This same total has been used by *Congressional Quarterly, Presidential Elections since 1789*, 4th ed. (Washington, D.C.: *Congressional Quarterly*, 1975); and by www.uselectionatlas.org. However, Richard Scammon, in *America at the Polls* (Pittsburgh: University of Pittsburgh Press, 1965), used the total for the highest-polling anti-Kennedy elector, 324,050, as the basis for the Kennedy vote. Perhaps Scammon was influenced to adopt this odd policy by the fact that he was appointed to a post in the Kennedy administration. This total is also cited by William G. Shade and Ballard C. Campbell, eds., *American Presidential Elections and Campaigns* (Armonk, N.Y.: M. E. Sharpe, 2003). Further, in this table, minor discrepancies among these five sources have been reconciled in favor of the consensus, always noting the preliminary nature of the December 1960 report. Texas is the only state other than Alabama that poses a serious problem, but the official Texas canvas, as reported in December 1960, is online at www.sos.state.tx.us/elections/historical/index.shtml. One reason that so many variations are reported is that different states use quite different counting rules. In some states, write-in votes are only counted if the candidate has filed a petition. In other states, the counting of write-in votes is at the discretion of the local counting board. The type of ballot used also can affect the ease or difficulty of casting a write-in vote. Finally, one might note that, regardless of which number is used for Kennedy in Alabama, the total Republican vote was greater than the total Democratic vote. Kennedy's 406,176 votes on the Liberal Party line in New York greatly exceeded the margin by which Kennedy topped Nixon. In other words, Nixon got more votes as a Republican than Kennedy got as a Democrat. However, because of the Liberal Party vote, Kennedy did outpoll Nixon. Still, it was an exceptionally close election. *AL: The top Kennedy elector polled 318,303; the top unpledged elector polled 324,050. All unpledged electors outpolled all Kennedy electors. LA: The "other" vote is for the States' Rights Party. NY: Kennedy's total includes 406,176 Liberal Party votes.

JOHN F. KENNEDY'S INAUGURAL ADDRESS, JANUARY 20, 1961

Vice President Johnson, Mr. Speaker, Mr. Chief Justice, President Eisenhower, Vice President Nixon, President Truman, Reverend Clergy, fellow citizens:

We observe today not a victory of party but a celebration of freedom—symbolizing an end as well as a beginning—signifying renewal as well as change. For I have sworn before you and Almighty God the same solemn oath our forbears prescribed nearly a century and three-quarters ago.

The world is very different now. For man holds in his mortal hands the power to abolish all forms of human poverty and all forms of human life. And yet the same revolutionary beliefs for which our forbears fought are still at issue around the globe—the belief that the rights of man come not from the generosity of the state but from the hand of God.

We dare not forget today that we are the heirs of that first revolution. Let the word go forth from this time and place, to friend and foe alike, that the torch has been passed to a new generation of Americans—born in this century, tempered by war, disciplined by a hard and bitter peace, proud of our ancient heritage—and unwilling to witness or permit the slow undoing of those human rights to which this nation has always been committed, and to which we are committed today at home and around the world.

Let every nation know, whether it wishes us well or ill, that we shall pay any price, bear any burden, meet any hardship, support any friend, oppose any foe to assure the survival and the success of liberty.

This much we pledge—and more.

To those old allies whose cultural and spiritual origins we share, we pledge the loyalty of faithful friends. United there is little we cannot do in a host of cooperative ventures. Divided there is little we can do—for we dare not meet a powerful challenge at odds and split asunder.

To those new states whom we welcome to the ranks of the free, we pledge our word that one form of colonial control shall not have passed away merely to be replaced by a far more iron tyranny. We shall not always expect to find them supporting our view. But we shall always hope to find them strongly supporting their own freedom—and to remember that, in the past, those who foolishly sought power by riding the back of the tiger ended up inside.

To those people in the huts and villages of half the globe struggling to break the bonds of mass misery, we pledge our best efforts to help them help themselves, for whatever period is required—not because the communists may be doing it, not because we seek their votes, but because it is right. If a free society cannot help the many who are poor, it cannot save the few who are rich.

To our sister republics south of our border, we offer a special pledge—to convert our good words into good deeds—in a new alliance for progress—to assist free men and free governments in casting off the chains of poverty. But this peaceful revolution of hope cannot become the prey of hostile powers. Let all our neighbors know that we shall join with them to oppose aggression or subversion anywhere in the Americas. And let every other power know that this Hemisphere intends to remain the master in its own house.

To that world assembly of sovereign states, the United Nations, our last best hope in an age where the instruments of war have far outpaced the instruments of peace, we renew our pledge of support—to prevent it from becoming merely a forum for invective—to strengthen its shield of the new and the weak—and to enlarge the area in which its writ may run.

Finally, to those nations who would make themselves our adversary, we offer not a pledge but a request: that both sides begin anew the quest for peace, before the dark powers of destruction unleashed by science engulf all humanity in planned or accidental self-destruction.

We dare not tempt them with weakness. For only when our arms are sufficient beyond doubt can we be certain beyond doubt that they will never be employed.

But neither can two great and powerful groups of nations take comfort from our present course—both sides overburdened by the cost of modern weapons, both rightly alarmed by the steady spread of the deadly atom, yet both racing to alter that uncertain balance of terror that stays the hand of mankind's final war.

So let us begin anew—remembering on both sides that civility is not a sign of weakness, and sincerity is always subject to proof. Let us never negotiate out of fear. But let us never fear to negotiate.

Let both sides explore what problems unite us instead of belaboring those problems which divide us.

Let both sides, for the first time, formulate serious and precise proposals for the inspection and control of arms—and bring the absolute power to destroy other nations under the absolute control of all nations.

Let both sides seek to invoke the wonders of science instead of its terrors. Together let us explore the stars, conquer the deserts, eradicate disease, tap the ocean depths and encourage the arts and commerce.

Let both sides unite to heed in all corners of the earth the command of Isaiah—to "undo the heavy burdens . . . [and] let the oppressed go free."

And if a beachhead of cooperation may push back the jungle of suspicion, let both sides join in creating a new endeavor, not a new balance of power, but a new world of law, where the strong are just and the weak secure and the peace preserved.

All this will not be finished in the first one hundred days. Nor will it be finished in the first one thousand days, nor in the life of this Administration, nor even perhaps in our lifetime on this planet. But let us begin.

In your hands, my fellow citizens, more than mine, will rest the final success or failure of our course. Since this country was founded, each generation of Americans has been summoned to give testimony to its national loyalty. The graves of young Americans who answered the call to service surround the globe.

Now the trumpet summons us again—not as a call to bear arms, though arms we need—not as a call to battle, though embattled we are— but a call to bear the burden of a long twilight struggle, year in and year out, "rejoicing in hope, patient in tribulation"—a struggle against the common enemies of man: tyranny, poverty, disease and war itself.

Can we forge against these enemies a grand and global alliance, North and South, East and West, that can assure a more fruitful life for all mankind? Will you join in that historic effort?

In the long history of the world, only a few generations have been granted the role of defending freedom in its hour of maximum danger. I do not shrink from this responsibility—I welcome it. I do not believe that any of us would exchange places with any other people or any other generation. The energy, the faith, the devotion which we bring to this endeavor will light our country and all who serve it—and the glow from that fire can truly light the world.

And so, my fellow Americans: ask not what your country can do for you—ask what you can do for your country.

My fellow citizens of the world: ask not what America will do for you, but what together we can do for the freedom of man.

Finally, whether you are citizens of America or citizens of the world, ask of us here the same high standards of strength and sacrifice which we ask of you. With a good conscience our only sure reward, with history the final judge of our deeds, let us go forth to lead the land we love, asking His blessing and His help, but knowing that here on earth God's work must truly be our own.

Source: "Transcript of President John F. Kennedy's Inaugural Address (1961)," www.ourdocuments.gov/doc.php?doc=91&page=transcript.

NOTES

ABBREVIATIONS

AES	Adlai E. Stevenson
COH	Columbia University Oral History, New York
CT	*Chicago Tribune*
HCL	Henry Cabot Lodge
HHH	Hubert H. Humphrey
HHHP	HHH Papers, Minnesota Historical Society, St. Paul
HOHP	Humphrey Oral History Program, Minnesota Historical Society, St. Paul
JFK	John F. Kennedy
JOH	Johnson Library Oral History, Austin, Texas
JPK	Joseph P. Kennedy Sr.
KOH	Kennedy Library Oral History, Boston
LAT	*Los Angeles Times*
LBJ	Lyndon B. Johnson
NR	Nelson Rockefeller
NYT	*New York Times*
RBROH	Richard B. Russell Library Oral History, Athens, Georgia
RFK	Robert F. Kennedy
RN	Richard Nixon
RNP	RN Papers, National Archives, Laguna Niguel, California
WP	*Washington Post*
WSJ	*Wall Street Journal*

CHAPTER 1 EISENHOWER'S AMERICA

1 For different versions, see Barry M. Goldwater, *With No Apologies: The Personal and Political Memoirs of United States Senator Barry M. Goldwater* (New York: Morrow, 1979), 71; Stephen E. Ambrose, *Eisenhower: The President* (New York: Simon & Schuster, 1984), 2:128–129; Irwin F. Gellman, *The Contender: Richard Nixon: The Congress Years, 1946–1952* (New York: Free Press, 1999), 423–442, 448; Patrick J. Buchanan, *Where the Right Went Wrong* (New York: Thomas Dunne Books, 2004), 220; and David A. Nichols, *A Matter of Justice: Eisenhower and the Beginning of the Civil Rights Movement* (New York: Simon & Schuster, 2007), 55–57, 296n10.

2 RN in Fawn M. Brodie, *Richard Nixon: The Shaping of His Character* (New York: Norton, 1981), 242.

3 Eisenhower in William Costello, *The Facts about Nixon: An Unauthorized Biography* (New York: Viking, 1960), 292; RN in Garry Wills, *Nixon Agonistes: The Crisis of the Self-Made Man* (Boston: Houghton Mifflin, 1970), 139;

Eisenhower in Stephen E. Ambrose, *Nixon: The Education of a Politician, 1913–1962* (New York: Simon & Schuster, 1987), 292.

4 RN in *Saturday Evening Post*, July 12, 1958, 27; RN in Brodie, *Richard Nixon*, 83; Taft in Costello, *The Facts about Nixon*, 7; RN, AES, and RN in Brodie, *Richard Nixon*, 247, 306, 307; Truman in John A. Farrell, *Tip O'Neill and the Democratic Century* (Boston: Little, Brown, 2001), 140.

5 Eisenhower in Byron C. Hulsey, *Everett Dirksen and His Presidents: How a Senate Giant Shaped American Politics* (Lawrence: University Press of Kansas, 2000), 109.

6 AES in John B. Martin, *Adlai Stevenson and the World* (Garden City, N.Y.: Doubleday, 1977), 342.

7 Reuther in Kevin Boyle, *The UAW and the Heyday of American Liberalism, 1945–1968* (Ithaca, N.Y.: Cornell University Press, 1995), 139.

8 Rayburn in Martin, *Adlai Stevenson and the World*, 344; LBJ in Robert Dallek, *Lone Star Rising: Lyndon Johnson and His Times, 1908–1960* (New York: Oxford University Press, 1991), 504.

9 For a summary of the nonexistent Missile Gap, see Michael R. Beschloss, *The Crisis Years: Kennedy and Khrushchev, 1960–1963* (New York: HarperCollins, 1991), 25–27.

10 Barry Goldwater to Harry F. Byrd, November 28, 1958, box 244, Byrd Papers, University of Virginia.

11 Eisenhower in Emmet J. Hughes, *The Ordeal of Power: A Political Memoir of the Eisenhower Years* (New York: Atheneum, 1963), 319; Eisenhower in Christopher Matthews, *Kennedy and Nixon: The Rivalry That Shaped Postwar America* (New York: Simon & Schuster, 1996), 112.

12 Eisenhower in Arthur Krock, April 7, 1960, Memoranda Book II, no. 335, and July 7, 1960, Memoranda Book III, no. 339, both in box 1, Krock Papers, Mudd Library, Princeton University; Eisenhower in William Robinson Diary, July 1960, in Ambrose, *Eisenhower*, 2:597.

CHAPTER 2 THE DEMOCRATIC PRIMARIES

1 George H. Gallup, *The Gallup Poll: Public Opinion, 1935–1971* (New York: Random House, 1972), 3:1658.

2 HHH, *The Education of a Public Man: My Life in Politics* (2nd ed., Minneapolis: University of Minnesota Press, 1991), 353.

3 LBJ in Edgar Berman, *Hubert: The Triumph and Tragedy of the Humphrey I Knew* (New York: Putnam's, 1979), 55.

4 Roosevelt in Joseph P. Lash, *Eleanor: The Years Alone* (New York: Norton, 1972), 279; Luce quoted in William Benton to HHH, March 23, 1959, box 89, HHHP.

5 HHH in Albert Eisele, *Almost to the Presidency: A Biography of Two American Politicians* (Blue Earth, Minn.: Piper, 1972), 137.

6 AES in Stewart Alsop, "Kennedy vs. Humphrey," *Saturday Evening Post*, April 2, 1960, 93; eastern boss in Winthrop Griffith, *Humphrey: A Candid Biography* (New York: Morrow, 1965), 102.

7 JFK in Paul Fay ms, chap. 2, p. 4, JFK Library.

8 JFK in Kenneth P. O'Donnell and David F. Powers, *Johnny, We Hardly Knew Ye: Memories of John Fitzgerald Kennedy* (Boston: Little, Brown, 1972), 98.

9 Jacqueline Kennedy in Gore Vidal, *Palimpsest: A Memoir* (New York: Random House, 1995), 310.

10 JFK in David Powers COH, 40; JPK in Richard J. Whalen, *The Founding Father: The Story of Joseph P. Kennedy* (New York: New American Library, 1964), 446; Gore Vidal, "The Holy Family," *Esquire,* April 1967, 204.

11 On the Pulitzer Prize, see Christopher Matthews, *Kennedy and Nixon: The Rivalry That Shaped Postwar America* (New York: Simon & Schuster, 1996), 15. On the *Time* cover, see Ronald Kessler, *The Sins of the Father: Joseph P. Kennedy and the Dynasty He Founded* (New York: Warner Books, 1996), 365. Walt Rostow KOH, 2.

12 Walter Lippmann KOH, 8; Turnure in Nancy Tuckerman and Pamela Turnure KOH, 17; Jacqueline Kennedy in Victor Lasky, *J.F.K.: The Man and the Myth* (New York: Macmillan, 1963), 160.

13 JPK in *Time,* April 18, 1960, 16.

14 India Edwards to Eugenie Anderson, December 15 [1958], Anderson Papers, Minnesota Historical Society, St. Paul; HHH in Michael V. DiSalle, *Second Choice* (New York: Hawthorn Books, 1966), 201.

15 Lytton and JFK in Bart Lytton KOH, 8–9.

16 HHH in Theodore C. Sorensen, *Kennedy* (New York: Harper & Row, 1965), 135; JFK in O'Donnell and Powers, *Johnny, We Hardly Knew Ye,* 155.

17 Frank Wallace memo to HHH, October 27, 1959, box 25, HHHP; HHH in Allan H. Ryskind, *Hubert: An Unauthorized Biography of the Vice President* (New Rochelle, N.Y.: Arlington House, 1968), 238; HHH in Robert Mann, *The Walls of Jericho: Lyndon Johnson, Hubert Humphrey, Richard Russell, and the Struggle for Civil Rights* (New York: Harcourt, 1996), 266.

18 HHH memo to Bill Sturdevant, February 2, 1960, box 185, HHHP. The cash payment to Krock is in Nigel Hamilton, *JFK: Reckless Youth* (New York: Random House, 1992), 212.

19 HHH memo to Phil Stern, January 20, 1960, box 185, HHHP.

20 JFK in Pierre Salinger, *P.S.: A Memoir* (New York: St. Martin's Press, 1995), 73.

21 Barry M. Goldwater, *With No Apologies: The Personal and Political Memoirs of United States Senator Barry M. Goldwater* (New York: Morrow, 1979), 104.

22 In 1971, only 40.5 percent of West Virginians had church affiliations; the national figure was 49.6 percent. Douglas W. Johnson et al., *Churches and Church Membership in the United States, 1971* (Washington, D.C.: Glenmary Research Center, 1974), 1, 9.

23 Catholics were estimated to be 5 percent of the population but 15 percent of the primary vote, in Alliston Craig to William O. Douglas, May 15, 1960, box 36, HHHP.

24 JFK in Sorensen, *Kennedy,* 142.

25 HHH in Chalmers M. Roberts, *First Rough Draft: A Journalist's Journal of Our Times* (New York: Praeger, 1973), 178.

26 On the draft-dodging charge, see Richard N. Goodwin, *Remembering America: A Voice from the Sixties* (Boston: Little, Brown, 1988), 88; Laurence Leamer, *The Kennedy Men, 1901–1963* (New York: Morrow, 2001), 425–427; Carl Solberg, *Hubert Humphrey: A Biography* (New York: Norton, 1984), 209.

27 On money, see Harry W. Ernst, *The Primary That Made a President: West Virginia, 1960* (New York: McGraw-Hill, 1962), 16–18, 30; Dan B. Fleming Jr., *Kennedy vs. Humphrey, West Virginia, 1960: The Pivotal Battle for the Democratic Presidential Nomination* (Jefferson, N.C.: McFarland, 1992), 89, 93, 105, 120, 155–156; Tip O'Neill with William Novak, *Man of the House: The Life and Political Memoirs of Speaker Tip O'Neill* (New York: Random House, 1987), 92; *Pittsburgh Post-Gazette*, May 31, 1960, 9; David Ginsburg memo, March 15, 1960, and "The Meaning of the West Virginia Primary" (n.d.), both in box 35, and Paul S. Mingus to HHH, May 23, 1960, box 36, all in HHHP. On Cushing, see Ronald Kessler, *The Sins of the Father*, 379–380; and Humphrey, *The Education of a Public Man*, 158–159.

28 Igor Cassini with Jeanne Molli, *I'd Do It All Over Again* (New York: Putnam's, 1977), 224; HHH to Elmo Roper, May 31, 1960, box 36, HHHP; Edward T. Folliard KOH, 19; Brinkley in the film, *The Great Campaign of 1960* (2000).

29 Miner in Peter Collier and David Horowitz, *The Kennedys: An American Drama* (New York: Summit, 1984), 237.

30 HHH in O'Donnell and Powers, *Johnny, We Hardly Knew Ye*, 170.

31 JPK in Stewart Alsop, "Kennedy's Magic Formula," *Saturday Evening Post*, August 13, 1960, 58.

32 Novak in Theodore H. White, *The Making of the President, 1960* (New York: Atheneum, 1961), 127; Bradlee in *Newsweek*, May 9, 1960, 31; William S. White, "Symington: The Last Choice for President," *Harper's Magazine*, July 1959, 80; Palmer in *LAT*, July 10, 1960, A17.

33 Frank Church JOH, 12; Lasker and Roosevelt in Lash, *Eleanor*, 279.

34 Reporter in Marquis W. Childs, *Witness to Power* (New York: McGraw-Hill, 1975), 206; LBJ in Jeff Shesol, *Mutual Contempt: Lyndon Johnson, Robert Kennedy, and the Feud That Defined a Decade* (New York: Norton, 1997), 10.

35 JFK in Joseph Rauh JOH, 2:3; Joseph Rauh to Carl Auerbach, February 13, 1960, box 23, Rauh Papers, Library of Congress; Rayburn in Robert G. Baker, *Wheeling and Dealing: Confessions of a Capitol Hill Operator* (New York: Norton, 1978), 119.

36 O'Neill, *Man of the House*, 181.

37 LBJ in LeRoy Ashby and Rod Gramer, *Fighting the Odds: The Life of Senator Frank Church* (Pullman: Washington State University Press, 1994), 134.

38 AES to Allan Nevins, February 4, 1960, box 64, AES Papers, Mudd Library, Princeton University.

39 AES in Jeff Broadwater, *Adlai Stevenson and American Politics: The Odyssey of a Cold War Liberal* (New York: Twayne, 1994), 183; Ball in Katie Louchheim, *By the Political Sea* (Garden City, N.Y.: Doubleday, 1970), 91; McGrory in Eric Sevareid, ed., *Candidates 1960: Behind the Headlines in the Presidential Race* (New York: Basic Books, 1959), 241.

40 AES diary in Adlai E. Stevenson, *The Papers of Adlai E. Stevenson, 1957–1961* (Boston: Little, Brown, 1977), 7:424; AES in John B. Martin, *Adlai Stevenson and the World* (Garden City, N.Y.: Doubleday, 1977), 482.

41 Agnes Meyer to AES, May 2, 1960, box 62, AES Papers; LBJ in Mann, *The Walls of Jericho*, 275; LBJ in Michael R. Beschloss, *The Crisis Years: Kennedy and Khrushchev, 1960–1963* (New York: HarperCollins, 1991), 463.

42 JFK in Beschloss, *The Crisis Years*, 463–464; JFK in ibid., 464; LBJ in ibid., 464n.

43 JFK and Minow in Martin, *Adlai Stevenson and the World*, 506; Arthur M. Schlesinger Jr., *Journals, 1952–2000* (New York: Penguin, 2007), 68.

44 JFK in Charles Bartlett KOH, 59; JFK in O'Donnell and Powers, *Johnny, We Hardly Knew Ye*, 178; AES in Schlesinger, *Journals*, 69; JFK in Gerald S. Strober and Deborah H. Strober, ed., *Let Us Begin Anew: An Oral History of the Kennedy Presidency* (New York: HarperCollins, 1993), 9; AES in George W. Ball, *The Past Has Another Pattern: Memoirs* (New York: Norton, 1982), 158; JFK in William McC. Blair Jr. COH, 49.

45 AES in Newton Minow COH, 86; Arthur Krock memo no. 337, May 26, 1960, Krock Papers, Mudd Library, Princeton University; AES in Stevenson, *The Papers of Adlai E. Stevenson*, 7:521; AES in Kenneth S. Davis, *The Politics of Honor: A Biography of Adlai E. Stevenson* (New York: Putnam's, 1967), 444; JFK in William S. White, *The Making of a Journalist* (Lexington: University Press of Kentucky, 1986), 151; Alsop in David Halberstam, *The Best and the Brightest* (New York: Random House, 1972), 34; Clinton P. Anderson with Milton Viorst, *Outsider in the Senate: Senator Clinton Anderson's Memoirs* (New York: World, 1970), 141; John Sharon COH, 4.

CHAPTER 3 THE DEMOCRATIC CONVENTION

1 Gallup in *Time*, July 11, 1960, 17; Janeway–Walter Jenkins call, May 16, 1960, box 2, Walter Jenkins ser. 2, LBJ Papers, LBJ Library; JFK in Michael R. Beschloss, *The Crisis Years: Kennedy and Khrushchev, 1960–1963* (New York: HarperCollins, 1991), 21; RN and LBJ in ibid., 22.

2 Brown in *NYT*, May 11, 1960, 22; AES in *Time*, May 30, 1960, quoted in Emmet J. Hughes, *The Ordeal of Power: A Political Memoir of the Eisenhower Years* (New York: Atheneum, 1963), 302; AES, RNC, and RN in *WP*, May 22, 1960, A4; Farley in *WP*, May 26, 1960, A25.

3 JFK in Arthur M. Schlesinger Jr., *Journals, 1952–2000* (New York: Penguin, 2007), 67, 84.

4 Truman in *NYT*, July 3, 1960, 19; JFK in Kathleen H. Jamieson, *Packaging the Presidency: A History and Criticism of Presidential Campaign Advertising* (New York: Oxford University Press, 1984), 141; Truman in John H. Davis, *The Kennedys: Dynasty and Disaster, 1848–1984* (New York: McGraw-Hill, 1984), 292.

5 Schlesinger, *Journals*, 58, 78.

6 LBJ in Gore Vidal, *Palimpsest: A Memoir* (New York: Random House, 1995), 16; RFK in Robert G. Baker, *Wheeling and Dealing: Confessions of a Capitol Hill Operator* (New York: Norton, 1978), 118.

7   Gallup in *LAT*, July 10, 1960, C1.

8   David E. Lilienthal, *The Journals of David E. Lilienthal, 1959–1963* (New York: Harper & Row, 1971), 5:100, 101; *NYT*, July 10, 1960, 46; Rayburn in Alfred Steinberg, *Sam Rayburn, a Biography* (New York: Hawthorn Books, 1975), 328.

9   LBJ in William W. Prochnau and Richard W. Larsen, *A Certain Democrat: Senator Henry M. Jackson, a Political Biography* (Englewood Cliffs, N.J.: Prentice-Hall, 1972), 190.

10 F. Richard Ciccone, *Daley: Power and Presidential Politics* (Chicago: Contemporary Books, 1996), 40.

11 David Powers COH, 43; Daley in Michael V. DiSalle, *Second Choice* (New York: Hawthorn Books, 1966), 204; Averell Harriman KOH, 12.

12 LBJ in Booth Mooney, *LBJ: An Irreverent Chronicle* (New York: Crowell, 1976), 10; Geraldine Joseph HOHP, 30; AES in *LAT*, July 13, 1960, pt. 1, 3; Meyer in John B. Martin, *Adlai Stevenson and the World* (Garden City, N.Y.: Doubleday, 1977), 525; RFK, *In His Own Words: The Unpublished Recollections of the Kennedy Years* (New York: Bantam, 1988), 38.

13 JFK in Kenneth P. O'Donnell and David F. Powers, *Johnny, We Hardly Knew Ye: Memories of John Fitzgerald Kennedy* (Boston: Little, Brown, 1972), 183; Connally and Sharon in John Sharon COH, 51; RFK and HHH in Winthrop Griffith, *Humphrey: A Candid Biography* (New York: Morrow, 1965), 247.

14 Tennessee and Alabama in Guy P. Land, "John F. Kennedy's Southern Strategy, 1956–1960," *North Carolina Historical Review* 56:1 (January 1979): 55–57; RFK in C. David Heymann, *RFK: A Candid Biography of Robert F. Kennedy* (New York: Dutton, 1998), 166.

15 Brown in Ethan Rarick, *California Rising: The Life and Times of Pat Brown* (Berkeley: University of California Press, 2005), 197.

16 McCarthy in *Time*, November 9, 1959, 22.

17 McCarthy in *LAT*, July 14, 1960, pt. 1, 3; police chief in James W. Symington KOH, 5.

18 Democrat in Robert W. Merry, *Taking on the World: Joseph and Stewart Alsop—Guardians of the American Century* (New York: Viking, 1996), 350; Norman Mailer, *Some Honorable Men: Political Conventions, 1960–1972* (Boston: Little, Brown, 1976), 15; Aiken in *LAT*, July 15, 1960, pt. 1, 4.

19 Reston in *NYT*, July 13, 1960, 34, and July 15, 1960, 22; Lippmann in *Seattle Times*, July 13, 1960, 8.

20 Baker in Arthur Krock, *Memoirs: Sixty Years on the Firing Line* (New York: Funk & Wagnalls, 1968), 394.

21 Anne H. Morgan, *Robert S. Kerr: The Senate Years* (Norman: University of Oklahoma Press, 1977), 291n83.

22 LBJ and JFK in Booth Mooney JOH, 34.

23 JFK in William White JOH, 1:11; LBJ in Ernest Vandiver RBROH, 44.

24 Kerr in Baker, *Wheeling and Dealing*, 126; Rayburn in ibid., 127–128; Rayburn in Steinberg, *Sam Rayburn*, 350.

25 Helen O'Donnell, *A Common Good: The Friendship of Robert F. Kennedy and Kenneth P. O'Donnell* (New York: Morrow, 1998), 214; O'Donnell and JFK in ibid., 215.

26 Union official in *WSJ*, July 15, 1960, 2.

27 Goldberg and JFK in David L. Stebenne, *Arthur J. Goldberg: New Deal Liberal* (New York: Oxford University Press, 1996), 224; Harriman and Meany in *WSJ*, July 18, 1960, 15.

28 RFK, *In His Own Words*, 26; LBJ in Beschloss, *The Crisis Years*, 296.

29 Rayburn in Baker, *Wheeling and Dealing*, 128.

30 LBJ and JFK in James Rowe JOH, 2:20; JFK in Graham memo in Theodore H. White, *The Making of the President, 1964* (New York: Atheneum, 1965), 414.

31 LBJ in Heyman, *RFK*, 169; Rayburn in Stebenne, *Arthur J. Goldberg*, 471n134.

32 LBJ in *Washington Star*, July 15, 1960; JFK in *LAT*, July 16, 1960, pt. 1, 3.

33 JFK "New Frontier" speech text in *WP*, July 16, 1960, A11.

34 Dirksen in Edward L. Schapsmeier and Frederick H. Schapsmeier, *Dirksen of Illinois: Senatorial Statesman* (Urbana: University of Illinois Press, 1985), 129; *WSJ* editorial, July 18, 1960, 8; Reagan to RN, July 15, 1960, in Stephen E. Ambrose, *Nixon: The Education of a Politician, 1913–1962* (New York: Simon & Schuster, 1987), 1:546.

35 Schlesinger, *Journals*, 78.

CHAPTER 4 THE REPUBLICANS

1 Chairs in George H. Gallup, *The Gallup Poll: Public Opinion, 1935–1971* (New York: Random House, 1972), 3:1634.

2 Primary voters in Gallup, *Gallup Poll*, 3:1631.

3 JPK in Christopher Matthews, *Kennedy and Nixon: The Rivalry That Shaped Postwar America* (New York: Simon & Schuster, 1996), 133; JFK in *WP*, February 24, 1957, B9.

4 Claude Robinson to RN, December 31, 1959, ser. 320, box 647, RNP.

5 The 300,000 figure in Joe A. Morris, *Nelson Rockefeller: A Biography* (New York: Harper, 1960), 327.

6 Taxi driver in Herbert S. Parmet, *Richard Nixon and His America* (Boston: Little, Brown, 1990), 369.

7 NR in *WP*, November 16, 1959, A2; *Fortune* poll in *NYT*, October 26, 1959, 59.

8 Eisenhower in *WP*, July 31, 1959, A4.

9 NR in *WP*, December 27, 1959, A7; Claude Robinson to RN, December 31, 1959, ser. 320, box 647, RNP.

10 RN in *NYT*, April 24, 1960, 1; Raymond Moley to RN, December 29, 1959, ser. 320, box 524, RNP.

11 South Carolinian in *NYT*, July 23, 1960, 8.

12 Hatfield in *WP*, May 18, 1960, A12.

13 Eisenhower in Stephen E. Ambrose, *Nixon: The Education of a Politician, 1913–1962* (New York: Simon & Schuster, 1987), 540.

14 NR in *Meet the Press*, June 12, 1960; Moley in *Newsweek*, June 27, 1960, 108.

15 Lawrence in *NYT*, June 19, 1960, E5; Claude Robinson to RN [received June 13, 1960], ser. 320, box 647, RNP; Robert H. Finch to Jack Kuhris, June 13, 1960, and to Robert F. Spindell, June 16, 1960, both in ser. 320, box 258, RNP.

16 *Winchester Evening Star*, June 11, 1960.

17 Kissinger in Arthur M. Schlesinger Jr., *Journals, 1952–2000* (New York: Penguin, 2007), 84.

18 Emmet J. Hughes, *The Ordeal of Power: A Political Memoir of the Eisenhower Years* (New York: Atheneum, 1963), 315.

19 *Human Events*, June 16, 1960, pt. 3, 4; Earl H. Blaik to RN, November 10, 1960, ser. 320, box 86, RNP.

20 *WSJ* editorial, June 27, 1960, 12.

21 Eisenhower in *NYT*, July 28, 1960, 14.

22 NR in *CT*, July 19, 1960, 5.

23 Reagan to RN, September 7, 1959, ser. 320, box 621, RNP.

24 Hall in Barry M. Goldwater, *With No Apologies: The Personal and Political Memoirs of United States Senator Barry M. Goldwater* (New York: Morrow, 1979), 112.

25 RN in Hughes, *The Ordeal of Power*, 318; RN, *RN: The Memoirs of Richard Nixon* (New York: Grosset & Dunlap, 1978), 215.

26 Graham in *CT*, July 26, 1960, 4.

27 NR in *WP*, May 2, 1960, A1.

28 Dwight D. Eisenhower, *Waging Peace, 1956–1961* (Garden City, N.Y.: Doubleday, 1965), 593; Republican in *WSJ*, June 13, 1960, 2.

29 Eisenhower in *NYT*, July 28, 1960, 14; Eisenhower in Jonathan Aitken, *Nixon: A Life* (Washington, D.C.: Regnery, 1993), 270; Eisenhower in Stephen E. Ambrose, *Eisenhower: The President* (New York: Simon & Schuster, 1984), 2:598.

30 Republican in *NYT*, July 30, 1960, 6; Goldwater in Earl Mazo and Stephen Hess, *Nixon: A Political Portrait* (New York: Harper & Row, 1968), 226.

31 Goldwater in *WP*, July 27, 1960, A6.

32 NR in *WSJ*, July 28, 1960, 2.

33 Texan in Parmet, *Richard Nixon and His America*, 387; Barry M. Goldwater with Jack Casserly, *Goldwater* (New York: Doubleday, 1988), 119; Buchanan in Robert A. Goldberg, *Barry Goldwater* (New Haven: Yale University Press, 1995), 145.

34 Goldwater in Aitken, *Nixon*, 271; Illinois delegate in *CT*, July 24, 1960, 6.

35 JFK in Matthews, *Kennedy and Nixon*, 136.

36 RN to Clare Boothe Luce, September 9, 1960, ser. 320, box 464, RNP; *CT*, July 27, 1960, 5. On the pajamas, see Jack W. Germond, *Fat Man in a Middle Seat: Forty Years of Covering Politics* (New York: Random House, 1999), 49.

37 Sorensen in Matthews, *Kennedy and Nixon*, 136.

38 Text in *NYT*, July 29, 1960, 9.
39 Ibid.; RN, *Six Crises* (New York: Doubleday, 1962), 319.
40 Hall in *NYT*, July 28, 1960, 13.
41 Text in *NYT*, July 29, 1960, 9.
42 RN, *RN*, 219.

CHAPTER 5 THE SOUTH

1 Reporter and Barnett in Charles M. Hills column, *Jackson Clarion Ledger*, September 30, 1960, 12.
2 John J. Synon to James J. Kilpatrick, August 15, 1960, box 6, Kilpatrick Papers, University of Virginia.
3 Barnett in *Jackson Clarion Ledger*, September 4, 1960, A9.
4 Eastland in Neil R. McMillen, *The Citizens' Council* (2nd ed., Urbana: University of Illinois Press, 1994), 331; Byrd to James F. Byrnes, August 25, 1960, box 242, Byrd Papers, University of Virginia.
5 Goldwater in *Richmond Times Dispatch*, August 31, 1960, 1; Byrd to Goldwater, November 28, 1958, box 244, Byrd Papers, University of Virginia.
6 Richard B. Russell to John J. Jones, July 18, 1960, ser. 6, box 26, Russell Collection, University of Georgia, Athens; Harris in *Augusta Chronicle*, July 19, 1960; Vandiver in *CQ Weekly Report*, September 2, 1960, 1524.
7 Harris in *Atlanta Daily World*, August 23, 1960, 1; Harris in *Atlanta Constitution*, September 16, 1960, 1; *Atlanta Journal*, November 6, 1960, in Patrick Novotny, "John F. Kennedy, the 1960 Election, and Georgia's Unpledged Electors in the Electoral College," *Georgia Historical Quarterly* 88:3 (Fall 2004): 388.
8 Russell to James B. Polhill Jr., August 24, 1960, ser. 6, box 26, Russell Collection, University of Georgia, Athens.
9 Thurmond in *CQ Weekly Report*, September 2, 1960, 1524.
10 Rayburn to RFK, September 19, 1960, in Sam Rayburn, *Speak, Mister Speaker*, ed. H. G. Dulaney and Edward H. Phillips (Bonham, Tex.: Sam Rayburn Foundation, 1978), 412.
11 LBJ in Drew Pearson column, *WP*, November 5, 1960, D3.
12 Rayburn to Barefoot Sanders, July 20, 1960, in Rayburn, *Speak, Mister Speaker*, 404.
13 LBJ in *Time*, October 24, 1960, 26.
14 LBJ in *WSJ*, October 14, 1960, 10; George Reedy, *Lyndon B. Johnson: A Memoir* (New York: Andrews and McMeel, 1982), 130–131.
15 LBJ in *Jackson Clarion Ledger*, October 15, 1960, 1.
16 LBJ in *WSJ*, October 14, 1960, 10; LBJ in *NYT*, October 7, 1960, 3; LBJ in *Jackson Clarion Ledger*, October 15, 1960, 1.
17 *Jackson Clarion Ledger*, October 17, 1960, 1.
18 Daniel in *Newsweek*, October 3, 1960, 41; LBJ in Robert Dallek, *Lone Star Rising: Lyndon Johnson and His Times, 1908–1960* (New York: Oxford University Press, 1991), 586; Rayburn to J. B. Skinner, October 13, 1960, in Rayburn, *Speak, Mister Speaker*, 416.

19 Chants in *Jackson Clarion Ledger*, November 5, 1960, 1; signs in Booth Mooney, *The Politicians, 1945–1960* (Philadelphia: J. B. Lippincott, 1970), 350, and in Drew Pearson column, *Jackson Clarion Ledger*, November 10, 1960, A12; LBJ and Alger in *WP*, November 6, 1960, A20; RFK in Jeff Shesol, *Mutual Contempt: Lyndon Johnson, Robert Kennedy, and the Feud That Defined a Decade* (New York: Norton, 1997), 60.

20 Russell to Edwin T. Smith, April 5, 1963, ser. 1, box 7, Russell Collection, University of Georgia, Athens; Russell to Thomas J. Purdom, November 11, 1960, ser. 6, box 28, ibid.

21 Rayburn to Mrs. Dallas Scarborough, August 12, 1960, in Rayburn, *Speak, Mister Speaker*, 408.

22 Byrd in *Richmond Times Dispatch*, August 28, 1960, A1; Byrd to David Lawrence, September 1, 1960, box 245, Byrd Papers, University of Virginia; Shivers in *Richmond Times Dispatch*, November 2, 1960, 1.

CHAPTER 6 THE FALL CAMPAIGN

1 George H. Gallup, *The Gallup Poll: Public Opinion, 1935–1971* (New York: Random House, 1972), 3:1681, 1687.

2 RN in *WP*, August 27, 1960, A2.

3 H. R. Haldeman with Joseph DiMona, *The Ends of Power* (New York: Times Books, 1978), 74–75.

4 Earl H. Blaik to RN, July 31, 1960, ser. 320, box 86, RNP.

5 3,700 preachers in *LAT*, September 12, 1960, 10.

6 RN to Clare Boothe Luce, September 9, 1960, ser. 320, box 464, RNP; RN in *NYT*, September 12, 1960, 19.

7 AES in Stephen E. Ambrose, *Nixon: The Education of a Politician, 1913–1962* (New York: Simon & Schuster, 1987), 564; RFK in *CT*, September 8, 1960, 8; Democrat in *WSJ*, September 19, 1960, 2; Peale in *Newsweek*, September 26, 1960, 42.

8 Gallup undated September data in *LAT*, October 7, 1960, 2.

9 Kenneth P. O'Donnell JOH, 1:22.

10 JFK in Theodore C. Sorensen, *Kennedy* (New York: Harper & Row, 1965), 191; Rayburn in ibid., 193; Californian in *WSJ*, October 19, 1960, 18.

11 Statistics in Kathleen H. Jamieson, *Packaging the Presidency: A History and Criticism of Presidential Campaign Advertising* (New York: Oxford University Press, 1984), 134–135.

12 RN in Stewart Alsop, *Nixon and Rockefeller: A Double Portrait* (Garden City, N.Y.: Doubleday, 1960), 200; RN in Leonard Lyons column, *Chicago Defender*, November 5, 1960, 6.

13 Poll in Warren E. Miller et al., *American National Election Studies Data Sourcebook, 1952–1978* (Cambridge: Harvard University Press, 1980), 306–308; media statistics in John H. Runyon et al., eds., *Source Book of American Presidential Campaign and Election Statistics, 1948–1968* (New York: Frederick Ungar, 1971), 184, 194, 197.

14 JFK and O'Neill in John A. Farrell, *Tip O'Neill and the Democratic Century* (Boston: Little, Brown, 2001), 183; JFK to Healy in ibid., 706n10.

15 Adviser in Theodore H. White, *The Making of the President, 1960* (New York: Atheneum, 1961), 283; Gallup, *Gallup Poll*, 3:1684.

16 Eisenhower in *Newsweek*, October 24, 1960, 35; RN in Mary A. Watson, *The Expanding Vista: American Television in the Kennedy Years* (New York: Oxford University Press, 1990), 9.

17 JFK in Sidney Kraus, ed., *The Great Debates: Background, Perspective, Effects* (Bloomington: Indiana University Press, 1962), 348–350.

18 RN in Kraus, *The Great Debates*, 350–353.

19 Chotiner in *Chicago Sun-Times*, October 21, 1960; Alexander in *LAT*, October 18, 1960, B5; Meade Alcorn to RN, October 3, 1960, ser. 320, box 25, RNP.

20 Daley quoted by Roman Puchinski in Gerald S. Strober and Deborah H. Strober, eds., *Let Us Begin Anew: An Oral History of the Kennedy Presidency* (New York: HarperCollins, 1993), 31; Ralph Barstow to RN, September 27, 1960, ser. 320, box 65, RNP; Longworth in Joseph W. Alsop with Adam Platt, *I've Seen the Best of It: Memoirs* (New York: Norton, 1992), 430; HCL in Fawn M. Brodie, *Richard Nixon: The Shaping of His Character* (New York: Norton, 1981), 427; Hannah Nixon in Julie N. Eisenhower, *Pat Nixon: The Untold Story* (New York: Simon & Schuster, 1986), 191; Klein in Earl Mazo and Stephen Hess, *Nixon: A Political Portrait* (New York: Harper & Row, 1968), 236.

21 JFK in Helen O'Donnell, *A Common Good: The Friendship of Robert F. Kennedy and Kenneth P. O'Donnell* (New York: Morrow, 1998), 252; LBJ in *WP*, October 7, 1960, A17; AES in John B. Martin, *Adlai Stevenson and the World* (Garden City, N.Y.: Doubleday, 1977), 547; Long in Robert Mann, *Legacy to Power: Senator Russell Long of Louisiana* (New York: Paragon, 1992), 205; Almond in *Time*, October 10, 1960, 20.

22 Roper data in White, *The Making of the President, 1960*, 294.

23 80 percent in Kraus, *The Great Debates*, 190; telegrams in *CT*, October 9, 1960, 12; JFK in Arthur M. Schlesinger Jr., *Journals, 1952–2000* (New York: Penguin, 2007), 87.

24 Earl H. Blaik to Fred A. Seaton, October 21, 1960, ser. 320, box 86, RNP.

25 Data in White, *The Making of the President, 1960*, 247.

26 Data in *Newsweek*, October 24, 1960, 35; William L. Rivers, "The Margin of Victory," *Reporter*, October 27, 1960, 21; *WP*, August 9, 1960, A2.

27 JFK in *Time*, November 7, 1960, 29; JFK in Sorensen, *Kennedy*, 178.

28 TRB column, August 8, 1960, in Richard L. Strout, *TRB: Views and Perspectives on the Presidency* (New York: Macmillan, 1979), 205; Lippmann in *WP*, October 27, 1960, A27.

29 Both in Kraus, *The Great Debates*, 154.

30 Gallup, *Gallup Poll*, 3:1688; registrations in *NYT*, October 23, 1960, 49; Long Island Catholics in *NYT*, August 1, 1960, 16.

31 JFK in Sorensen, *Kennedy*, 180; RFK in White, *The Making of the President, 1960*, 320.

32 McGill in *Atlanta Constitution*, October 22, 1960, 1.

33 RN in *Time*, October 31, 1960, 16.

34 *National Review*, October 8, 1960, 204; Charles W. Briggs to RN, October 31, 1960, ser. 320, box 102, RNP; Raymond Moley to RN, May 10, 1960, ser. 320, box 524, RNP; Claude Robinson to RN, May 3, 1960, ser. 320, box 647, RNP; Eisenhower to RN, October 1, 1960, in Dwight D. Eisenhower, *The Papers of Dwight D. Eisenhower* (Baltimore: Johns Hopkins University Press, 2001), 21:2109.

35 Alsop, *Nixon and Rockefeller*, 177; Lerner in *LAT*, October 7, 1960, B4; Schlesinger in Joseph Alsop column, *WP*, October 3, 1960, A15.

36 JFK in Theodore H. White, *Breach of Faith: The Fall of Richard Nixon* (New York: Atheneum, 1975), 69; Barry M. Goldwater, *With No Apologies: The Personal and Political Memoirs of United States Senator Barry M. Goldwater* (New York: Morrow, 1979), 110; Emmet J. Hughes, *The Ordeal of Power: A Political Memoir of the Eisenhower Years* (New York: Atheneum, 1963), 317.

37 RN to Earl H. Blaik, September 8, 1960, ser. 320, box 86, RNP; *WP*, November 6, 1960, E1.

38 Lubell column, *LAT*, September 27, 1960, pt. 1, 22.

39 Bridges in *LAT*, September 30, 1960, pt. 1, 3; RN in *LAT*, October 23, 1960, F1; LBJ in *LAT*, November 1, 1960, 5.

40 RN to Raymond Moley, March 31, 1960, ser. 320, box 524, RNP; Roosevelt to JFK, October 24, 1960, in Joseph P. Lash, *Eleanor: The Years Alone* (New York: Norton, 1972), 299; RN in *NYT*, November 1, 1960, 32.

41 HCL in *NYT*, October 13, 1960, 1; Republican in *NYT*, October 14, 1960, 1.

42 RN in *NYT*, October 13, 1960, 1; HCL in *NYT*, October 14, 1960, 1.

43 Coretta Scott King in Scott Stossel, *Sarge: The Life and Times of Sargent Shriver* (Washington, D.C.: Smithsonian, 2004), 163.

44 Horne in *Chicago Defender*, October 8, 1960, 19.

45 Shriver in Harris Wofford, *Of Kennedys and Kings: Making Sense of the Sixties* (New York: Farrar, Straus, Giroux, 1980), 18; JFK in *Jackson Clarion Ledger*, October 28, 1960, 1; Coretta Scott King in *Atlanta Constitution*, October 27, 1960, 14; O'Donnell in Stossel, *Sarge*, 165.

46 RFK in Arthur M. Schlesinger Jr., *A Thousand Days: John F. Kennedy in the White House* (Boston: Houghton Mifflin, 1965), 74.

47 RN in *NYT*, March 27, 1962, 52.

48 King Sr. in *Atlanta Constitution*, October 28, 1960, 1; King Sr. in White, *The Making of the President, 1960*, 323.

49 Leaflet title in *NYT*, December 14, 1960, 24; Tallahassee data in Russell Middleton, "The Civil Rights Issue and Presidential Voting among Southern Negroes and Whites," *Social Forces* 40:3 (March 1962): 210, 212.

50 Data in Runyon, *Source Book*, 246–251.

51 RFK in *LAT*, November 6, 1960, D2; signs, balloons, and RN in *NYT*, November 3, 1960, 24; RN in *CT*, November 3, 1960, 1; workers in *NYT*, November 3, 1960, 25.

52 JFK in Richard N. Goodwin, *Remembering America: A Voice from the Sixties* (Boston: Little, Brown, 1988), 123.

53 Eisenhower in *CT*, November 5, 1960, 1; Eisenhower in *NYT*, November 5, 1960, 1; JFK in Schlesinger, *A Thousand Days*, 76.

54 Housewife in *LAT*, October 25, 1960, 7.

55 Graham to Isaiah Berlin, October 9, 1960, in Katharine Graham, *Personal History* (New York: Knopf, 1997), 269; Krock in David Halberstam, *The Best and the Brightest* (New York: Random House, 1972), 36; Schlesinger, *Journals*, 88; Lawrence in Robert D. Novak, *The Prince of Darkness: 50 Years Reporting in Washington* (New York: Crown Forum, 2007), 73; Russell Baker, *The Good Times* (New York: Morrow, 1989), 319; Michael V. DiSalle, *Second Choice* (New York: Hawthorn Books, 1966), 221; Goldwater, *With No Apologies*, 105.

56 RN to Claude Robinson, April 9, 1960, ser. 320, box 647, RNP; RN to Dillon Anderson, January 14, 1961, ser. 320, box 40, RNP; JFK in Sorensen, *Kennedy*, 169.

57 Finances in Herbert E. Alexander, *Financing the 1960 Election* (Princeton, N.J.: Citizens' Research Foundation, 1962), 10–12, 38, 44; Benjamin C. Bradlee, *Conversations with Kennedy* (New York: Norton, 1975), 201; Harris in Evan Thomas, *Robert Kennedy: His Life* (New York: Simon & Schuster, 2000), 92.

58 Polls in *NYT*, November 8, 1960, 18.

CHAPTER 7 KENNEDY'S VICTORY

1 Bridges in *Whittier Daily News*, February 27, 1961; LBJ in Theodore H. White, *The Making of the President, 1960* (New York: Atheneum, 1961), 23.

2 RN in RN, *RN: The Memoirs of Richard Nixon* (New York: Grosset & Dunlap, 1978), 223; JFK in White, *The Making of the President, 1960*, 25.

3 Statistics in Richard M. Scammon, ed., *America Votes 2, 1956* (Pittsburgh: University of Pittsburgh Press, 1958); and *America Votes 4, 1960* (Pittsburgh: University of Pittsburgh Press, 1962); *WP*, November 13, 1960, A1.

4 Party preference in Warren E. Miller et al., *American National Election Studies Data Sourcebook, 1952–1978* (Cambridge, Mass.: Harvard University Press, 1980), 94; votes in George H. Gallup, *The Gallup Poll: Public Opinion, 1935–1971* (New York: Random House, 1972), 3:1692. On other elections, see http://cara.georgetown.edu/Presidential%20Vote%20Only.pdf.

5 HHH, *The Education of a Public Man: My Life in Politics* (2nd ed., Minneapolis: University of Minnesota Press, 1991), 171.

6 4.4 million computed from Philip E. Converse et al., "Stability and Change in 1960," *American Political Science Review* 55:2 (June 1961): 278; religious statistics in U.S. Bureau of the Census, *Current Population Reports*, ser. P-20, no. 79 (February 2, 1958); Harlow in Drew Pearson column, *WP*, December 30, 1960, B19.

7 Statistics from *WP*, December 9, 1960, A2; James Reston in *NYT*, November 9, 1960, 20; Ohioan in *Jet*, October 27, 1960, 15; Gallup, *Gallup Poll*, 3:1694–1695.

8   *WP*, December 7, 1960, A11; December 9, 1960, A2; December 11, 1960, 36; Gallup, *Gallup Poll*, 3:1694–1695.

9   Goldwater in *Seattle Post-Intelligencer*, November 10, 1960, 1.

10 Georgian in *WSJ*, November 25, 1960, 6.

11 Statistics in *CQ Weekly Report*, Supplement, March 10, 1961, 1–45.

12 Many statistics on both states are in *WP*, December 4, 1960, A1, and December 11, 1960, E1. These two articles are condensed from Earl Mazo's articles in the *New York Herald Tribune*, December 4–7, 1960. More statistics are in *CT*, December 1, 1960, 5, December 5, 1960, 1, December 7, 1960, 2, and December 8, 1960, pt. 1, 2; and in *Houston Chronicle*, November 29, 1960, 3.

13 Precinct captain in F. Richard Ciccone, *Daley: Power and Presidential Politics* (Chicago: Contemporary Books, 1996), 10.

14 Politician in *CT*, December 1, 1960, 16; Holzman in Edmund F. Kallina Jr., *Courthouse over White House: Chicago and the Presidential Election of 1960* (Orlando: University of Central Florida Press, 1988), 262n46.

15 *CT*, December 14, 1960, 18.

16 Rayburn in Jim F. Heath, *Decade of Disillusionment: The Kennedy-Johnson Years* (Bloomington: Indiana University Press, 1975), 60.

17 JFK in Theodore C. Sorensen, *Kennedy* (New York: Harper & Row, 1965), 262.

18 LBJ in Robert G. Baker, *Wheeling and Dealing: Confessions of a Capitol Hill Operator* (New York: Norton, 1978), 142.

19 Haddad in Scott Stossel, *Sarge: The Life and Times of Sargent Shriver* (Washington, D.C.: Smithsonian, 2004), 191.

20 Inaugural Address in Sorensen, *Kennedy*, 245–248.

21 Morse in Clinton P. Anderson with Milton Viorst, *Outsider in the Senate: Senator Clinton Anderson's Memoirs* (New York: World, 1970), 306; RN in Jonathan Aitken, *Nixon: A Life* (Washington, D.C.: Regnery, 1993), 293; Richard L. Strout, *TRB: Views and Perspectives on the Presidency* (New York: Macmillan, 1979), 218; Truman in *NYT*, January 21, 1961, 8; Gallup, *Gallup Poll*, 3:1707.

BIBLIOGRAPHIC ESSAY

The classic account of the 1960 election is the now badly dated Theodore H. White, *The Making of the President, 1960* (New York: Atheneum, 1961). The book was filmed for ABC television in 1963. Added material is in White's appendix to *The Making of the President, 1964* (New York: Atheneum, 1965); and in *Breach of Faith: The Fall of Richard Nixon* (New York: Atheneum, 1975). A short overview is Gary A. Donaldson, *The First Modern Campaign: Kennedy, Nixon, and the Election of 1960* (Lanham, Md.: Rowman & Littlefield, 2007). Important studies of American politics are Michael Barone, *Our Country: The Shaping of America from Roosevelt to Reagan* (New York: Free Press, 1990); Michael R. Beschloss, *The Crisis Years: Kennedy and Khrushchev, 1960–1963* (New York: HarperCollins, 1991); and Christopher Matthews, *Kennedy and Nixon: The Rivalry That Shaped Postwar America* (New York: Simon & Schuster, 1996).

On postwar liberals, see Steven M. Gillon, *Politics and Vision: The ADA and American Liberalism, 1947–1985* (New York: Oxford University Press, 1987); and Nicol C. Rae, *The Decline and Fall of the Liberal Republicans from 1952 to the Present* (New York: Oxford University Press, 1989).

On labor, see Kevin Boyle, *The UAW and the Heyday of American Liberalism, 1945–1968* (Ithaca, N.Y.: Cornell University Press, 1995); Taylor E. Dark, *The Unions and the Democrats: An Enduring Alliance* (Ithaca, N.Y.: ILR Press, 1999); and David L. Stebenne, *Arthur J. Goldberg: New Deal Liberal* (New York: Oxford University Press, 1996).

On race, see Taylor Branch, *Parting the Waters: America in the King Years, 1954–63* (New York: Simon & Schuster, 1988); and Robert Mann, *The Walls of Jericho: Lyndon Johnson, Hubert Humphrey, Richard Russell, and the Struggle for Civil Rights* (New York: Harcourt, 1996).

On conservatives, see Mary C. Brennan, *Turning Right in the Sixties: The Conservative Capture of the GOP* (Chapel Hill: University of North Carolina Press, 1995); and Donald T. Critchlow, *The Conservative Ascendancy: How the GOP Right Made Political History* (Cambridge, Mass.: Harvard University Press, 2007).

Dwight D. Eisenhower dominated the 1950s. See Stephen E. Ambrose, *Eisenhower: The President, Volume 2* (New York: Simon & Schuster, 1984). Eisenhower's aide, Emmet J. Hughes, wrote the insightful *The Ordeal of Power: A Political Memoir of the Eisenhower Years* (New York: Atheneum, 1963). The 1956 Democratic Convention is covered in Ralph G. Martin, *Ballots and Bandwagons* (Chicago: Rand McNally, 1964).

Many accounts by or about journalists are important. See Joseph W. Alsop with Adam Platt, *I've Seen the Best of It: Memoirs* (New York: Norton, 1992); Benjamin C. Bradlee, *Conversations with Kennedy* (New York: Norton, 1975); Katharine Graham, *Personal History* (New York: Knopf, 1997); Arthur Krock, *Memoirs:*

Sixty Years on the Firing Line (New York: Funk & Wagnalls, 1968); Chalmers M. Roberts, *First Rough Draft: A Journalist's Journal of Our Times* (New York: Praeger, 1973); and William S. White, *The Making of a Journalist* (Lexington: University Press of Kentucky, 1986). *New Republic* columns are collected in Richard L. Strout, *TRB: Views and Perspectives on the Presidency* (New York: Macmillan, 1979). An excellent dual biography is Robert W. Merry, *Taking on the World: Joseph and Stewart Alsop—Guardians of the American Century* (New York: Viking, 1996). Arthur Krock's papers at Princeton University are valuable.

On John F. Kennedy, see especially Arthur M. Schlesinger Jr., *A Thousand Days: John F. Kennedy in the White House* (Boston: Houghton Mifflin, 1965); and Theodore C. Sorensen, *Kennedy* (New York: Harper & Row, 1965). More critical accounts include Henry Fairlie, *The Kennedy Promise: The Politics of Expectation* (Garden City, N.Y.: Doubleday, 1973); Herbert S. Parmet, *Jack: The Struggles of John F. Kennedy* (New York: Dial Press, 1980); and Garry Wills, *The Kennedy Imprisonment: A Meditation on Power* (Boston: Little, Brown, 1981).

Associates' memoirs include Paul B. Fay Jr., *The Pleasure of His Company* (New York: Harper & Row, 1966); Richard N. Goodwin, *Remembering America: A Voice from the Sixties* (Boston: Little, Brown, 1988); Lawrence F. O'Brien, *No Final Victories: A Life in Politics—From John F. Kennedy to Watergate* (Garden City, N.Y.: Doubleday, 1974); and Kenneth P. O'Donnell and David F. Powers, *Johnny, We Hardly Knew Ye: Memories of John Fitzgerald Kennedy* (Boston: Little, Brown, 1972). Pierre Salinger has published *With Kennedy* (Garden City, N.Y.: Doubleday, 1966); and *P.S.: A Memoir* (New York: St. Martin's Press, 1995). Also valuable are Arthur M. Schlesinger Jr., *Journals, 1952–2000* (New York: Penguin, 2007); and Ted Sorensen, *Counselor: A Life at the Edge of History* (New York: HarperCollins, 2008). On appointees, see David Halberstam, *The Best and the Brightest* (New York: Random House, 1972).

For a collection of interviews, see Gerald S. Strober and Deborah H. Strober, eds., *Let Us Begin Anew: An Oral History of the Kennedy Presidency* (New York: HarperCollins, 1993). Uncut typescripts of Schlesinger's 1965 book and Fay's 1966 book are available at the John F. Kennedy Library, Boston, which also contains John Kennedy's prepresidential papers, Robert Kennedy's campaign papers, Arthur M. Schlesinger Jr.'s papers, and Theodore Sorensen's papers, as well as Louis Harris polls and many oral histories. The materials are often disappointing because John Kennedy kept the most important information in his head, and the assassination warped the oral accounts produced afterward.

On the Kennedy family, see Peter Collier and David Horowitz, *The Kennedys: An American Drama* (New York: Summit, 1984); and John H. Davis, *The Kennedys: Dynasty and Disaster, 1848–1984* (New York: McGraw-Hill, 1984).

On Joseph P. Kennedy, see *Hostage to Fortune: The Letters of Joseph P. Kennedy*, ed. Amanda Smith (New York: Viking, 2001). The best biography remains Richard J. Whalen, *The Founding Father: The Story of Joseph P. Kennedy* (New York: New American Library, 1964).

Two excellent studies of Robert Kennedy are Arthur M. Schlesinger Jr., *Robert F. Kennedy and His Times* (Boston: Houghton Mifflin, 1978); and Evan Thomas,

Robert Kennedy: His Life (New York: Simon & Schuster, 2000). Robert Kennedy's oral histories have been published as *In His Own Words: The Unpublished Recollections of the Kennedy Years* (New York: Bantam, 1988). See also C. David Heymann, *RFK: A Candid Biography of Robert F. Kennedy* (New York: Dutton, 1998). A valuable related book is Helen O'Donnell, *A Common Good: The Friendship of Robert F. Kennedy and Kenneth P. O'Donnell* (New York: Morrow, 1998).

On other members of the Kennedy family, see Scott Stossel, *Sarge: The Life and Times of Sargent Shriver* (Washington, D.C.: Smithsonian, 2004); and Gore Vidal, *Palimpsest: A Memoir* (New York: Random House, 1995).

The best biography of Mayor Richard J. Daley is F. Richard Ciccone, *Daley: Power and Presidential Politics* (Chicago: Contemporary Books, 1996).

On Tip O'Neill, see Tip O'Neill with William Novak, *Man of the House: The Life and Political Memoirs of Speaker Tip O'Neill* (New York: Random House, 1987); and John A. Farrell, *Tip O'Neill and the Democratic Century* (Boston: Little, Brown, 2001).

On Catholicism, see Thomas J. Carty, *A Catholic in the White House? Religion, Politics, and John F. Kennedy's Presidential Campaign* (New York: Palgrave Macmillan, 2004).

An excellent documentary film on Wisconsin is *Primary* (1960), produced by Robert Drew for Time-Life Films.

On West Virginia, see Harry W. Ernst, *The Primary That Made a President: West Virginia, 1960* (New York: McGraw-Hill, 1962); Dan B. Fleming Jr., *Kennedy vs. Humphrey, West Virginia, 1960: The Pivotal Battle for the Democratic Presidential Nomination* (Jefferson, N.C.: McFarland, 1992); and Charles Peters, *Tilting at Windmills: An Autobiography* (Reading, Mass.: Addison-Wesley, 1988).

On Hubert H. Humphrey, see his fine memoir, *The Education of a Public Man: My Life in Politics* (2nd ed., Minneapolis: University of Minnesota Press, 1991). See also Winthrop Griffith, *Humphrey: A Candid Biography* (New York: Morrow, 1965); and Carl Solberg, *Hubert Humphrey: A Biography* (New York: Norton, 1984). Humphrey's excellent papers are at the Minnesota Historical Society, St. Paul.

Humphrey and Eugene McCarthy are shrewdly compared in Albert Eisele, *Almost to the Presidency: A Biography of Two American Politicians* (Blue Earth, Minn.: Piper, 1972). On McCarthy, see Eugene J. McCarthy, *Up 'til Now: A Memoir* (San Diego: Harcourt Brace Jovanovich, 1987). A superb biography is Dominic Sandbrook, *Eugene McCarthy: The Rise and Fall of Postwar American Liberalism* (New York: Knopf, 2004).

On Stuart Symington, the best biography is James C. Olson, *Stuart Symington: A Life* (Columbia: University of Missouri Press, 2003). A devastating critique is William S. White, "Symington: The Last Choice for President," *Harper's Magazine*, July 1959, pp. 78–81.

The best study of Lyndon Johnson is Robert Dallek's two-volume biography: *Lone Star Rising: Lyndon Johnson and His Times, 1908–1960* (New York: Oxford University Press, 1991); and *Flawed Giant: Lyndon Johnson and His Times, 1961–1973* (New York: Oxford University Press, 1998). See also Booth Mooney, *LBJ: An*

Irreverent Chronicle (New York: Crowell, 1976). Two Johnson aides have written revealing books: Robert G. Baker, *Wheeling and Dealing: Confessions of a Capitol Hill Operator* (New York: Norton, 1978); and George Reedy, *Lyndon B. Johnson: A Memoir* (New York: Andrews and McMeel, 1982). Also valuable are the Johnson Papers and numerous oral histories (many online) at the Lyndon B. Johnson Library, Austin.

On Sam Rayburn, see Alfred Steinberg, *Sam Rayburn, a Biography* (New York: Hawthorn Books, 1975). An excellent collection of letters is Sam Rayburn, *Speak, Mister Speaker*, ed. H. G. Dulaney and Edward H. Phillips (Bonham, Tex.: Sam Rayburn Foundation, 1978).

The definitive biography for Adlai E. Stevenson is John B. Martin, *Adlai Stevenson and the World* (Garden City, N.Y.: Doubleday, 1977). Excellent letters are in Adlai E. Stevenson, *The Papers of Adlai E. Stevenson, 1957–1961*, vol. 7 (Boston: Little, Brown, 1977). Additional letters are in Stevenson's papers at Princeton University. Many oral histories are at Columbia University.

Memoirs of prominent Democrats include Clinton P. Anderson with Milton Viorst, *Outsider in the Senate: Senator Clinton Anderson's Memoirs* (New York: World, 1970); Michael V. DiSalle, *Second Choice* (New York: Hawthorn Books, 1966); and Harry McPherson, *A Political Education: A Washington Memoir* (Boston: Little, Brown, 1972).

Major studies of Democrats include Alonzo Hamby, *Man of the People: A Life of Harry S. Truman* (New York: Oxford University Press, 1995); Joseph P. Lash, *Eleanor: The Years Alone* (New York: Norton, 1972); Ethan Rarick, *California Rising: The Life and Times of Pat Brown* (Berkeley: University of California Press, 2005); and Jeff Shesol, *Mutual Contempt: Lyndon Johnson, Robert Kennedy, and the Feud That Defined a Decade* (New York: Norton, 1997).

Richard Nixon authored two compelling memoirs: *Six Crises* (New York: Doubleday, 1962); and *RN: The Memoirs of Richard Nixon* (New York: Grosset & Dunlap, 1978). The best biographies are Jonathan Aitken, *Nixon: A Life* (Washington, D.C.: Regnery, 1993); and Stephen E. Ambrose, *Nixon: The Education of a Politician, 1913–1962* (New York: Simon & Schuster, 1987). See also Stewart Alsop, *Nixon and Rockefeller: A Double Portrait* (Garden City, N.Y.: Doubleday, 1960); Fawn M. Brodie, *Richard Nixon: The Shaping of His Character* (New York: Norton, 1981); William Costello, *The Facts about Nixon: An Unauthorized Biography* (New York: Viking, 1960); Earl Mazo and Stephen Hess, *Nixon: A Political Portrait* (New York: Harper & Row, 1968); and Herbert S. Parmet, *Richard Nixon and His America* (Boston: Little, Brown, 1990). Nixon's aide, Herbert Klein, wrote the valuable *Making It Perfectly Clear* (Garden City, N.Y.: Doubleday, 1980). Much can be learned from Nixon's papers, now transferred from the National Archives, Laguna Niguel, California, to the Nixon Library at Yorba Linda, California.

On Nelson Rockefeller, see Frank Gervasi, *The Real Rockefeller: The Story of the Rise, Decline and Resurgence of the Presidential Aspirations of Nelson Rockefeller* (New York: Atheneum, 1964); and Joseph E. Persico, *The Imperial Rockefeller: A Biography of Nelson A. Rockefeller* (New York: Simon & Schuster, 1982).

Barry M. Goldwater has a feisty memoir: *With No Apologies: The Personal and Political Memoirs of United States Senator Barry M. Goldwater* (New York: Morrow, 1979).

On the South, see Guy P. Land, "John F. Kennedy's Southern Strategy, 1956–1960," *North Carolina Historical Review* 56:1 (January 1979): 41–63.

On Mississippi, see Neil R. McMillen, *The Citizens' Council* (2nd ed., Urbana: University of Illinois Press, 1994); and Guy P. Land, "Mississippi Republicanism and the 1960 Presidential Election," *Journal of Mississippi History* 40:1 (February 1978): 33–48.

On Alabama, see Brian J. Gaines, "Popular Myths about Popular Vote–Electoral College Splits," *PS: Political Science and Politics* 34:1 (March 2001): 70–75.

On Georgia, see Gilbert C. Fite, *Richard B. Russell, Jr.: Senator from Georgia* (Chapel Hill: University of North Carolina Press, 1991); Herman E. Talmadge with Mark R. Winchell, *Talmadge: A Political Legacy, a Politician's Life: A Memoir* (Atlanta: Peachtree, 1987); and Patrick Novotny, "John F. Kennedy, the 1960 Election, and Georgia's Unpledged Electors in the Electoral College," *Georgia Historical Quarterly* 88:3 (Fall 2004): 375–397. Russell's excellent papers and a number of oral histories are at the University of Georgia, Athens.

On Virginia, see Robert L. Heinemann, *Harry Byrd of Virginia* (Charlottesville: University Press of Virginia, 1996); James R. Sweeney, "Whispers in the Golden Silence: Harry F. Byrd, Sr., John F. Kennedy, and Virginia Democrats in the 1960 Presidential Election," *Virginia Magazine of History and Biography* 99:1 (1991): 3–44. Byrd's exceptionally fine papers are at the University of Virginia, Charlottesville.

The Kennedy-Nixon debate transcripts are in Sidney Kraus, ed., *The Great Debates: Background, Perspective, Effects* (Bloomington: Indiana University Press, 1962). On campaign finance, see Herbert E. Alexander, *Financing the 1960 Election* (Princeton, N.J.: Citizens' Research Foundation, 1962). On political advertising, see Kathleen H. Jamieson, *Packaging the Presidency: A History and Criticism of Presidential Campaign Advertising* (New York: Oxford University Press, 1984). On television, see Mary A. Watson, *The Expanding Vista: American Television in the Kennedy Years* (New York: Oxford University Press, 1990).

For election data, see Numan V. Bartley and Hugh D. Graham, *Southern Elections: County and Precinct Data, 1950–1972* (Baton Rouge: Louisiana State University Press, 1978); Warren E. Miller et al., *American National Election Studies Data Sourcebook, 1952–1978* (Cambridge, Mass.: Harvard University Press, 1980); Ithiel de S. Pool et al., *Candidates, Issues, and Strategies: A Computer Simulation of the 1960 Presidential Election* (Cambridge, Mass.: MIT Press, 1964); and John H. Runyon et al., eds., *Source Book of American Presidential Campaign and Election Statistics, 1948–1968* (New York: Frederick Ungar, 1971). Three volumes edited by Richard M. Scammon are important: *America Votes 2, 1956* (Pittsburgh: University of Pittsburgh Press, 1958); *America Votes 4, 1960* (Pittsburgh: University of Pittsburgh Press, 1962); and *America at the Polls: A Handbook of American Presidential Election Statistics, 1920–1964* (Pittsburgh: University of Pittsburgh Press, 1965). Also useful is www.uselectionatlas.org.

For polls, see George H. Gallup, *The Gallup Poll: Public Opinion, 1935–1971* (New York: Random House, 1972). Religious statistics are in Douglas W. Johnson et al., *Churches and Church Membership in the United States, 1971* (Washington, D.C.: Glenmary Research Center, 1974). On ethnic analysis, see Philip E. Converse et al., "Stability and Change in 1960: A Reinstating Election," *American Political Science Review* 55:2 (June 1961): 269–280; and Russell Middleton, "The Civil Rights Issue and Presidential Voting among Southern Negroes and Whites," *Social Forces* 40:3 (March 1962): 209–215.

cabinet, 176, 192–193
as a Catholic, 7, 180–182
and Catholics, 7, 20–22
civil rights, 41–42, 91–92
debates with Nixon, 9, 140, 147–152, 154–155, 157
Democratic Convention, 73, 75, 76–77, 80–81
early life, 38–40
election night, 176–178
election results, 179–184, 209–210
electoral math, 82–83
fall campaign, 9, 140–175, 203
front runner, 66–68, 72
Houston speech, 9, 144–146, 201
and Humphrey, 7, 45
without ideology, 4, 10
Inaugural Address, 176, 195–196, 212–215
issues, 158–159
and Johnson, 64–65, 83–91
and King, 168–170, 175
as a liberal, 41–42, 84
and liberals, 69–70
and Lodge, 40–41, 116
and McCarthy, Joseph, 40–41, 42, 203
and media, 4, 7–8, 49–50, 81–82, 173–174, 202
Missile Gap, 22, 24
and money, 8, 147, 174–175, 198–200, 205
and Mountain West, 61–63
"moving again" theme, 3, 9, 24, 152, 158, 159, 175
and Nixon, 96, 121, 140, 147–152, 154–155, 157, 163, 171
nomination ballot by state, 207–208
polls, 202
primaries, 7–8, 199, 203–204, 205
Pulitzer prize, 43, 44
religious issue, 7–9, 144–146, 198–199
and Rockefeller, 97, 98
in Senate, 40–44, 122

and South campaign, 124–132, 134–135
and Stevenson, 64–66
strategy, 119–120, 157–159
on television, 4, 146–148, 198, 201, 204
and U-2 incident, 68–69
vice presidency, 11–12, 20–22
victory, 176–196
West Virginia, 7, 51–55
Wisconsin, 7, 47, 49–51, 102
World War II, 1, 4, 39–40
Kennedy, Joseph P., 4, 38–41, 44, 47, 57, 71, 75
for Johnson for vice president, 84
and Kennedy, John, 22, 43
and money, 170, 200
for Nixon, 96
Kennedy, Joseph P., Jr., 39–40, 52, 133
Kennedy, Robert F., 5, 21, 40, 41, 42, 43, 118, 177–178
attorney general, 193
campaign manager, 47, 54, 57, 72, 118, 137, 144, 157, 160, 200
Democratic Convention, 75, 76–77, 78–79
and Johnson, 61, 87–91
Kennedy, Rose, 39, 40, 41, 47
Kennedy, Ted, 44, 47, 62, 63
Kennedy family, 39–40, 41, 47, 199–200
Kennedy staff, 81, 154, 157, 199–200, 201, 204
and King arrest, 168–170
in primaries, 44–45, 49, 53, 56
Kentucky, 181, 183
Kerr, Robert, 85, 87
Kerry, John, 199
Khrushchev, Nikita, 35, 68–69, 164,
and Nixon, 99–100, 104, 105
King, Coretta Scott, 167–170, 200
King, Martin Luther, Jr., 25, 167–170
Kissinger, Henry, 106
Klein, Herb, 109, 154
Knowland, William, 19, 27